Victor de Lange was born and raised in the Netherlands. At the age of twenty-two, he moved abroad to study and work to the Caribbean, the United States and China. An immersion with different cultures and people enriched him with a million experiences and inspiration to write about. Today he lives in Sydney, Australia with his Chinese wife and daughter. You can always lure him with good coffee and the beach. *The Shanghai Expat* is his debut memoir.

The Shanghai Expat

a memoir

Victor de Lange

First published by Victor de Lange in 2021
This edition published in 2021 by Victor de Lange

Copyright © Victor de Lange 2020
www.victordelange.com
The moral right of the author has been asserted.

All rights reserved. This publication (or any part of it may not be reproduced or transmitted, copied, stored, distributed or otherwise made available by any person or entity (including Google, Amazon or similar organisations, in any form (electronic, digital, optical, mechanical or by any means (photocopying, recording, scanning or otherwise without prior written permission from the publisher.

The Shanghai Expat

ISBN: 9789464351774

Cover design by Red Tally Studios

Publishing services provided by Critical Mass
www.critmassconsulting.com

This book is entirely a memoir. Some of the characters, names, conversations and story sequences portrayed in it are the work of the author's imagination.

1

Shanghai International Airport, 9:30

There I stood. Back in Shanghai. The city where I lived and completed my graduation internship from January till June. After graduation, I spent the summer travelling in France and Spain, divided in two weeks with friends and two weeks with my parents. I went abroad to get an understanding of what the next step in my life could be. Heading back to Shanghai was the result of a well-weighted decision between moving back to America, Aruba or China, where I spent a significant part of my time as an International Business and Management Student. The marketing professor at Texas State University offered me help with a job in a software company in Austin, but soon after that, dark skies appeared above America's economy.

Aruba, an island lying in the southern Caribbean Sea would have been pleasant to return to as well, but after living there for eight months, the island started to feel small to me. Not sure whether I would settle well and besides that, the opportunities of an internationally exposed career are relatively small. About seventy-five per cent of the economy and services are dominated by tourism. As a result, Shanghai would be the most logical place to return to. My professional network is most fresh and China is economically booming. At the time of my arrival in Shanghai, the Beijing Olympics had just finished. In August, as a result of the Olympics, it was nearly impossible to apply for a Chinese visa. But it gave me the chance to work at a local music festival in the

Netherlands to build a financial buffer to cover myself for the first months to come.

Meanwhile more people surrounded the luggage belt now, and the first luggage arrived on luggage belt number ten. White, black, grey and yellow luggage in different sizes passed my eyes, some of them with distinctive recognition tags or labels attached. Even though the suitcases only just arrived, some people already seemed annoyed by the time it required to get their luggage. But I was not in a hurry. There was no office to go to, and it was just 07:25 in the morning. The entire day was still in front of me.

Suddenly I saw my blue luggage within reaching distance. I pulled it from the luggage belt onto the trolley and followed my way to the customs. As I had nothing to declare I could walk through and after passing a few counters that offered last-minute hotel, car and travel packages, the big diffused glass doors to the arrival hall of Terminal 1 opened. Already at this early time of the day - a midweek day at least a hundred people were waiting for their beloved family or friends. Others came to pick up colleagues, and I saw a line of Chinese men in suits carrying whiteboards and paper sheets with Chinese and Western names written on it. They are probably company drivers to pick up executives or hotel staff to collect their guests.

As I passed through the door, I could feel a couple of hundred eyes looking at me. Avoiding eye contact with all of them, I pushed my trolley forward to the middle of the arrival hall where an illegal taxi driver approached me for a drive into the city. With only a few words of English, they try to make you think they are qualified taxi drivers while approved taxis are lined-up outside the arrival hall. With a direct but kind "bu yao" I made clear that I wasn't interested in his service. Instead, I walked to the bus stop from where busses departure to several locations in Shanghai. On the spot I bought a single ticket to People Square as it would make a convenient location to walk to the hotel I booked for the first three days.

It was an old looking bus, with a green colour affected by the sun. Soon after I found a seat on the window side, the bus started moving. It wasn't even half-full, but they depart on a twenty-minute schedule. While Pudong Airport disappeared at the horizon, we passed by factories and small villages. Some were old, while others were still in construction. In this area, people are still free to build their own home as long as they own a piece of land. Often, the homes are narrow and just have three or four floors because it accommodates the entire family and often as many as three generations together.

Many of the people know that one day a property developer will be knocking on their door to buy the land. They pay a price depending on the size of the home. The compensation to receive is higher if the homeowner can claim that the home comes with nine rooms instead of four. With higher compensation, they hope to improve their lifestyle by buying a new apartment. Right at that moment, the Maglev train passed by, blocking my view for a second or two. It's one of the contradictions you see in China today. There is capitalism resulting in a magnetic levitation high-speed train to connect the city with the airport with a variating speed of up to four hundred thirty one kilometres per hour. The Maglev's rail route cut straight through villages where people live with only one aim: survive. They often depend on the vegetables or fruit they grow on their land. Or the collection of plastic bottles, carton or iron. After collection, they drive their tricycles to an assembly point where they receive compensation for every kilo of material they bring in. The carton collectors would cheat a bit by pouring water over their carton, resulting in a heavier load so they can ultimately bring more cash home. The money they earn with this presumably provides enough daily to pay for a single trip ticket of the Maglev train, costing fifty RMB.

When I looked further in front of me, we neared a crossroad and even further in the far distance I could see the skyline of the city. Always an impressive view, with on the left side the Grand Gateway twin towers. When I looked to the right, I could see the futuristic Marriott hotel on People's Square with on the top the iconic four spikes with a resting ball in the middle. The Jin Mao Tower emphasised the Pudong skyline. We passed the Lupu Bridge over the Huangpu river, connecting Shanghai's Huangpu and Pudong districts. It is an impressive construction and the world's second-longest steel arch bridge after the Chaotianmen Bridge in

Chongqing. It's even possible to climb the bridge and see, obviously on a clear day an unforgettable three hundred sixty degrees view on one hundred meter high.

While we crossed the bridge with the bus, I had to think about the clear but cold winter day I climbed the bridge with a German friend of mine. The temperature on top of the arch must have been minus ten degrees caused by a strong wind. I ended up suffering three days of heavy cold and fever as a result of this little adventure. When driving on the descending highway from the Lupu Bridge into the city, I instantly felt the feeling of arriving in my second hometown. The bus continued the elevated highway in the north direction, and all I could see were hundreds of residential and office buildings on both sides of the highway. Most of them at least a thirty-meter high with some balconies only twenty meters away from the thousands of cars passing by every day. From the second level, I could watch into the streets below, where Shanghai life continued as normal. As usual, many people walking down the street. Groups of them waiting in front of red traffic lights. All with a destination in mind. I heard cars horning and noticed street sellers offering books and clothes on a busy corner of Nanjing Road. It seemed to me life was still the same compared to when I left three months ago. Even in a city with twenty-four million people, things can stay the same.

As we were nearing People's Square the bus slowed its speed, preparing to make a right curve onto the designated bus stop. People's Square was the first stop for the bus to take and from looking around, I could conclude that nearly everybody had the same plan to depart from the bus at this moment. Already before the bus came to a stop, most passengers lined up in the passage so that they could be out of the bus first. I always considered this to be a survival instinct shared by many locals. In a society where everything evolves around rankings starting from kindergarten and onwards, you better make sure to be the first or at least be part of the top three. Otherwise, somebody else for sure will take your place, and you may end up with nothing at all. In the Shanghai subway, it sometimes leads to funny situations as people entering and departing the subway at the same moment. When the door opens, only the strongest will survive.

I stepped out of the bus, and I could instantly feel and smell the humid air. Different compared to the cool and dry air in the Netherlands. Shanghai in September offers on average a temperature of nearly twenty-eight degrees with seventy-five per cent humidity. I let the other people go out first and took my suitcase out of the luggage compartment. It felt good to be back. I had an enormous feeling of freedom. Shanghai and China lay wide open for me. When I think back to that moment, I never feared that I could possibly end up failing as well. The drift to survive was much stronger. Before booking the flight, I had given myself three months to find a job in Shanghai. If this didn't work out, I would be home for Christmas to find a job in the Netherlands.

Energised with this feeling, I walked up north towards East Nanjing Road. The hotel I booked for the first three days was located in a side street of East Nanjing Road and Fuzhou Road. A simple but decent hotel and good enough spend the first few days acclimatising while hunting for an apartment. While walking on the street, I remembered that it is not possible to access East Nanjing Road directly from West Nanjing Road. To do so, you have to cross the People's Square subway station and follow the tunnel under Xizang Middle Road and ultimately walk the stairs up. This will bring you to a slightly higher part of the street, which is an ideal location for tourists to take pictures. East Nanjing Road is a massive tourist attraction and perhaps the most famous and busy commercial streets in China, if not in the world. As it is pedestrianised, it is a nice walk to the Bund. Many movies have been recorded on East Nanjing Road, and at night the building facades are all light up with neon.

As I had my luggage with me, it was easier to take the escalator up to the street level. While I stood there slowly the street entrance became more visible. East Nanjing Road did not change either since I left Shanghai in June. There is always an incredible mass of people, no matter on which day of the week you're visiting. During my internship days, I tried to avoid East Nanjing Road as much as possible. Especially in the weekends. As a foreigner, you're an easy target for street sellers and other individuals offering massages or sex with pretty girls in town. While overlooking East Nanjing

Road, I suddenly realised that the entire population of my hometown Koudekerke in the south west of the Netherlands counts three thousand people. The first part of East Nanjing Road accommodated already at least three thousand people. The contrast here is so much different. When I grew up in Koudekerke, I always considered Amsterdam a big city located on the other side of the world while in fact, it was only a two and a half-hour drive. When measured in the total size of the population, Amsterdam comes close to just Shanghai's Yangpu district. Although the world's highest people density is claimed to be in the Netherlands as a country, Yangpu district's people density is twenty-two thousand per square kilometre. No surprise considering all the high residential towers around me.

While I walked on East Nanjing Road in Northern direction, it started to rain. People were looking for shelter in nearby shops. The rain came with this typical humid smell. Luckily for me and as I was not carrying an umbrella, it disappeared pretty soon so I could follow my way to the hotel. After arriving in the hotel lobby, I hoped to check in but it was only eleven o'clock in the morning. It did not seem to be an issue, so I handed over my passport to the receptionist lady.

"Good morning and welcome to our hotel. Did you have a nice trip, sir?" she asked in flawless English.

"Yes, I surely had. Thank you for asking." That seemed like quite a nice welcome.

"I have booked a single room for two nights." She checked the hotel's booking system. "Let me check. V... Victor... Ah yes, here I see your reservation." As required by every hotel, she made a copy of my passport and the visa on which I entered China. This is for registration with the local police station. For convenience the hotel will do this for tourists but once you find a place to live for yourself you have seventy-two hours after the first entry on your visa in China or address change to register yourself in the nearest police station. When I first arrived in China, I considered this strange. Or it made me cautious, even though I had nothing to hide. Can you imagine something like that in the Netherlands?

"All done," the reception lady said.

"Here is your room key; your room is on the fourth floor."

I found the way to the elevators and pressed four. It was not crowded in the hotel. Perhaps because it was a Tuesday morning in September. Business traveller check-in and out behaviour usually peaks on Mondays, Wednesdays and Fridays. And everybody on a business trip would be in an office or meetings by now.

I heard a ping and the door opened on the fourth floor. Luckily my room wasn't right next to or in front of the elevators. Those rooms are usually noisy with hotel guests passing by and having conversations while they wait for the elevator. Not this time. I walked down the corridor and once in front of room number four hundred and twelve, I swiped the card through the room door lock. I heard a soft beep and unlocking sound. I opened the door. Immediately after walking in, I could feel the air-conditioning. I immediately raised the temperature to twenty-two and I looked through the room. The room looked decent and maintained, as I expected after booking a superior room. As a student, I once visited Hong Kong for a visa extension and stayed in a hotel in Kowloon where the room was basically the size of the king bed and the bathroom the size of the toilet. The most comfortable position while taking a shower would have been standing with one leg actually in the toilet. And not to mention the dodgy alley leading to the hotel entrance with what I considered true drugs dealers. After this gruelling experience, I promised myself that after graduation I would never stay in this type of hotel anymore.

I opened my luggage to take my toiletry bag out and prepared for a shower. I truly enjoy getting out of my clothes after a long trip to take a shower and refresh. I entered the cabin and felt the warm water streaming over my body. Shanghai tab water always comes with a chloral smell. Still, it felt wonderful when it touched my skin. It just gives you an instant kick of energy. While showering, I brushed my teeth. I avoided drinking the water as it maintains an unusually high number of irons and in some cases, chemicals. Most hotels offer complimentary water bottles in the room which is good for reasonable high water consumers like me.

After refreshing, I went out and had a walk in one of the department stores nearby East Nanjing Road. Many of these stores would represent an unknown Western brand name and sell fashionable goods at a high price, but they are all Made in China. They make an enormous margin by selling a pair of shoes for not less than two thousand RMB or not to mention the coats. Back in the days, these "Western" brands would attract Chinese consumers as in their perception it would come with high quality. In some cases it would have a good quality, but if I could spend two thousand RMB on shoes I would rather do so in the Netherlands. I had lunch in one of the many food courts around People's Square. It's a concentrated area in a shopping mall with many food outlets in a market set-up. There are tables in the middle of the "court" where people eat their lunch, dinner or snack. The food is often good and not expensive. As there is a high turn-over of guests, they only work with fresh ingredients. It's a perfect location if you're in for Chinese, Malaysian, Singaporean or Indonesian food.

After lunch I walked towards Bund, one of the main attractions in Shanghai. After arrival, I continued walking in the north direction and turned my head to the left. I noticed a few early 1900 architectural style buildings. Today they are mainly occupied by Chinese banks, hotels, luxury retailers and high-end restaurants. Another eye-catcher is the customs building, easy to recognise with the clock on top of the building. This clock is the biggest in Asia and plays the Chinese Communist song *East is Red* during every daylight hour of the day. And sometimes at night as well. Over my other shoulder, I saw Pudong's financial district. The Shanghai World Financial Centre determined the top of the skyline. When I first arrived in Shanghai for my internship, the top of the Shanghai World Financial Center was still in construction and was surrounded by cranes to construct the glass windows to the skyscraper. It just opened a month ago. I saw the Oriental Pearl Tower and the Jin Mao Tower. The Bund in Shanghai has its uniqueness. By times it can be incredibly crowded, so avoid the Bund during the weekend and public holidays.

While I was walking there this early afternoon in September, I remember walking over the Bund at night. It has its own charm. The buildings on the Puxi district side of the Bund are illuminated in such way that the architecture remains visible at night. Most buildings have a yellowish look at evening hours. The Lujiazui area is dominated by the RGB colours of the Pearl Tower and the thousands of residential and office lights. The aircraft warning lights on top of the skyscrapers and high-rise buildings turn on and off slowly in a cycle of a few seconds. It provides a twinkling effect, stretched out over the entire Pudong Skyline. Furthermore, tens of Illuminated boats will cross the Huang Pu River and host tours and buffet dinners for tourists. The only boat tour I ever took over the Huang Pu river was the ferry from Puxi to Lujiazui. It's a cheap and short one; just two RMB which was roughly twenty Euro cents. That gives you a wonderful view for roughly seven minutes while crossing the river. Those are all memories of evening walks on the Bund. Sometimes alone, sometimes accompanied by friends. Right now, it was the sun coming through the clouds, and I heard the clock of the Customs Building playing the song that defines the Bund. While passing each other, hundreds of people looked at me. Wondering where that tall Foreigner was going to.

2

Park Hotel Shanghai - 8:00

After breakfast the next morning, I planned to do some research to find an apartment to live in for at least the next three months. As there are two ways to do do this, I first went online as there are numerous websites offering apartments to rent and sell. I called one of the property managers on the first website that popped up on my screen. The phone ringed for a couple of times before it was answered with "Wei?!". That means "Hello" in Mandarin Chinese. In addition to most Westerners, Chinese people never say their name when answering the phone. But I am Western.

"Good morning, my name is Victor. Am I talking to Mr Jeremy from Shanghai Properties?

A faltering "Yes...?" was the answer.

"Good," I continued. "I'm searching for an apartment to rent, and I saw one listed on your website with reference number 9003845. Is it still available?"

There was a silent moment on the other side of the line as if he did not expect this cal to be in English. "Let me check," he ultimately answered. I heard him typing on the keyboard of his PC. "No," was the answer. "It was rented just yesterday. But we do have other properties."

"Yes, I'm sure you have. But I like this apartment, and it looks well designed for a reasonable price."

I suddenly remembered the moment when I first arrived in Shanghai to start my internship. I called a few property companies, but they are generally hard to trust. The apartments you like are always "just signed to somebody else", and most of the apartments have a too good to be true rental price for what looks like a very nice deal. So in the rule, you call them and ask for a particular apartment, but it is most likely unavailable. Meanwhile, they have your number and know you're in the market for a rental apartment. They will call you a couple of times over the next few days with available apartments which are most often not meeting your requirements. Easy lead generation.

I decided not to waste my entire day with Jeremy from Shanghai Properties and told him I would continue my online search. The next website I saw was the same story. I saw two nice apartments and called the agent, which was a lady this time. Against Chinese traditions, she introduced herself as Ping and her English was significantly better compared to Jeremy. Unfortunately, she delivered the same story, or at least the same tactics.

"Those apartments are rented Sir; we did not update the website yet."

So, this is how it really works. She invited me to come over to their property agency so we could visit available apartments, but I refused. The next website I saw was a Shanghai Classified website where supply and demand in a variety of buy, sell, and rental categories can meet. It reminded me of the individual - often rubbish - property agents offering homes on a free website. No need to pay for Google ads or other registration fees. I should better stay away from this kind of websites.

My thoughts went back to the landlord I had during my internship in Shanghai earlier this year. The classmate I did my internship in Shanghai with found this individual property agent online, causing issues more than once over the total six-month period of our rental contract. During my internship I lived with two guys. One from Switzerland and from Ireland. All of us had issues to contact her in case something had to be fixed in the apartment.

I remember when the Irish guy moved out in May, he actually never got his down payment of two months' rent back. And I almost did not get anything back either. We had to pay our rent for three months in advance and after that in cash for the remaining contract duration. So in June, I was leaving Shanghai to return to the Netherlands, and she owed me two months of rent I paid for deposit at the start of our contract. Three days before my return flight, I passed by her office in Jingan district which was actually a residential apartment where she used to live and work to collect my deposit. After getting up to the tenth floor of the building an unknown Western guy opened the door and told me that Kathy, which was her name, did not live there anymore. He invited me in, and I had a small talk with his two roommates. One of them was dating Kathy. I wondered what kind of relationship that would be. It was nothing new for her to move her office to a new location without any notification. At least her boyfriend could tell me the address where she lived now. When I left their apartment, I started to worry a little bit about the whereabouts of my deposit.

After arriving at the address I was given earlier, I was facing five enormous residential towers, containing five apartments on each of the twenty-four floors. That would be like searching for the proverbial needle in a haystack. The needle named Kathy could be hiding in one of each of the six hundred apartments haystack in front of me. Suddenly I realised that if she is causing so much trouble, I wouldn't be the first person here looking for her. I decided to ask the security guard of the compound. In my best Chinese I explained to him that I was looking for a lady named Kathy, who was my property agent, and whether he had any idea where she lived. Those security officers work like a magnet when it comes to tracking needles in haystacks. They know most of the people living in their compound, which apartment is empty or will become available for rent soon. For a small compensation, they are often willing to help you out or link you with the owner of an apartment. This security officer knew who I was looking for and without the need to bribe him, he told me the building number, floor and apartment number in which he thought my property agent must be living. While I was walking to building number three, I thought to myself:

"Wow. Kathy must be living here for a short time only, but she made herself famous already. That can't be a coincidence."

I walked into the residential tower, first entering the lobby with yellow, blue and orange bikes parked on the left side, while the other side was a wall equipped with hundreds of mailboxes. I walked towards the elevator. It was on the way down from the fourteenth floor, not the floor Kathy lived. That would eliminate a possible surprise factor in case we would meet here in the building's lobby. The elevator doors slowly opened, and I pressed the button with number eighteen, which was according to the security guard the floor Kathy must be living. While I felt the air pressure as a result of the moving elevator, I stared at the advertisements on both walls. One was a local shampoo brand, where a model or famous movie star showed a beautiful glans in her hair. Although I couldn't recognise the person itself, there was an autograph in the right corner of the advertisement. That means she must be famous. The other advertisement was from a local Sichuan restaurant chain. Probably with the aim to increase the people's appetite and I have to confess it somehow worked on me. The pictures with well-prepared dishes made me feel hungry.

Meanwhile, the elevator came to a stop and the door opened slowly. I was on the eighteenth floor now. There was a little map with the location of each apartment, and I searched for number C where Kathy should be living. When I stood in front of the door I pressed the doorbell, and a girl in her early twenties opened the door. It wasn't Kathy.

"Excuse me," I started, "My name is Victor and was told Kathy should be living here right now? She is my landlord, and she owes me a deposit."

She didn't introduce herself and without saying anything, she let me in. It didn't look like a residential apartment, as the living room was filled with a couple of desks.

"Is Kathy here?" I asked again.

"Yes, let me find her for you."

I waited in the living room while she walked to the back of the apartment. I heard short arguing before the girl returned. She seemed embarrassed.

"Kathy is here, but she locked herself in her bathroom." She continued: "I can't open the door."

Damned, I thought. She must have heard me when I introduced myself at the front door. On the other side, I felt relieved that I found Kathy among twenty-four million people in this metropole city. I told the girl I could wait for Kathy to come out eventually. She didn't object and continued her work on an old-looking desktop. I navigated the room. The atmosphere was sober. Colours were dark and grey. No flowers to find and all windows were closed. I wondered whether there was any source of fresh air in this room.

Meanwhile, ten minutes passed by and the girl was solely focussed on her desktop. She continued working as if I wasn't even there anymore. Her body language indicated that she didn't want to be involved in my ugly deposit dispute. I could probably wait here all afternoon while Kathy inside the bathroom hoped I would give up and leave.

"Ehm, sorry? Would you mind if I talk to Kathy directly?" I said. The girl was still focussing on her screen. As if it took five seconds for my words to travel with the time of sound for her to hear me, she looked up from her screen.

"Yeah, sure," she said. "Go ahead." She pointed towards the direction of the bathroom.

I followed a small corridor with open doors leading to two bedrooms. One door at the end of the corridor was closed. I knocked, but that did not result in any reaction. I turned the door handle and realised it was still locked. This must be the bathroom where Kathy is hiding.

"Hello?" I tried. I could hear a movement inside the bathroom as if she increased the distance between her and the door.

"Hello?" I tried it again.

"Is this Kathy?"

She was now a rat trapped in a maze. I thumped against the bathroom door.

"Kathy, please open the door." Silence.

"I am at the end of my rental contract, and you owe me two months' rent I paid for the deposit."

I decided to put a bit more pressure on her.

"I need it now as I am leaving the country tomorrow morning. Please open the door!" Still no reaction.

"Listen, Kathy," I tried again.

"I have nothing to do anymore this afternoon, so I'm just going to wait here for you to come out." and I added: "And at some point, I may decide to involve the police in this."

That threat made her move. I heard her rummaging in the bathroom. She suddenly unlocked the door. I waited for her to open it. It did not take long until I saw Kathy standing wearing pink pyjamas as if she just got out of bed. To my surprise, she had a collection of banknotes in her hand. I realised she might be using this bathroom periodically as a safe room when renters knocked on her door to demand deposit back.

"How... how did you find me?" She had a vitriolic expression on her face.

"It wasn't as difficult as I expected beforehand." I answered. "You may start by asking your boyfriend."

I didn't mind ruining a relationship at this point. Her boyfriend anyway deserved better than Kathy. She looked away and handed me the deposit. I counted the money, which surprisingly ended up with the right amount of Renminbi Kathy owed me. She remembered this damn well. Thank you, I said, and I walked to the front door of the apartment. The girl was still working at her desk. She stared at her screen as if she didn't absorb anything of what just happened. I honestly felt a bit sorry for her. It must not be easy to have Kathy as your employer.

While I walked through the door, I looked over my shoulder to make sure Kathy did not follow me with an axe to attack me. I realised that this must be part of a solid strategy. She must, on purpose, change her office location frequently to avoid facing the mess she left behind. During the rental period, she often promised things but never delivered. Not just with me. My two housemates and another friend who rented from her told me to have similar experiences. A relocation strategy could only work if Kathy bribed the people surrounding her to guarantee protection. She was a self-claimed queen, high in a palace but all the doors and stairs leading to her room were unsecured. Although a queen status would be too much prestige for her. An unsecured Narcos suits her better.

Slowly my thoughts went back to the present. I've learned from this bad experience with Kathy so let's not try to do this again. The rule of thumb is to go with a recommended property agency and if possible one with chain locations all over the city. But even recommended property agencies sometimes change location from one to another district. In case you have any issues with your contract or landlord, one of the other locations can back you up. I decided to go outside. Everything looks better online. Apartments look bigger and nicer and always for a low price. The best thing you can do is walk-in and ask which apartments they have available within your budget. Usually, when you pass by a property agency, at least eight employees are working behind their desk set up in classroom formation. For sure they would not mind helping a foreigner looking for an apartment?

I went out and took the subway from People Square to Shanghai Railway Station. From there I took line 3 in south direction towards Yishan Road. This line is entirely above ground except for Tieli Road Station. It's providing passengers with good views of the city. There are just buildings everywhere in Shanghai. I carried a small notebook with me in which I listed down the stations I passed. In between the stations, I made notes of nice apartment buildings I saw. Next time I could get out at one of the stations to walk into that particular neighbourhood and search for a property agency.

The plan worked. After getting out in Yishan Road to take the same line back to Shanghai North Railway Station, I got out in Zhenping Road. There were a couple of nice compounds near the Suzhou Creek. Recently built compounds always have empty apartments for rent as some of the apartments are sold solely to investors who aim to rent out the place. Once I took the elevator down from the subway platform back to street level, I saw at least a hundred bikes parked in front of the station. At least in an organised manner. The interesting difference with Amsterdam is that at least half of the bikes are electric bikes. I just suddenly wondered how many electric bikes Shanghai would have.

With this question still in my mind, I suddenly recognised a powerful smell. I could hardly imagine this to be food. I looked around and saw a street seller baking sweet potatoes on the side of the subway station. Some other street sellers offered clothes and small accessories for mobile phones. I crossed Kaixuan North Road and walked into Putuo Park. Nice to see this sudden greenery in a city full of brick. Colourful flowers in yellow and orange smiled at me. Some of the trees started to have brown leaves, indicating that the fall season would arrive soon. I enjoyed watching young people and older couples appreciating this little piece of green. Imagine you were born in this enormous city and parks are the only opportunity to escape from the busy streets to witness some green?

I left the park from the Guangfu Road exit and followed a small promenade build beside the Suzhou Creek. I still didn't see any property agents. It's just like McDonald's. If you're not hungry, you see that big yellow "M" everywhere, but once you feel about eating some junk food, they are nowhere to find. Nevertheless, I was still walking in the direction of the residential compound I saw from the subway. It was relatively easy to find my way, as the three towers peaked above the average height of surrounding buildings. After walking for another ten minutes, I arrived at a T crossing where Guangfu Road meets Dongxin road. This was as close as I could get to the compound. Dongxin Road had a couple of shops in nice-looking retail spaces. I was lucky. Among some shops and restaurants, there was one property agent. This "on the spot" agent must be able to show me a couple of apartments in the compound I could see me living in. The promenade, retail spaces and the compound must have been recently built. All in the same architecture. I was easy to tell from the dusty facade, and some of the retailers seemed still in the process of moving in.

While I stood in front of the shop window, I could see through the advertisements that this property agency consisted of a small team but representing a long list of available properties. It did not take long for one of the sales representatives to come out while I looked for available properties in the window shelf.

"Are you looking for an apartment?" a young lady asked.

"Yes," I answered. "I was hoping for an available apartment in the compound here across the street." and I pointed in the right direction.

Without reaction to my question, she handed me her business card. Next to a Chinese name consisting out of three characters I couldn't read, her English name was Cherry. Cherry is quite a common name for girls to name themselves in University. Just like Apple, Snow, Candy, Super or Fish. That is supposed to sound cute until graduation, but once they start working, they should be restricted to find themselves a serious name. Mentioning an English name like Foggy on your resume might not help to score a new job. Anyway, Cherry was apparently one of them who decided not to change her name after graduation.

"Are you looking to rent a place by yourself or do you mind sharing?" She asked.

"I don't mind sharing with a clean and neat person."

"Alright," She added. "In that case, we have a couple of places available."

Property agents often have keys from available apartments in their office. If not, they will call the landlord to ask whether they are available to open the apartment. Cherry grabbed a pair of keys and put on her coat.

"Let's go." She said.

We walked outside and crossed the street to the compound.

"How long are you in China?"

"I did my internship here in Shanghai from January till June. I graduated from University in the Netherlands this Summer, and now I'm back with the aim to find a job."

"Wow," she reacted. "You're Dutch? And you are looking for a job so far away from home?" She seemed impressed.

Meanwhile, we arrived at the gate of the compound. It had a signage logo that said *Xinhu Riverside Residence* in English. She talked in Chinese to the security guard, who swiped his card over a sensor to unlock the door. I thought this is amazing, while entering the compound. Lots of plants and grass. There was a small lake in the middle of the compound. I could see the fountain heads reaching just above the surface of the water. I could see three tall residential towers were in front of us, while there were three lower buildings on our right side. Somehow it does not seem like many people live here yet. We crossed a red-brown coloured wooden bridge with red and purple veining over a puddle connected to the main lake. Cherry mentioned that building number three had a shared apartment for rent. I noticed that in order to enter the building, an access card was required, but the door stood open, so we could just walk in. The lobby looked a bit dark because all the lights were turned off. It smelled new but humid. Both the floor and the walls had a marble-like finish which provided the lobby with an exclusive look. Still, it seemed the developer did not feel responsible for cleaning the place before delivering the building. There was a layer of concrete dust all over the floor. This is China. The developer invests over a billion RMB to build this compound but hiring a team to clean the tower lobbies was too much to ask. Apartments are delivered like bunkers, with nothing inside but grey concrete walls. Once you move in, you need to go through an entire process of construction. That's probably why at this stage nobody cares too much about flying dust. Two corridors were leading to the elevators. One of them was already waiting for us. The walls were covered with a wooden layer for protection against any damage by newcomers moving in their household equipment and furniture. Cherry pressed the button to bring us to the tenth floor. As if I hadn't noticed yet she added that this was a very new compound. We left the elevator on the tenth floor. Cherry walked immediately to the right side. From a map between the elevators, I could see that each floor contained six apartments in an oval-shaped building. Even though Cherry was carrying a key, she first pressed the doorbell.

"I know that the brother of the landlord is living here." She explained. "But he stays in the second bedroom. The master bedroom is available for rent."

I could hear somebody approaching on the other side of the door. A gentleman in his early forties opened the door. Cherry explained him in Chinese regarding my interest to rent the master bedroom. He smiled at me and introduced himself as Mr Lu. The apartment looked simple but nice. Instead of covered with any carpet, the floor was painted in a purplish colour. Combined with the white walls, it created a basic but fashionable interior design. The dining table had a shining glass surface, and I walked to the front window in the living room. Right in front of us was one of the two other residential towers belonging to this compound. I could see some of the apartments in the other building occupied with residents. Windows were covered with linen cloths used as curtains. The balconies looked extremely messy, equipped with laundry and furniture. One of them even had a fridge. The residents probably moved from nearby cities into Shanghai but lacking the decoration skills that suit this brand-new compound.

Cherry proposed to show the master bedroom. She opened the door that led us into a spacious room in the same style as the living room and equipped with a closet, queen size bed and a desk. There was a mat glass door to connect the bathroom directly with the bedroom while on the other side of the room, a roll-door provided access to the balcony. I checked the view once again. The right side provided a clear view of Zhongshan Park, which must be five kilometres away. I asked Cherry what it would cost me to live here.

"Two thousand and eight hundred RMB per month, all included." she answered. "There is an ayi visiting twice per week to clean the apartment."

Ayi in pinyin means aunt, but it is a widely used description for cleaning lady.

"Is renting for three months at first an option?"

I wanted the freedom to move out without losing my deposit if I wasn't able to find a job by Christmas. Cherry looked at Mr Lu and asked him my question in Chinese. He nodded yes. While we were still in the master bedroom, I looked around. This apartment is brand-new. The price is good, but considering I share the place with the brother of my future landlord, I may need to reduce the number of parties at home. On the other hand, Cherry explained to me that Mr Lu works for his sister and is therefore not at home frequently.

I realised that this was a unique opportunity. Usually, you need roughly fifteen to twenty apartments before you see something that meets your requirements. This time it was different. Maybe because I pointed Cherry on this particular compound, and so giving her no other options to show me. I could save myself a lot of time and frustration by accepting this apartment.

"Alright," I said. "I think this is a nice place to live."

I could see an appeasing expression on both Cherry and Mr Lu's face. I shook the hand of Mr Lu, and we went back to the property agent office to finalise the agreement. I asked Cherry whether there was much interest for Xinhu Riverside Apartments.

"Not much right now, but people increasingly ask for the possibility to live here." I carefully read through the contract before putting my signature on the bottom of the page and put a small staple of one hundred yuan banknotes on the table to cover for deposit. Good timing, I concluded to myself. Tomorrow I will check out from the hotel and move straight to my new apartment where I will be living in for at least the next three months.

3

Xinhu Riverside Residence - 7:43

One of the things about moving into a new place is the need to visit IKEA. I woke up early to witness the crowd in the morning jam but at the same time avoid a crowd in IKEA. I closed and locked the heavy hardwood apartment door. I followed the marble tiles in the dusty corridor towards the elevator and pressed the elevator button. One of the two elevators was waiting for me a couple of floors away. The moment the doors opened, I realised that my wallet was still on the table in the living room. There is not much I could do in IKEA without a wallet. I walked back to the front door, opened it and collected my wallet.

Once back at the elevators, I pressed the button and looked outside from the window. Down on the street, I saw people on their way to work. They commuted by car, bike or walking their way to the nearest subway station. The property agencies were still closed. A couple of street sellers offered breakfast. Some of them are actually quite good. During my internship, I remember riding a bike to the office, and I purchased a pancake with two eggs and green onion and parsley for breakfast at the side of the street. They are prepared in front of you for just three RMB.

Meanwhile, I could hear the elevator coming closer. Once it stopped, I turned around and after the doors opened, I saw a chubby Western guy. He was dressed well, clearly on the way to work. I smiled and walked in. He smiled and looked a bit surprised by another foreigner in the elevator. For a few floors we stood there, silently staring at the elevator's wall.

"When did you move in here?" he asked all out of nothing.

"Oh, just yesterday." I answered. "But I lived in Shanghai from January till June earlier this year, went back to the Netherlands to graduate from University and now I'm back to find a job and start my career. How about yourself?" I asked in return.

"I'm originally from Brazil and finished a master's degree at Tsinghua University in Beijing, and now I'm working for a multinational company here in Shanghai."

"How long do you live in Shanghai?" I asked.

"Just a couple of months, I graduated last June."

He introduced himself as Raphael.

"My name is Victor. Good to meet you here."

Meanwhile, the elevator doors opened, and we walked outside.

"Do you have any friends you hang out with here?" Raphael asked.

"Not really," I admitted. "Most of the people I hung out with during my internship meanwhile left the city."

Raphael nodded in agreement. "Yes," he said. "Shanghai is like a bird's nest. People are constantly moving in and out." He grabbed his phone and continued: "Let me know if you like to hang out sometime. I have a couple of Western friends. We usually go out for dinner, drinks or cook at home and have a party." He offered his phone for me to add my number. I pressed the call button to make sure I had his number as well.

"This weekend we plan to have a couple of drinks in a nice salsa bar on Yongjia Road near Hengshan Road. You should join us if you like."

"That sounds like a nice idea; I'll send you a text message in the next few days." I confirmed.

At the entrance of the compound, we both waived a taxi to the side of the street. Raphael to another day in office, while I asked the taxi driver to drive me to IKEA. It was just after eight in the morning. The worst effect of the morning traffic is usually visible around nine in the morning when highways are occupied with endless traffic jams.

After driving out of Dongxin Road, I asked the driver to take the elevated highway south so we could avoid a hundred red traffic lights on our way to IKEA. It's amazing how this city comes to life. Most people leave their compound walking to the nearest subway or bus station. The Shanghai subway system absorbs millions of passengers per day on their way to work. It's better to be in the subway before seven-thirty in the morning unless you want to experience the feeling of being packed like a sardine in a tin. Propounding a Shanghai subway ride around eight-thirty in the morning usually gives you that satisfaction.

Meanwhile, the taxi continued the way onto the elevated highway, providing me with a clear city view. The weather was nice, with the sun comfortably decorating the Pudong horizon. Closer, I could distinguish commercial and residential building construction sites helping to fuel the fourteen per cent economic growth the set by the government for this year. Soon I saw the Grand Gateway towers getting closer. Easy to recognise with their iconic diagonally chopped rooftops, so you're always able to locate yourself in this concrete jungle called Shanghai.

The taxi driver sorted to the left side of the highway and reverted to street level. He stopped the taxi at the designated taxi drop-off location. From there it's easy to enter IKEA directly. For me, a visit to IKEA consists of as many as possible shortcuts to minimise the number of impulse purchases. I avoid just following the endless shopping route exhibiting every dark corner of the IKEA building. And how many times did I intent to visit IKEA just to purchase one or two things and came home with a bag full? Way too many times.

While I walked up the stairs, I remembered the one time I came up with the brilliant idea to visit IKEA on a Saturday afternoon. New and naive as I was at that time, I never expected to witness the thousands of people wandering around the shopping floor that afternoon. I mean, I just arrived from a three thousand inhabitant village located in the south west of the Netherlands. Oddly enough though the majority of people had no purchase intentions at all. One long human traffic jam was caused by visitors moving utterly slow from one to the next home display. Throughout this spectacle, people sleep ungraciously on beds and couches or just sit and watch other people slowly moving by. Sometimes three generations worth of family would occupy an entire IKEA living room to make plenty of pictures of the grandparents, parents and children in what is considered for many a luxury living environment. Witnessing this on a Saturday afternoon can be quite entertaining, or at least if you're not in a hurry for your next appointment.

Interestingly enough IKEA doesn't do anything against the army of people sleeping on showroom beds and couches. Yes, it can be a bit annoying if the bed you were looking for is occupied by two people who randomly choose that bed to do a nap. But IKEA understands as well that this is the best promotion a company can get. This Friday morning was different. Despite some older people chatting and enjoying a cup of tea in the restaurant area, there were not many people sharing the same idea as me. I followed the map to the products I was looking for but using as many as possible shortcuts towards the cash desks.

4

Huangpu District, Shanghai - 20:10

The subway was nearly empty on this Tuesday evening. The time was heading towards nine o'clock, and possibly most people were home already. The white TL light provided me with an unhealthy and tired look in the window in front of me, even though I dressed up and did not feel tired at all. To kill time, I tried to read and understand some of the Chinese characters in paper commercials on the wall. The air was now clearly fresher compared to a subway full of people in rush hour. The only sound I heard came from the driving subway, accelerating after a short stop and the scratching sound of the wheels changing to another rail. The computerised voice mentioned that we just left South Huangpi Road station, an indication for me that I almost arrived in Hengshan Road. The third stop from now would be the moment for me to depart from this train. Earlier today, I received a text message from Cecile that she is in Shanghai for a few days, and whether I was free to meet tonight.

Cecile was among the first the people I met after I arrived in Shanghai for my internship. Originally, she came from the city of Shantou, in the south Chinese province of Guangdong. Her dad owns a company in Shanghai, and she was visiting him during Chinese New Year together with a girlfriend. On the evening we first met I was having a drink with a girl in a Xintiandi bar. Cecile was confident enough to approach us directly and ask Chrissy whether she could dance with me for a while. Chrissy must have felt awkward, but her moderate intentions with me made her agree with that, so we danced and talked for a while. We exchanged numbers and agreed to meet again for dinner within the next few days. We first did so together with her friend in a Western restaurant in Grand Gateway, which was a nice evening to get to know each other. Both Cecile and her friend Susy had the intention to study in America and had a clear target in mind to make the American dream happen.

After this, I recall a dinner alone with Cecile in Shangri-la on the Pudong side of the Bund, where we, among other dishes enjoyed a hundred Euro lobster in soft cheese sauce. This culinary highlight added significantly to the restaurant bill, but never mind. I was on a student pension from the Netherlands and earned money out of my internship so actually had more money to spend back then compared to now. Throughout her Chinese New Year holiday in Shanghai, we grew closer to each other, leading to her staying over one night at my shared apartment where we had sex for the first time. It only happened once as her dad was a bit protective, and she would be leaving Shanghai back to Shantou to start her second semester in school. By text message and an occasional call, we stayed in touch over the next couple of weeks.

That was even when she confessed that at the time we met, she was actually still in her last year of high school and just sixteen years old. This, in addition to her claiming to be eighteen years old. She was scared I considered her too young, was her explanation. I was twenty-four at that time. Later I learned that in addition to America, where laws can be stringent - the Chinese law defines the age of consent for sexual activity to be fourteen years, regardless of gender or sexual orientation.

Meanwhile, the subway slowed down, and I heard the computerised voice mentioning that we were nearing Hengshan Road. The subway was basically empty now. Probably the next stop in Xujiahui people who finished dinner will float the subway to follow their way home in the Southern part of Shanghai. I stood up and kept myself in balance while the subway came to a stop. The door lights started flickering, and a beep sound made clear that the doors would open soon. While I step onto the subway station platform, the same voice reminded passengers once again that we arrived in Hengshan Road. It seemed I was the only one on the platform. How could a city like Shanghai be so quiet? While the subway gained speed and left the station, I saw one more person with Hengshan Road as destination. In the bright white platform lights, I could identify her as a female person. She was about fifty meters away. While I was looking for an exit to leave the platform, I heard

"Hey Victor!" When I heard the voice, I realised it was Cecile.

We walked towards each other, still the only persons on the subway platform.

"Wow, what a coincidence," Cecile remarked while she gave me a quick but firm hug.

"I already knew you were in the same subway because I could smell your Aqua Di Gio fragrance."

There must have been three wagons in between us. Cecile remarkably matured to a young adult in the six months that we did not see each other. Or was it possibly the way she dressed-up tonight - wearing black high heels, which enabled her to reach my shoulder now? She was wearing a skinny black and sleeveless dress, short but not too short and she backed her necklines under a layer of black curly hair. She held a tiny and glimmery handbag in her right hand, just big enough for a phone and some cash. I recognised Dior's J'adore as her choice of perfume for tonight.

"You look stunning, Cecile." I complimented. She looked up and smiled at me, a little bit shy. "What brought you to Shanghai this time?"

"I am visiting my dad. I'm only here for a couple of days, though." Her English is remarkably good as the result of her hard work to score high grades in English. That will make it easier for her to be selected by good universities in America.

"How have you been?" I informed while we were standing on the escalator on our way up to street level. Cecile was one step in front of me, making her almost as tall as I.

"I am doing fine," Cecile answered. "Tired of school, though, I just had to get out of Shantou for a while."

I remembered Cecile as a bit more outrageous compared to an average Chinese high school student. She didn't mind drinking and occasionally smoked those super slim sized cigarettes. She had her clear opinion on politics and other big world issues we couldn't actually change anything about. She was clever and full of confidence. Why would she otherwise approach a guy in a bar while he is having a drink with another girl? Many other girls would give up by only the picture of that.

"Where would you like to go for dinner?" I asked.

"Do you know any nice dinner spots around here? It's quite late already, and it's Tuesday evening, so I am not sure what is still open."

While looking at her high-heels, I could imagine Cecile not to be in for endless walks in search of a restaurant. We could do two things: or walk a few blocks with the hope that something is still open, or take a taxi and drive to a restaurant of which I know it's good and still open.

"Let's grab a taxi," I proposed. "Let's go to Plaza 66. There is a nice restaurant nearby."

After arriving on street level, the reasonably quiet Hengshan Road provided a surplus of taxis. We only had to raise our arm in the sky, and the first taxi stopped. We got in and Cecile explained in Chinese that we were heading to Plaza 66. The preconception was all written over the taxi drivers' face: that foreign guy must be her sugar daddy. It was the most expensive shopping mall in Shanghai, if not in China. One could only find the top of luxury brands inside such as Chanel, Emporio Armani, Dior, Louis Vuitton and Gucci. Only walking there makes people think you are rich.

I saw Cecile looking outside the taxi window. The neon lights of retail building facades lighted up her face, while she was witnessing people on the street.

"There are so many people in Shanghai," she said and asked: "Since when are you back, and why you decided to come back here?"

I thought for a second.

"It's been three weeks now. I came back because I realised that Shanghai could represent the best opportunity for me to start my career. America and Europe are affected by that as well. Headcounts are frozen in most multinational companies, but

China's economy still shows growth. China could, in fact, even benefit from a crisis in the Western world as demand for cheaper products will increase."

Cecile looked to me as if I explained her the principles of economics.

"Yes, you may be right in that. But supply could be affected as well."

"Correct, but there is still a growth prediction of nine point six per cent this year. As a result of the global crisis, this will be lower than last year when the Chinese economy still grew with fourteen per cent, but it is so much better compared to the shrinking economies in the West."

This is what I liked about her. Not many Chinese high school students would survive in a talk like this. I'm sure she will be doing well in America.

"How's the university selection going?" I informed.

"Oh, no outcome yet. I applied for three universities. The first one is New York University, as I told you before. The other two are in Los Angeles and Chicago. But I really hope I can go to NYU."

I remembered that. Although she never visited the United States, she is a big fan of New York. During my internship, we used to talk about New York sometimes, while I shared pictures of the six days I spend there before my exchange semester at Texas State University.

"When will you hear whether you are accepted or not?" I asked.

Cecile stared for a couple of seconds at the driver seat in front of her.

"Within now and three months, I should have the answer."

It is interesting to consider that many Chinese have an American dream when it comes to studying. Many of them will stay in the country after they graduate and move on for a master's degree. It's been estimated that seventy per cent of the Chinese students who study abroad won't come back to China anymore. I'm not too sure whether I see Cecile ever again after her relocation to the United States. Probably not.

"What makes you want to go to study in America?"

"Well, the education system is much better compared to China, and I will be able to improve my English significantly."

Cecile replied while I recognised the neighbourhood close to Plaza 66. I had to pay attention now to direct the driver to the right location.

"Yes, I agree. But you can go to Canada or the United Kingdom as well. Or Australia? By moving to the United Kingdom, you will learn traditional English."

"I just love America," Cecile interrupted me. "From what I have seen in the movies, it looks like a wonderful country to me."

That is how American dreams are created these days. Out of movies.

"Why don't you consider studying in Europe?" I asked.

"It will be much more interesting from a travelling point of view. America is just America. One country with fifty-one states. Europe is a Union with twenty-six countries. While driving through Europe, you will experience the culture and change of the landscape with every country you pass." And I continued;

"A two-hour flight from Amsterdam brings you to Vienna, Rome, Barcelona, or for example Marseille. All those places have their own distinguished culture, food and language."

"The individual States in America represent a different culture too," said Cecile.

"Yes, but not so insignificant compared to European countries. For sure, Texas is like no other state in America and will be hard to compare with California or New York. But after all you are still in the same country."

"You know?" I continued, "I honestly think the attractive force of the American Dream led many Chinese not realising that once you are in the European Union - which means with either a passport or permanent resident status - you can enjoy the systems and benefits of living and working in twenty-six member countries. That opportunity would be much more appealing to me, personally."

Cecile looked at me as if I just told her something completely new.

"That's true," she said. "But Europe is still not like America."

"Europe is looking good in movies too, have you seen *Oceans Twelve* with Brad Pitt and George Clooney? Or *The Tourist* with Angelina Jolie and Johnny Depp? Just to name a few. They are recorded in Italy." I continued: "The Bourne movies will take you all over Europe, as Jason Bourne is a former secret agent on the run and looking for his identity."

It seems I was giving too much information for Cecile to do something with.

"No," was her only answer. "But I watched *Vicky Christina Barcelona* a couple of times. I really love that movie."

"I've seen that one too, it is nice indeed."

Meanwhile, the taxi slowed down, indicating that he was looking for the right street number to drop us off.

"It's there,"

I pointed to a white and green logo light-up logo on the facade of the restaurant. The taxi stopped, and the driver told us the price we had to pay, while the fapiao - which is pinyin for receipt was still being printed. I paid the driver and opened the door. We were in one of the side streets near Plaza 66. There was noise above us caused by the air-conditioning systems of the shopping mall releasing their heat. The street had some trash laying around, mostly plastic cups and paper napkins, probably from the takeaway counter of a fast-food restaurant a couple of locations away. From judging this street, nothing looked like you stood next to Shanghai's most expensive shopping mall. This looked more like a backstreet of Bangkok. I offered my hand to let Cecile go out of the car.

"Thank you. You are still a gentleman."

Once she got out, she was standing right in front of me, still holding my right hand and our bodies were touching as if we would start a dance together. I could feel her breathing. She looked up and stared me in the eyes for a couple of seconds, as if she was looking for the right words to say during an intimate moment like this. I stepped back and softly pulled Cecile towards me, said thanks to the driver in Mandarin and closed the taxi door.

"There is the restaurant,"

I said while I felt a little bit bad to break the flow of this moment. I developed quite a big appetite as it was nearly ten o'clock already. Cecile firmly held my hand while we walked over the uneven sidewalk. Holding hands now occurred rather from safety than from an intimacy point of view. Some tiles were broken or even missing, but it did not seem like any construction was going on here. Many roads are facing construction sites to upgrade the city for the upcoming Shanghai Expo; this street could actually use such a metamorphose. The people who saw us walking could only assume we were just another couple finding our way to a bar to enjoy a drink. And even though Shanghai is pretty safe to walk around late at night, this was one of the streets I would not let Cecile walk by herself. Tonight, she was quite an eye-catcher with her high heels and skinny dress. Some people might have bad intentions with her.

I opened the restaurant door and let Cecile go in first. Given this time of the night, there were enough tables for us to choose from. Both walls of the restaurant were completely made out of historical orange bricks, giving it an authentic look. Both sides of the restaurant had a chain of tables where couples could eat, while in the middle a couple of tables were based for groups of four people. There was a little stage in the back of the restaurant with a big black shiny piano. It looked unplayed now but usually from ten o'clock onwards somebody would be playing live piano music for guests to enjoy during their dinner. The atmosphere was intimate as a result of the dimmed lights and candles on each of every table.

"Where would you like to take a seat?" I asked Cecile. "In the middle, or the side section?"

Cecile looked around.

"Let's take the table there in the middle section. The seats look more comfortable." After we were seated, the waitress approached us with two menus.

"Can I first offer you a drink?"

"What would you like to drink to start with?" I passed the question on to Cecile.

"Are you in for wine? Red wine?" Cecile nodded. I browsed the menu.

"Can we have two glasses of the Poliziano Chianti please?" The waitress confirmed our choice of wine and gave us some more time to choose our food.

"Are you familiar with red wines?" I asked Cecile. Actually, a stupid question, I realised the moment the words came out of my mouth. How can you expect a Chinese girl, just seventeen years old to know something about European wines? Cecile looked at me with a similar expression on her face.

"Not really," she said while she went with her hand through her long-curled hair.

"Ok," as I tried to explain;

"The reason I choose this one is that usually, Chianti represents a very drinkable fresh, fruity and versatile wine. They go very well with antipasto, pasta dishes, risotto and pizza. Easy to combine."

Unlike my brother who is working in the wine business, I wasn't very much into wine neither. I just tried to act like I knew my way around in a wine list. Don't get me wrong; I can distinguish a couple of good ones on a wine menu based on the grape type. I could well pair a wine with a dish.

"Personally, I love red wine with characteristics of berry fruit, cassis, chocolate and cigar box." Cecile frowned her eyebrows.

"Cigar box characteristics?"

I nodded. "More powerful than Chianti."

"How do you know about wines?" Cecile asked as if she could read my mind.

"As a student, I used to work in restaurants, both in kitchens and as a waiter. That provided a good environment for me to try and learn about wines. I started working at age fourteen in the kitchen as a dishwasher, continued this in several restaurants until I was twenty-two and moved to America for my study."

"So, you were already drinking wine when you were fourteen years old?" Cecile asked with a smile on her face.

"No, probably not. At that age, I had a beer or Coca Cola after work."

"Chinese students usually don't have part-time jobs while they are studying." Cecile explained, "The Chinese education system forces us to score high grades, which is only possible if you fully commit to studying. The reason I love to visit Shanghai is that I can leave my boring life in Shantou. Do you know I only have Sunday afternoon off? We literally study six and a half days per week from the early morning till late evening. Even if there are no classes, there is enough homework to do, or my parents send me to after-school study groups."

"Really? That is in such a different contrast with how students live in Europe."

"The reason is that we have an annual exam to take, usually around June. The score of this single exam determines to which school you have access. The better your score, the better your school. Basically, the only thing Chinese parents care about is the well-being of their child in school. Their only child represents the future of the family. The better the education, the better job and marriage partner they find in life. This is what Chinese parents care about. Actually, my mum doesn't like me to go to Shanghai. She prefers that I just stay in Shantou and focus on my school. But my dad lives here, so I want to see him sometimes."

"Yes, I can understand that."

"You live here for a while now Victor, how long in total?"

"Nearly one year, if you include my internship time. Shanghai is… special, I guess? It's like no other city in the world I lived in before. This city has so incredibly much to offer, yet you can feel totally lonely and lost sometimes. I wonder how that is possible. I grew up in a village with nearly three thousand people and I never felt like that."

"That is because villages are more like small communities," Cecile said.

"In cities, there is much more competition. Everybody wants the best and in order to get it, people become competitive. See how the housing price in Shanghai is increasing?

It is high now, but there will be a day that only the absurd rich can afford to live in downtown."

I realised that this was quite a clever conclusion from a seventeen-year-old. What are they teaching the kids here in school nowadays? In the corner of my eye, I saw the waitress approaching our table with two glasses of wine. After she placed them on the table and left, I lifted one of the glasses and said:

"To what do we cheer tonight?"

"To us, and our friendship," Cecile said.

"That sounds like something worth cheering for."

We both took a sip from our wine.

"How do you like it?" I asked.

"It tastes nice, a bit like grape juice," Cecile smiled.

"Oh, don't tell that to the Italian vineyard owners, they might not appreciate this kind of comments so much."

"Hey, let's decide on what to order, otherwise the kitchen will be closed soon."

The pianist started playing on the background. I recognised the tones of a piano version of *Mad World*, a song by Gary Jules. I hummed the lyrics of the song on the rhythm of the piano tones. By doing so, I somehow realised a Shanghai scene in this song. People travel to nowhere and everywhere with no expression on their faces. As well, you'd be surprised how in a city of twenty-four million people, you still see familiar faces.

"What food would you like to order?" I asked Cecile.

"What are you into?" Her dark eyes were browsing the menu.

"I'm considering between a Caesar salad and the scallops," She concluded.

"But I'm not very hungry."

No surprise when considering her skinny body, I thought to myself. She did not appeal voracious to me.

"If the Caesar salad is a meal salad, I will choose that one," Cecile concluded.

"That's alright, I will go for the roasted lamb ribs."

I needed a bit more protein and layer in case we would still have a drink afterwards. Since Cecile left Shanghai, we did not have frequent contact. Maybe because she was busy with school, or possibly because I belonged to her Shanghai world.

"How often do you see your dad?"

"A few times per year only, my mum stays in Shantou to take care of my sister and me. Chinese New Year is the only time per year our family is together."

That's how many Chinese families are often divided. Either the husband or the wife is working elsewhere, earning money for the family. This is what is causing the Chinese insurrection twice per year, once during Chinese New Year, and the second time during the October holidays. During each of these national holidays, hundreds of millions of people will travel to their beloved hometown to stay with their family. Imagine how the train and bus stations and airports look like the days before Chinese New Year. Meanwhile, the waitress found our table again to get our orders.

"We would like to have the Caesar salad, and the roasted lamb ribs please,"

The waitress nodded and left again. All out of nothing, Cecile asked:

"Did you sleep with any other girls since I stayed over in your apartment?"

I took a sip of wine. Why is she asking this? Didn't we just cheer on our friendship? Why is she leading our conversation into this awkward direction?

"I know you must get a lot of attention from girls here in Shanghai, Victor. Back in Holland you are the thirteenth in a dozen of Western faces. Don't get me wrong, you're handsome. But here you are standing out, catching attention by just crossing the street, or while paying for groceries. And not just because of your height." Cecile continued.

"Are girls approaching you in public?"

"Yes sometimes, I have to admit."

I looked away, trying to give Cecile an impression that I didn't want to continue the recent course of our conversation.

"Then do you take advantage of it?"

"How do you mean; do I take advantage of it?" I tried.

"Do you invite them over to your apartment, just like you did with me? Do you have sex with them if they offer themselves to you?"

"Listen, Cecile, I am sure there were numerous occasions I could have done that yes. But unlike other expats or students who work and study here temporarily, I have a long-term focus when it comes to relationships. It's easy to have pointless sex with a girl you don't care about, but what will you gain from that?"

I felt embarrassed to have this type of conversation with a seventeen-year-old girl. But she asked for it. She started it for God's sake. She suddenly floated our table with suspicion. What would be the easiest way to get out of this uncomfortable conversation?

Just confess by saying yes? Although there is actually nothing to confess. We never had a serious relationship. Provided the distance between Shanghai and Shantou, and Cecile's American dream I always considered the long-term success of a relationship quite small. If I say no she wouldn't believe me anyway, probably suspecting me of trying to look good in front of her.

"If I decide to sleep with a girl, it's none of anybody's business," I started.

"I have no responsibility to pay to anybody."

"So you did?"

"Yes, I did."

Cecile looked away, searching for distance which she found in a spot on one of the restaurant walls. I could see a disillusioned expression on her face. I hove a sigh.

"Did you come here with any objectives Cecile?"

She swigged a large portion of her wine, leaving only a bit there to enjoy while eating food. Having our dinner served would probably give me a chance to change the course of our conversation.

"What do you mean with do I come here with any objectives?" Cecile asked.

"Well, testing grounds for anything more than friendship?"

She didn't say anything. And thank God, there arrived my opportunity to change the unenviable topic of our conversation. I saw the waitress walking into our direction, carrying two plates in her hands.

"The Caesar salad is for...?"

"The lady please."

"The roasted lamb rack is for me."

The top of the lamb rack was still sizzling, creating a wonderful smell of herbs and garlic. It was even served on a warm plate, pretty uncommon in China. The dish came with two side dishes. Mushed potatoes and sprouts, together with gravy to pore in case one wished to add extra taste. Cecile stared at her dish. She didn't say anything after I asked her whether there was any other particular reason for us to meet tonight beyond friendship.

"It's looking delicious, don't you think Cecile?"

I said in a first attempt to push our conversation back to the comfortable level during the beginning of the evening. It started so well.

"Yes, I think so."

"Hey," she continued, "Why don't you tell me about America?"

As radically as she changed the conversation topic from which food to choose to how many girls I recently slept with, she bounced back to a safe left-wing topic - probably as she realised that we wouldn't enjoy a long evening out if we continued like this.

"What would you like to know about America? Travel, food, people, cities, university life?"

"University life," Cecile answered while she tasted her Caesar salad.

"But before that, shall we order another glass of wine?"

I looked at our glasses. The conversation we had a couple of minutes ago absorbed a significant amount of Cecile's wine.

"Will you be okay with another glass of wine? I'm not going to carry you home, you know that, right?"

"Yes, I can drink wine, Victor. Don't you worry."

As the waitress passed by, I ordered two glasses of the same and we continued the conversation.

"University life in America was possibly the best time in my life from a social aspect. You know I grew up in a village with three thousand people, in addition to this Texas State University enrolled around twenty-seven thousand students back in 2006. Roughly twenty per cent of them live on campus or in University-owned homes. It's a small village itself. You probably never going to have so many friends in your life again, even though a university campus would vanish in comparison with Shantou, counting a population of 5 million. There are so many parties, where outsiders are often welcome as well. The best are home and fraternity parties. I remember one in a decent neighbourhood, where there must have been at least a hundred fifty people spread out through the garden and home.

"They must have many friends," Cecile added.

"No, people hear about it and invite other friends, everybody brings their own drinks, and you have a good time together. I remember that particular party had a huge block of ice, diagonally installed with a trench in the middle. There were people with bottles of liquor at the top side, poring the liquor from the top on the ice block. It poured down through that trench, and on the down part you only had to open your mouth, and the liquor just flowed into your mouth. I never saw anything like that in my life. Eventually, the cops came to break up the party. Probably after noise complaints from the neighbours. We've had probably three or four parties per week." Cecile looked amazed.

"With such a lifestyle, how did you manage to study well?"

"By applying one simple rule. Study when everybody else is studying, party when everybody else is partying. That helped me through the semester."

Cecile giggled while I continued:

"What I liked as well was the food, not the quality in particular, but the choice we had every day. The University offered a buffet for breakfast, lunch and dinner. Would you believe that I gained about eight kilos' during my time abroad in Texas?"

"No. You're so skinny," Cecile replied.

"Within one year after America, where I spent six months in the Netherlands to finish my seventh semester at the HZ University and another six months in Shanghai for my internship at Philips, I lost twelve kilos'."

"How did you do that? Did you stop eating?" Cecile asked.

"No, but I obviously consumed fewer calories. I went from an egg, bacon and brownies with syrup breakfast in America to a three RMB egg with a vegetable pancake in Shanghai. Then a three-course buffet lunch was replaced by a small selection of rice, veggies, and fish or meat in the Philips canteen. It must have been only ten per cent of the calories I took in for lunch before. Do you see? That's why you Chinese are so skinny."

"Most of us are yes," Cecile agreed. "But the younger generations are getting fatter now. For one reason that overweighted children are considered a sign of prosperity, the other reason is that grandparents are often raising the children because the parents both have to work. Those grandparents are spoiling them so much by taking them out for lunch or dinner to KFC or McDonald's."

"Ah yes, I suddenly remind a chart I once saw where the Chinese obesity trend today shows exactly the same trend during the eighties in America. Sooner or later, China will have the most overweighted people in the world. But that's a relative fact of course as China represents one point three billion people."

I suddenly realised we were the only guests still in the restaurant. One other table with four people just left. Two other couples left too. The pianist still played songs, creating a comfortable environment to enjoy dinner. The roasted lamb was just perfect, a bit crispy on the outside but soft and medium-rare on the inside. The warm plate kept the lamb warm but did not overcook it.

"Would you like to try a piece of the lamb Cecile?" I asked.

"It's really delicious." Cecile looked at my plate.

"Yes please, I'd love to." I cut off a slice of lamb and gave her a bite. Her face got the expression of a connoisseur while she was searching for the right words to describe the taste experience.

"That is indeed delicious," she concluded. "Next time we'll enjoy dinner together I will try this lamb dish as well."

But... next time? I realised that this might even be the last time we ever see each other. What are the chances that we will meet again after Cecile flies off to America? What are the chances she will anyway come back? She is not really the type to start working in China after her graduation. I checked my watch. It was just after ten-thirty, the evening was still reasonably young. I noticed that the restaurant manager already sent some of the staff home. Since the last twenty or so minutes, the pianist only played for us, as we were the only guests left in the restaurant. I appreciated the way how the restaurant manager dealt with this situation, where I am sure some staff or owners would become pushy by switching on the general lights or placing your bill on the table because they want to go home.

"Are you still in for a desert Cecile?"

"Hmm, maybe not here? There are some nice sweet Hong Kong dessert restaurants we can decide to go later. Are you still hungry?"

"Not really, I'm just alright now."

"Let's ask for the bill, so the restaurant staff can go home as well,"

Cecile waved to the waitress and said Mai Tan, which in Mandarin Chinese literally means buy bill. We raised our glasses in preparation to make a toast.

"On your time in America," I said.

"I'm sure you're going to do well out there." Cecile's eyes were sparkling.

"I can't wait to go there," she confirmed as if I did not understand that yet. Meanwhile, the waitress reached our table with the bill. I put four red bills of one hundred RMB on the table, and the waitress walked away to prepare my change.

"Do you know any of the desert restaurants around here?" I asked Cecile.

"No, but we can have a walk and see where we go next. Shanghai is a city that never sleeps. There is always somewhere we can go."

That's true, I thought. There are people on the street at any given the time of day. After midnight you see people leaving bars, restaurants and KTV's. From four o'clock in the morning and onwards, you see trash and raw material collectors driving around on their tricycles and the older generation doing morning exercises in groups or individually. The waitress came back with the change.

We stood up and said thanks to the staff and the piano player. I opened the door for Cecile and followed her path on the way out - or her perfume actually led me.

"Shall we go left or right?" Cecile asked when we were standing on the sidewalk. I thought for a few seconds. Given Cecile's high heels, we wouldn't be able to walk long distances, without taking another taxi.

"Let's have a look in Plaza 66," I suggested. "There is a nightclub called Muse; it must still be open."

"Have you been there before?" Cecile asked.

"Muse has several locations all over Shanghai. I haven't visited this particular one." As we walked the dark street behind Plaza 66, I looked upstairs to the characteristic towers. The illuminated transparent top reflected itself in the low hanging clouds.

"Are you still in for dessert?" I asked Cecile.

"No, I have had enough food."

While we walked to West Nanjing Road cars passed by, mostly taxis at this time of the evening. Shanghai counts roughly fifty thousand taxi's, shared by two drivers to pay the lease it cost to maintain a taxi. Every given driver takes a shift every other day, so you can always assume that most of the taxis are always in operation. I've once heard that drivers have to make six hundred RMB per day to break even on the lease expense, this won't include petrol yet. Including petrol, you're looking at nine hundred RMB. Based on one month where they work fifteen long days, not like you and I ten to twelve hours per day - they get a hard-earned six thousand RMB. Based on exchange rate currency in 2008, this was about six hundred Euro. While I was thinking about this, a cool breeze filled the street. Cecile grabbed my arm and held herself close to me.

"I'm feeling a bit cold," She said. Even though she felt cold, her warm hand had a soothing effect on my arm.

"Yes, it's becoming a bit chilly now. Would you like to wear my coat?" I offered.

"Won't you feel cold then?" Cecile said in return.

"I'll be fine, don't worry." I covered Cecile's shoulders with my coat.

"I like Shanghai by night," Cecile said.

"Why?"

"Because of the thousands of lights everywhere and there are not so many people on the street."

I could only agree with that. We were literally surrounded by lights, mostly from residential or office tower windows. The majority of them have white light, while you can distinguish the luxury hotels by their warm lights.

"Less cars, fewer people... Why can't Shanghai always be like this?"

"Then it wouldn't be Shanghai," I answered.

"This city is synonym to a certain degree of chaos. Most of the time, organized chaos, though. Not as disastrous as in Jakarta or Mumbai."

While we walked to the mall's entrance, I could see our reflection in the shop window between bags and accessories of Louis Vuitton. This part of the mall even looks like a giant Louis Vuitton suitcase. The edges of the wall were covered in the famous LV pattern in suitcase shape. Quite an eye-catcher. And so were we. Or at least Cecile was. When I opened the door of the Plaza 66 mall, the house music beats of the on the sixth floor welcomed us. Such in contrast with the live piano music performed in the shopping mall at daytime. Muse security pointed us to the elevators, and the higher the elevator went up, the noisier the house music became. When the doors opened, we entered a little hallway leading towards the main entrance of the club. It did not seem very crowded, but for sure it wouldn't just be the two of us out there. Even though we walked indoors now, Cecile continued to hold my arm as if it was something completely natural. As if we were in a relationship. While I looked at my arm, she turned her dark eyes up as if she silently asked for permission. I smiled but did not say anything. It felt comfortable.

Muse is a nightclub like every other nightclub in Shanghai. Lots of tables, a bar and a small dance floor. Smart choice considering that dancing people do not spend money. The tables usually come with a minimum charge. Depending on the size, which is from four to twelve or even sixteen persons. During weekends, all tables are booked. Walking in and hoping for a table is risky. As this was a Tuesday evening, not even half of the tables were occupied. As well the minimum charge was just two hundred RMB, so that's easy to cover with two persons without getting drunk. Our table provided a nice view of the bar and the dance floor. Nobody took an initiative to dance yet, as the guests all stayed at their table to play Common Jiuling, a simple drinking game with four dices and a cup. One person shakes the dimes under a cup, but not before the other table members guess the total number of accumulated dots. The persons guessing wrong will have to drink. Now you even understand why almost every bar and nightclub standard have a cup with dimes on the table. While I was witnessing this, one of the bar ladies approached us with a menu. I browsed through the cocktails.

"What are you into Cecile?" I asked. She asked me the same question in reverse.

"I am actually in for a cocktail of something."

My standard choice when it came to cocktails was Manhattan. It's made from whiskey mixed with red martini and a swimming cherry.

"I'll have the Manhattan," I answered.

"Me too," Cecile said.

"Do you know what a Manhattan is made from?"

She searched the menu directly, hoping to find the ingredients.

"No," She answered. "It's not exactly lemonade," I ensured her.

"But if you like to try it too, go ahead. Two Manhattan's, please."

The waitress nodded and walked back to the bar. It shouldn't take too long for the drinks to arrive as the six bartenders didn't have anything to do.

"Have you gone back to Xintiandi after we met each other there?" Cecile asked me.

"Yes, a couple of times."

"To visit a bar?"

"Yes, and I can remember enjoying a coffee on a Sunday afternoon."

"I like Xintiandi," Cecile said.

"I love the atmosphere of the traditional mid-nineteenth century Chinese homes. Now everybody lives in apartments. We don't have anything like this in Shantou."

"Xintiandi was actually the site location of the first congress of the Chinese Communist Party, did you know that?"

Cecile shook no.

"It used to be a normal neighbourhood like everywhere else. But these days the houses serve as bookstores, bars, restaurants, shops, and cafes. Some of the apartments in and around Xintiandi are among the most expensive properties in the world with prices higher than New York, Tokyo and London. For this, some redevelopment had to be done - as houses were renovated and some demolished and eventually rebuild. As a result, three and a half thousand Shanghainese families had to be relocated to other parts of the city."

Cecile looked up.

"This can only happen in China."

At the bar, I saw two Manhattan's waiting to be picked up by the waitress. She was talking to guests at one of the other tables. As they were laughing it probably had to be a funny topic. Cecile saw it as well and reacted a bit irritated.

"How long is she going to let our Manhattan's stand over there?"

"Let me try to catch her attention," I said, and I waved my hand into the air. It had an immediate effect. The waitress looked at me, and I pointed to the Manhattan's. She put her hand in front of her mouth and looked back at us. Immediately she walked to the bar to bring our drinks, with Cecile not giving her any look. Cecile took a big sip of her drink.

"Hey, this isn't lemonade ok?" I said.

"You have to learn to enjoy it by taking little sips."

Cecile looked at me but did not seem to care. She was searching in her purse. I could not imagine losing anything inside that purse, given the small size of it. Suddenly she threw a pack of super slim cigarettes on the table. She continued to search.

"Where is my lighter?" She asked.

"Otherwise use the matchbox on the table, laying over there." I pointed.

Cecile opened the pack of cigarettes and put one between her red lips. She scratched the match on the side of the matchbox, which instantly caught fire. The light of the flame illuminated her face. She instantly took a deep hit of her cigarette and released herself. The table was covered with smoke. Cecile just literally set the last chance of us kissing each other on fire, I thought. I'm not going to kiss and end up with an ashtray taste in my mouth.

"Do you want it?" Cecile asked and held her pack of cigarettes in front of me.

"No thanks," I said. "It's not healthy to smoke, and particularly not in Shanghai."

"Why?"

"Because the damaging effect on your lungs is more significant with the considerable air quality here."

Cecile looked at me and to her cigarette.

"Well, I am not smoking a lot actually. Just when I go out."

She took another sip of her Manhattan. And a new hit of her cigarette. It seemed she wanted to taste both as good as possible. She abruptly looked less clear out of her eyes. She looked me into the eye, but it was as if she looked behind me on the wall.

"Are you alright, Cecile?" She did not answer and bottomed up her Manhattan. Her cigarette was only finished half, but she pressed it out in the ashtray.

"I feel dizzy."

I thought about her diet tonight. Two glasses of red wine, a salad and a Manhattan. And a cigarette but that doesn't count on food or alcohol. She seemed fine until she lighted up that damn cigarette.

"Would you like me to order some water for you, Cecile?"

She looked at me, but her facial expression was even less clear compared to a minute ago.

"Nnno..." She said.

"What else did you eat today? Did you have breakfast or lunch?"

"Only... b... breakfast, a little."

This did not look good.

"You either should have eaten more today or with such little food in your body, don't drink alcohol at all Cecile."

She looked at me with a disapproving face as if I were her dad talking to her. The tough young lady from just two hours ago suddenly looked like a seventeen-year-old girl who had too much to drink.

"Let's go home. I think that'll be better for us and your safety."

It looked like Cecile agreed with me, she instantly searched for her bag, which was right next to her on the sofa. With a bit of difficulty, she stood up, but I could see that she had difficulties standing straight. And her high heels did not make it easier for her to walk normally.

"Let's go outside and find a taxi."

After all, Cecile was only able to walk with my support, so I put my arm around her, and we walked in moderate speed to the exit. Outside was a small line of taxi's waiting for drunks to arrive out of Muse. Taxi driver must be an awesome job around this time of the day. I opened the door and lifted Cecile inside on the backseat of the taxi.

"Bye…" She said and looked up.

"What?" I answered. "Do you think I just let you go like this?"

I would never forgive myself waking up the next morning and reading in the news about a taxi driver who sexually abused a drunk young lady on a desolate car park in a Shanghai suburb - before possibly killing her and dumping the body. I thought about her dad. He was probably waiting for Cecile to come home. Every dad would pray that nobody would harm his daughter in this condition. "Come on, move up to the other side of the couch. I will make sure you arrive home safely. That's the least I can do.

"Tell me, where do you stay?"

"In Xujiahui…" Cecile answered with a soft voice.

"Yes, but where in Xujiahui? Do you know the street or compound name?

She suddenly said something in Chinese to the taxi driver who obeyed and started his car to this for me unknown location.

"How do you feel now?"

No reaction. The taxi driver made a sharp turn onto West Nanjing Road, driving to the direction of Huaihai Road and Hengshan Road. She just stared in the distance. The day just turned to Wednesday morning, and there was almost nobody on the street anymore. The majority of the population on the street is now represented by taxi drivers looking for passengers to enjoy a ride home. Shanghai's night scene dimmed down a bit as well. Skyscrapers become large dark structures, only to be distinguished by a couple of office floors that remain light-up - either for city scenery purposes or cleaning teams that are doing their work. The skyscraper tops seemed dark now and only to be recognised by aircraft warning lights going off and on. Even Hengshan Road was quiet. People with a job or family should be in bed already.

I looked at Cecile. She fell asleep, with her head resting on her right shoulder. I hope she will sleep it off at least until we arrive at her home. Then it's up to her dad on how to deal with her. How will he respond when he sees his daughter dropped off completely drunk by a foreigner? Is he going to blame me for this? The taxi driver made a couple of rights and left turns, and I had no idea anymore where we drove. Suddenly the taxi driver stopped. He said

"Dàole" meaning arrived in Mandarin Chinese.

I looked outside. I could not recognise anything. I poked Cecile, but she was still sleeping.

"The taxi driver tells us you are home." Cecile looked up, but she did not show any recognition towards the buildings on the other side of the street.

"No…" She said now with a hoarse voice.

"It's not here." I sighted.

"Okay, then tell the driver where you actually stay, please."

A short story in Chinese followed to the driver. Maybe it was a misunderstanding. Quite well possible. Chinese people sometimes lose each other on a slip of the tongue when a tone is incorrectly misspelt. The taxi driver seemed to understand it now. We started driving again. After two left turns, Cecile said she did not feel well, followed by a noise as if she could vomit instantly. I asked the taxi driver to stop, which he did in the middle of the road. I opened the car door at Cecile's side. I quickly pulled her hair and let her hang out of the car. It was right on time; all the vomit ended up on the street. This would at least save me an angry taxi driver.

"Are you done?"

I asked Cecile. She said something like yes. I closed the door and opened the window a bit so she could at least have some fresh air. A cool breeze instantly filled the car. The taxi kept on driving. I looked at the meter. We were nearing the seventy RMB already, which is nothing in comparison to take a taxi in Europe. Within downtown Shanghai, most taxi rides will cost you between twenty and thirty RMB. Meanwhile, I noticed that Cecile didn't feel well again. She opened the window and vomited through the window opening, at least again out of the car. Now the taxi driver looked a bit irritated. I could only hope it did not end up on the car's surface. A couple of blocks further down the road he told us again that we arrived, or maybe just because he wanted Cecile out of his car. Cecile looked up.

"This is not where I live either."

"Then what are you telling him? Do you actually know where you live? We are pointlessly driving around now for forty minutes."

"But we are close to where I live... I can walk back home from here."

"I don't think that is such a good idea, Cecile. You're barely able to walk right now." I thought for a couple of seconds. Trusting Cecile on her instincts and leaving her behind on the street in this drunken state of mind would be riskier than leaving her with a taxi driver.

"How about you stay with me tonight? At least I will be able to take care of you. I am not looking forward to driving around much longer in search of your home."

"Okay..." Cecile said.

The taxi driver seemed a bit annoyed by us now and asked in Chinese whether this was our final destination.

"So, do you want to let your dad know that you won't come home tonight?" She grabbed her phone, but it fell out of her hands onto the car seat. She tried again and typed a message. But not being able to control her phone well. I'm not sure whatever she texted to her dad was going to make him feel less worried about the whereabouts of his daughter.

"What did you tell him?" I asked.

"Ohh... That I'm staying over at a friend's home... Don't worry. He is fine with that." I instructed the driver to drive to Wuning Road, crossing Dongxin Road, where my apartment was located. The car window was still open, and Cecile fell asleep again. If her dad called her now, he would hear that something is wrong. I stared in front of me. Maybe this is just her strategy? Acting like she doesn't know anymore where she lives, stay with a friend, so her dad doesn't have to see her in this drunk situation? I'm sure he would limit her freedom in going out next time. Or eliminate it. Well, she just had two glasses of wine and a cocktail, and I warned her already to be careful. Drinking a mix of wine, whiskey and martini on an empty stomach while having a salad as dinner isn't such a good idea.

Meanwhile, we were back in a familiar part of Shanghai, nearby where I lived. We crossed the bridge over the Suzhou River, and in the far distance I could see the apartment towers from my compound already. From now, it would only take about five minutes until we were home. I had to think about Mr Lu, would he still be awake? He usually does not sleep early. I checked my watch. Nearly one o'clock. Probably yes. What would he think when he witnesses Cecile like this? He might think that I did this on purpose so I could take advantage of her. When we drove into Dongxin Road, the night market was still open. Mostly food and snacks were consumed at this time of the day. A nice barbecue smell soon spread inside the car. At the same time, I was hoping it would not be a reason for Cecile to vomit for the third time.

I asked the driver in Chinese to bring us to the front of the residential tower where I lived. This would minimise the chance that neighbours would see me and I did not expect Cecile to walk all the way from the compound entrance to the tower. Once we arrived, I paid for the fare - nearly one hundred and fifty RMB and apologised for all what happened to the taxi driver. He did not look as annoyed anymore compared to twenty minutes ago, probably because he just made sure that he kept his car clean on the inside. I stepped out and checked the door on Cecile's side, which surprisingly seemed clean as well.

"Cecile, wake up... We just arrived at my place."

She opened her eyes and seemed blinded by the warm light coming from the welcome hall next to us. She stretched herself out, and I offered her a hand to get out of the car. She still did not look very sober.

"How do you feel now?" I asked.

"Still dizzy... and sick."

"Come, I will support you while you walk."

I put my arm around her, said thanks to the taxi driver, closed the door and walked towards the entrance of the residential building. I pressed the button to go up. At this time of the day, the elevator opened immediately.

"We'll be up soon," I said while I searched for my keys.

Cecile had support now from the elevator wall. She looked at us in the mirror. Probably not a view to remember, if she could remember anything at all from what happened after Muse. The elevator doors opened, and we walked around the corner to the front door of my apartment. From here, I could not tell whether Mr Lu was still awake. The door made a cracking noise when I opened it just a little bit to check whether there was anybody in the living room. No. Luckily it was dark. Only a beam of light came from under Mr Lu's bedroom door, indicating that he was still awake. I directed Cecile to my bedroom, turned the lights on and closed the door. I let her rest on the edge of my bed.

"Here we are," I said.

She looked at me but did not say anything.

"I'll give you nightclothes you can wear, and perhaps it's a good idea to put a barrel next to your side of the bed in case you still have to vomit."

Cecile nodded in agreement. I left a t-shirt next to her on the bed and walked to the kitchen for a barrel. Once I came back into the bedroom, Cecile fell asleep again.

"Come, take off your shoes and wear your nightclothes before you step in bed. I will take a shower now."

I collected everything I needed to shower and left to the bathroom. I closed the diffused glass door and undressed. After a couple of minutes under the shower, I heard vomiting noises again from the bedroom. I could only hope she managed to find the barrel, so I did not have to clean the bed or the floor. I patiently finished my shower, dried myself, got dressed and walked back into the bedroom. Cecile managed to wear the nightclothes I left for her on the side of the bed.

"I had to vomit again."

"Yes, I could hear that from the shower. I'm glad all ended up in the barrel."

"You can go to sleep first Cecile, and I will clean this up."

I put her down in bed and pulled the cover over her.

"Good night. I hope you feel better tomorrow. Let me know if you need anything."

After cleaning the barrel, I returned it on her side next to the bed, dimmed the light and joined Cecile under the cover. She came closer to me, so close that I could feel her body against mine.

"I'm so sorry Victor..." Cecile whispered.

"I'm so sorry for what happened..."

I exhaled through my nose.

"Don't worry Cecile. I am not angry with you. This happens to all of us. Just try to learn from it."

Cecile sighed in a release. Meanwhile, I felt her arm over my chest. She moved a little bit closer again. She started kissing me on my mouth and neck.

"Cecile… do you think this is such a good idea? You're still drunk…"

Without saying anything, she stopped and held me until she fell asleep. She was breathing slowly now. I stared in the darkness. What an evening. I was glad to be back home and that thus far, everything went quite well. Tomorrow we would wake up and laugh about it, with Cecile hopefully feeling much better.

5

Xinhu Riverside Apartments - 7:40

The mornings were usually most difficult to deal with during the first few weeks. Facing the reality of not having a job, you're looking at yourself in the bathroom mirror, and you know exactly how this entire day will look like. From the bathroom, I walked up to the balcony where a humid flow of air welcomed me after I opened the door. I walked towards the balcony fence and saw compound residents leaving for work. It was something I could only dream about right now.

I followed my way back inside where I noticed my laptop still in sleeping mode on my desk. Curiosity was taking the lead over me. Would I have any response on the job applications I send out? So far, the reaction on my applications was far from satisfactory. Or to be more specific; no reaction at all. Up to this moment, I mainly used Zhaopin to search for open positions. The disadvantage for me is that most employers require a couple of years of experience and fluency in Chinese. This results in me not suitable for roughly eighty per cent of the jobs. You can imagine the competition for the remaining twenty per cent. I'm speaking now four languages and graduated with a bachelor's in International Business and Management Studies from the Netherlands. I spent a business exchange semester abroad at Texas State University and successfully did two internships in PricewaterhouseCoopers and Philips.

Still, it seemed no company was interested in giving this foreigner a chance. I opened my laptop, browsed to my email account and scrolled through the list of un-replied emails. Most of them were focussed on positions as a business analyst, sales and marketing managers, junior client consultants or even a relocation specialist job. I opened one of the emails I send out the day before. As far as I could judge, it was job-specific and listed a link with the required experience for the position. Still, nobody even dares to send me a kind rejection email.

From: Victor de Lange
To: Sasa Zhao
Send: Thursday September 10, 2008
Subject: Application for the position of Junior Client Coordinator

Dear Sasa,

Regarding the vacancy on the Zhaopin website, I am writing to apply for the position of Junior Client Coordinator. I am a fresh International Business and Management graduate, who's trying to give his career a prospecting start in China. The core competencies mentioned in the vacancy suit my profile after I successfully finished my internships at PricewaterhouseCoopers on Aruba, Dutch Caribbean and Philips here in Shanghai.

As a result of my earlier internship at PricewaterhouseCoopers, I have experience in the gathering, controlling, analysing and concluding of financial and non-financial business information. As an auditor, I worked as a supervised individual with several clients in different industries. It required excellent skills in communication, planning, critical thinking and the achievement of agreements and deadlines. For my second internship, the execution of my qualitative research for Philips, a visit to several intermediaries in Shanghai, Hong Kong, Macau and Taipei was required. The result was a well-appreciated market research with market insights Philips used for a successful product launch. During both internships, a high degree of intensity, working in a team and providing an excellent contribution as an individual were prerequisites. Furthermore, several job-related courses during the execution of my study in the Netherlands and the United States of America expanded my skills in strategic management, marketing management, research methods and financial management. I feel therefore that the experience and knowledge gained during both internships and my International Business and Management major have given me invaluable skills which would benefit me in working as a Junior Client Coordinator for Acxiom Corporation.

Please find a copy of my resume attached. I would like to have the opportunity to discuss my resume with you further. You can always reach me by phone: 1500 034 7055. Thank you for your consideration.

Yours sincerely,

Victor de Lange

You can consider this good or weak but in China, people do not often include a cover letter with their job application. On the other hand, the human resources people promoting these jobs must receive hundreds of reactions per vacancy. Why would they even read or reply to everything? Besides mainly using Zhaopin, I browsed a couple of more job application websites. 51job, ChinaHR and Matchdragon offered many more opportunities. Still, the concept is the same, so chances are considerably low. To be more successful, I should change my job hunt from desk research to a more field research strategy. I mean, there must be plenty of network events in the city where you can talk directly to head-hunters or companies?

After a short research, I found the FC Club, an abbreviation for fortune connection club. I noticed the Shanghai Expat Show as well, which was coincidentally happening right now until Saturday. The Expat Show would represent an excellent opportunity to meet new people. I made up my plan for Saturday. I send a text message to Raphael as well, to ask whether the salsa night for Saturday night was still on. He replied with yes, and proposed to meet in Mural around ten o'clock. Hope to see you there. I smiled. Tomorrow is going to be an exciting day.

6

Shanghai Subway Line 2 towards Jingan Station - 9:53

The next morning I woke up at 7:30, had a quick breakfast at home and took the subway to People Square. After arrival there, I had to change lines to line two, which would bring me eventually to Jingan Temple. From there it would only be a short walk over West Nanjing Road to the Shanghai Exhibition Centre. Once the subway door opened, the air conditioning welcomed me in an almost empty subway. The few people occupying the seats weren't paying attention to what happened around them. They were either sleeping or reading. I felt a bit overdressed as I decided to wear a suit with a red tie. Not entirely usual for a Saturday morning. But still, it might increase the chance to find any job opportunity.

I stared in the distance in front of me. Maybe today would make a difference by actually meeting people face to face instead of sending hundreds of emails that probably won't be noticed at all. While I thought that, a cautious feeling took control of me. I was totally on my own in a twenty-four million people city. I am a fresh graduate with a bachelor's degree in International Business and Management studies. Instead of a secure job search in my home country, I decided to take an aeroplane back to Shanghai. I could have gone back to Aruba, where I did my first internship at PricewaterhouseCoopers.

One good reason to go back would be Katalina, living next door from the apartment I rented. She was the oldest daughter in a Colombian immigrant family. Especially during the last couple of months of my internship, we grew passionately close. She was funny, caring and above all incredibly pretty. Even though she preferred not to stay in touch anymore after I decided to move back to China, I still miss her and the times we spent together. But Aruba is a small island. A drive by car from the north to the south part takes about forty-five minutes. The economy is mainly focussed on tourism, aloe export, petroleum refining and offshore banking. And actually, about seventy-five per cent of the Aruban gross national product is earned through tourism and related activities. As a result of this, the closest I could get to an international career was a job in one of the big hotel chains on the beautiful west beaches.

America could have been an option too, but newspapers are currently signalling ultra-dark clouds above the American economy. Lehman Brothers is facing problems for a while now and last week's shares plunged forty-five per cent as a result of a non-successful acquisition by the Korea Development Bank. They restrained from this acquisition because of a sudden loss reporting of three-point nine billion US Dollar. The Dow Jones lost nearly three hundred points on the day investors started to get worried over the Lehman Brothers bank. In addition to all of this the housing market shows signals of a giant bubble, insurances have been unlawfully sold, and it was reported that Americans own an average of nine credit cards, where one card is used to pay off the debt of another. Probably not the best time for a foreigner to move back and start looking for a job.

Reality is that the Chinese economy still grows with an impressive annual fourteen per cent. Although the culture is completely different compared to Europe or America, it represents not the easiest but certainly the best option for now.

Abruptly I woke up from my dream bubble and noticed Jingan Temple was only one subway stop left. The people around me changed without me even realising it. Nothing changed in their behaviour, though. I wondered how many people in Shanghai on a daily basis miss their actual destination as a result of a subway nap. Must be plenty. A female voice announced in Chinese that we entered Jingan subway station, followed by a male voice delivering the same message but in English. I stood up and kept my balance while holding the handrail. Usually, during rush hour I am the only person who can see both ends of the subway. That's what you get when you're nearly two meters tall. Especially here in China my height is noticed. But that is a no-brainer in a country where people average between one point fifty and one point seventy meters.

The subway doors opened, and I followed the route to exit number two. Once I arrived at street level, I noticed the city had woken up. Taxi's in red, green, white and purple colours passed me by while I was waiting for the traffic lights. Once they changed to green, I checked whether both sides of the street were safe enough to walk. Especially bikes don't really take traffic lights seriously. They would still cross a red light while driving on the wrong side of the road, assuming that cars would let them go first. When walking on the sideway, I noticed three disabled beggars within one hundred meter distance. I remember reading an article on street beggars in China. In fact, they are often not naturally disabled, but sadly part of unwillingly organised crime.

When you walk on West Nanjing Road nearby Jingan Temple, it is common to see up to six disabled people laying on the street and begging for money. You would wonder how people without legs and wheelchairs can move themselves to the street. The story behind this is gruelling. Those people are victims of kidnappings either in the city or countryside. They return mutilated and have to earn money for an organised gang. You would expect the local authorities and police to deal with this, but it seems they can't or don't want to make any impact. Some argue that they are even part of the deal and enjoy financial benefits out of this. Others say that they do not want to be involved in this business. As a result, some of the streets in Shanghai are affected by this. Usually, during big events when many foreigners visit Shanghai you see them temporarily disappear. This is to give tourists the impression that it doesn't happen. What can we do about this? We can only impact the mafia's income by not giving the beggars any money. Or local authorities should start acting harder against this brutal crime. Till that moment, we still have to witness these unfortunate humans begging for money on the sidewalk.

The closer I got to the exhibition centre, I noticed that I wasn't the only person to offer a Saturday morning in search of a better future. When the Shanghai Exhibition Center appeared on the horizon, I noticed the old Soviet Union construction style. A bit out of contrast compared to the other buildings here. Where skyscrapers and hotels now surround the exhibition centre, it used to be the tallest building in Shanghai up till the nineties. Today that's hard to imagine. I collected the entrance paper with barcode I received after pre-registering for the expat show. It usually saves you a hundred RMB by doing so.

The entrance staff screened the barcode in front of a machine and wished me a nice day at the show. Curious as I was on what to expect, I followed the red carpet steps downstairs to the ground level. What I saw was a wide and long corridor with pillars and booths on both sides where companies exhibited their products or services. I instantly felt that this was not the right event to find a job. The confidence instantly sank to my shoes, but despite this, I decided to have a walk and see which companies choose to exhibit. This could be helpful as I technically just settled in Shanghai. I saw wine importers, relocation and financial consulting companies. All of them with the clear intention to score as many as business cards and increase their clientele.

All out of nothing a Chinese guy approached me. With an exciting tone in his voice, he introduced himself as James.

"I'm working for Jiao Tong University," he added. In his enthusiasm, he assumed that I exactly knew what Jiao Tong University was. But the name did not ring any bells to me.

"Do you want to be a teacher?" He asked.

"We are looking for a project management teacher." I took a few seconds to absorb his offer.

"But I am only recently graduated," I answered. "I do not think that I have the required experience to teach a project management course at a university."

I could better be honest immediately not to create any misunderstanding.

"That's no problem,"

"Is this a full-time position?"

"No. This is a part-time job. The course takes only three hours per week."

This wasn't going to solve my problem. I wouldn't be able to live from a three-hour working week.

"I'm not sure whether this is what I'm looking for at this moment," I concluded.

James didn't seem to accept this as an answer.

"Here is my business card. If you change your mind, please contact me again."

I accepted his business card and thanked him for the opportunity offered. That could always be handy. I continued my walk over the exhibition and recognised the logo of the Fortune Connection Club. When I came closer to the booth, one of the team members walked up to me and introduced herself.

"Hi, my name is Lara, I am working as a promotor for the Fortune Connection Club. By organising a diversity of events, we created a network for young business professionals to connect the international community in the cities of Shanghai, Beijing and Hong Kong."

I had a look at the first sentences of the leaflet she handed to me.

"I know the Fortune Connection Club," I confirmed. "Earlier this week, I was searching for jobs online and I ended up on your website."

Lara smiled and understood that I was part of their target group.

"Among all professionals who participate in our events, a vast number of human resource managers and head-hunters working for medium and big sized multinational firms. You might want to join our next event. They are free, so you have nothing to lose."

"When will the next event take place?" I informed. This upcoming Monday, starting at 19:00 in the Ritz Carlton Hotel. Follow the FC Club's banners in the lobby to the second floor."

"Alright, I will be there. Thank you Lara, for the introduction."

As I moved on, I realised that there must be a hundred and fifty companies exhibiting during the expat show. Not that you need all of their services right now, but it could surely be convenient for the near future.

7

Shanghai Subway Line 1 - 22:51

From Hengshan road subway exit two it is only a couple of minutes walking to Mural. It was a couple of minutes before ten, providing me with a bit of buffer to arrive on time to meet Raphael. It was Saturday evening, a perfect time for many to start a long night of drinking and bar hopping in Hengshan Road. Around me were mainly Chinese youngsters, some of them already tipsy or even beyond that, as they did not seem able anymore to walk in a straight line properly. They hung around each other's shoulders to stay balanced, talking understandably loudly.

To my surprise, I wasn't approached by strangers to sell me hash, cocaine or massages with a happy ending. All I had to be careful of now was to not to walk into a broiling street barbecue or table of one of the many people enjoying an evening snack or dinner. I crossed the street between two taxi's lined up in a traffic jam caused by a red light further in the street. The driver smiled and raised his hand to me to indicate that his taxi was empty. I greeted back and pointed in the intended direction I wanted to walk. Once I approached the entrance of Mural, I could hear the pervasive bass of salsa music. I paid a hundred RMB for the entrance cover and received a glow in the dark stamp on the inside of my right arm. The cover included one drink with a choice of either soft, beer or mixed drinks.

After getting the coupon, I followed the stairs down to the basement where Mural was situated. Although the stairs were pretty even, it looked like climbing down into a cave. The walls around me were grey and undulated. The closer I came to the door, the louder the music became. Suddenly the door smashed open, a Western couple just being able to balance each other walked out. I could grab the door before it would close again. Inside I saw a mass of people, gathered near the bar. In an aisle leading to the dance floor, even more people had a good time. I looked around whether I could find Raphael, which was not an easy task because of the dimmed lights. I checked my phone but no message from him with a word of location sharing. While I continued my search and walked towards the dance floor, I felt a hand on the backside of my shoulder. It was Raphael, approaching me from the back. He must have followed me a couple of steps before being able to catch my attention.

"You're so tall, Victor. Easy to recognise in a crazy crowd like here," Raphael shouted in my ear.

I nodded in agreement - I could usually find myself relatively easy back in crowd pictures taken during pop concerts or soccer games.

"Let's go to the other side of the bar, where we have a table with a couple of more friends." Raphael suggested.

"But not before we pass by the bar and get you a drink, what are you into tonight?"

I quickly checked the menu, handwritten on a black school board on the wall behind the bar.

"A rum coke for me please," I answered.

"Good choice, I'll join you with that one."

Between all people, Raphael found a space at the bar and ordered two rum cokes. With a smile on his face he returned, adding that he asked for an extra shot rum.

"This one is going to taste really good and set the tone for the evening," he said.

I didn't know what to expect from this, but I experienced ordering mixed drinks in Chinese bars while asking myself whether it contained any liquor. An extra shot of rum would probably not hurt. We continued our way to the table. A small group of mostly foreigners looked at us when we arrived, and Raphael took the opportunity to introduce me shortly:

"This is Victor, guys, he lives in the same compound as I do."

I nodded in reaction to their greetings. I sat down on one of the empty seats and looked around in Mural. The band stopped playing, and now it was the DJ taking over with upbeat music in addition to the salsa style before. In reaction to this, the tango and salsa couples on the dance floor were replaced by individuals now moving synchronically on the quick beats of the dance music. The rented table had a couple of snacks on it. I could see a fruit plate, some fries, chicken wings and peanuts. I knew that this is usually part of the table rent. Tables come with a minimum spend of let's say two thousand RMB, depending on the size of the table. It's easy to meet the minimum by ordering two or three bottles of liquor, but prudent minded people will order some food as well to avoid ending up completely wasted.

As I was back in Shanghai to start my career, it is a necessity to get in touch with people. I monitored the people around our table. What kind of background would they have? In what kind of industries are they working? I decided to introduce myself to the person right beside me.

"Hi, my name is Victor," I opened. The gentlemen looked at me, put his glass on the side and shook my hand.

"My name is Camilo," he answered.

"How long are you living in Shanghai for?" I asked.

"It has been a year now since I moved here from the middle of Italy."

"And how do you like it so far?"

It took him a few seconds to think.

"Well, it is work that actually brought me here. It was a good opportunity, so I decided to accept the offer." I nodded.

"How long is your contract here?" I informed.

"Three years in total."

"So you have two years left."

Camilo nodded yes.

"How about yourself?"

"I live in Shanghai since the end of February this year, so that makes nine months now. The first six months for an internship and after my graduation in the Netherlands I decided to come back to

Shanghai to start my career here. I'll give it a try for three months and if I'm successful I will stay. Otherwise, I may leave back to the Netherlands."

Camilo looked a little bit surprised.

"You are on an interesting journey," he concluded.

"Well," I added, "I have nothing to lose now, right? And as a result of the internship, my professional contacts in Shanghai are still fresh I feel I should give it a try. In the Netherlands, I know nobody outside of the restaurant industry, where I worked for nine years as a student."

Camilo nodded in agreement.

"You're absolutely right," he said.

"Which profession do you have?" I asked.

"I'm working in the automotive industry, for an Italian car manufacturer."

"Ah, Ferrari?" I joked. Camilo laughed.

"No. It is the other Italian car manufacturer starting with a F."

"Let me guess. Fiat?"

Camilo nodded yes. He continued.

"The automotive industry a big business now in China. On one hand, you increasingly see Western car manufactures, shifting their factories to China. On the other hand, the Chinese middle-class society getting richer and willing to buy a car. Unlike in Europe, cars here are considered a sign of wealth. Although the majority of people are borrowing money to buy a car from the bank or friends. This is leading to the fact that in the past four years, China nearly doubled the total annual vehicle production. Only Japan still produce more cars. Passenger vehicles, that needs to be said. In the commercial vehicle industry, China is already a world leader."

"So what are you exactly doing for Fiat?"

"I am a product manager with responsibility for a portfolio of car components produced at Fiat. They are either used in Fiat cars or some other car brands."

"Sounds interesting,"

I said while the DJ announced the final dance song before the salsa music would come back. I could see people's positive reaction. I looked around, where I saw Raphael on the other side of the table.

He was looking at two girls passing by our table. To get his attention, I threw a piece of popcorn into his direction, hitting him on his cheek. That must have been a rough wake-up call out of a possible imaginary threesome with the girls that just passed by. He looked up and laughed.

"Why don't you go after them?" I asked.

"There will be salsa music soon. Ask one of them for a dance!"

"Naah," He said, a bit shy.

I could see that directly approaching girls wasn't his style to get their attention.

"Come join us on this side of the table,"

I invited Raphael over. I've been talking with Camilo for the past ten or so minutes.

"You guys know each other?"

"Yes," Raphael answered.

"We know each other via work, as we both work in the automotive industry. I work for a multinational company producing tires."

"Ah yes." I concluded.

"Every car need tires, so it's easy peasy for you two to get to know each other."

"What is the background of the other friends of you around the table here?"

"Really a mix of nationalities and professional backgrounds," Raphael answered.

"They are French, Turkish, Chinese, Russian, one other Italian, American and Japanese."

I wondered how this collection of nationalities ever came together. Raphael explained:

"It started with two friends and they invited friends, those friends involved their friends again, that's how it went."

"Well," I joked, "Dutch doesn't seem to be part of your nationality portfolio yet. I can fit in perfectly!"

"I'll let you know when we will meet again in a group," Raphael said.

"Otherwise we can either meet for a drink in my place, or we hang out with Camilo."

"Sounds like a nice initiative," I added.

Camilo told us about JZ Club and The House of Blues and Jazz, places he regularly visits.

"And add Cotton Club to that list," I suggested.

"They have a genius guitar player there. It's a Westerner playing with different bands. He is tall and has long grey hair till just over his shoulders, usually in a tail."

Talking about guitar players, the band was back on the small stage. A few dancing couples filled the dance floor.

"Why don't you show us some of your salsa dance skills, Victor?" Raphael said.

I had to think about my time on Aruba. I was seriously considering salsa lessons, but I was just too late to sign up for classes so that never worked out.

"No... I'm too tall anyway to match with any dance partner. Look at all the girls here. They hardly reach my chest. How is that ever going to look good?"

Both Raphael and Camilo looked at me with an expression on their face as if they agreed with my explanation.

"How about you guys?" I tried with a mission to allocate attention to them.

"You two were raised in Brazil and Italy."

"Especially you, Raphael. I bet you could dance salsa before you even could properly walk."

Raphael laughed.

"Yes I can but I am not a dancing type. I rather just sit at the side of the bar and look at other people dancing and having fun."

"Let's have another drink," I suggested.

"As we both rather watch than dance, let's do that at least with a fresh drink in our hand. What would you like?" I asked.

"I'll go for a gin and tonic," Raphael said.

"For you as well, Camilo?"

"Yes please, why not." He answered.

As more people were dancing now, fewer people were at the bar to order drinks. I ordered three gin and tonics and found my way back through the crowd to Camilo and Raphael.

"Let's cheer on a nice evening," I said.

We clinked our glasses, and a second later, I felt the ice cubes touching my upper lip. It felt good and so fresh, in the middle of a hot salsa bar. I was making progress. Not professionally yet, but after a week in Shanghai, it looked like I've made some new friends. And that's fundamental to start the next chapter of your life in a new country.

8

Xinhu Riverside Apartments - 14:35

From: Victor de Lange
To: Gerald van Tatenhof
Send: 09/28/2008 - 14:33

Dear Gerald,

How are you? I hope everything's fine. I am back in Shanghai now for one and a half week. I published my resume online on four different websites, applied for some jobs, but without any success yet. It's a holiday now so I can only search for jobs… My main problem now is the lack of experience and the fact that I don't speak Mandarin fluently. I started learning, so that will only be a matter of time.

Of course, I didn't forget about Philips. We discussed a still to be created position with focus on the hotel sector, similar to what I did during my internship. Can I make a proposal? For me to invest in myself and gain experience, I am willing to start working for a lower salary, see it as an extended internship. As long as I can survive here, I'm fine. I think it can be a benefit for both Philips and myself.

Please let me know; I'm always willing to come over to your office to have a chat.

Kind regards,
Victor

9

Shanghai Ritz Carlton Hotel - 18:33

It was just after six-thirty when I entered the lobby from the Ritz Carlton hotel. I looked around for any signs of the FC Club event. This time must be peak hour for such a hotel. People were waiting for colleagues or friends to go out for dinner or used the lobby as a meeting point to continue the evening in one of the luxury restaurants located in the hotel. I noticed attractive young girls in short sexy dresses waiting for their sugar daddy to meet so they could go up into one of the rooms of opulence and enjoy an evening or a night together. I experienced how funny it is that people in such a situation can mistake you as the person they are waiting for. They look at you in search of recognition, but when the response is not mutual, quickly act normal again. Ironically enough, the attractive girls know exactly for who they were waiting. None of them mistook me as their partner for tonight.

Next thing I saw was the big FC Club banner with the message that the event would be organised in the ballroom located on the second floor. The easiest way up was to take the stairs. Events like this are often organised in luxury hotels. Easier to find for participants, and it surely adds to the brand recognition. I paid the entrance fee of a hundred RMB, that included a glass of wine and got a name batch that was waiting for me among a hundred other names. The lady at the entrance handed me a leaflet with the schedule of the evening, which included a couple of keynote speakers and a lucky draw. When I entered the ballroom, there must have been twenty or so people. In order not to stay there with empty hands, I proceeded to the bar to hand my voucher for a glass of red wine. Most of the people were already talking with somebody. I felt a bit awkward to join one of the conversations randomly. I could imagine that the number of people looking for a job or new opportunity must overrule the participants who could offer a job.

Visiting an event like this is no job guarantee at all. It is a sponsored platform for companies or speakers to put their name on the map. For us participants, it creates a nice opportunity to broaden your business network and perhaps friend circle. But for the good job opportunity, I can't imagine you'd have to be here. Meanwhile, more people walked in. I glanced at them. Gentlemen dressed in a business casual way like me. Ladies in dress or carefully ironed trousers with a blouse. A few dressed a bit too sexy as if they came here with another intention. As I was standing on the side of the room, I made an effort to walk more to the centre with the aim to start a conversation with somebody. It reminded me of high school disco's when I was thirteen years old. I usually spent most of the time standing on the side of the atrium nervously hoping that the girl I liked would come and ask me for a slow dance when "*My Heart Will Go On*" from Celine Dion played. Or at least talk to me. She never did. Instead, she ended up dancing with another guy who had the guts to walk up to her and start a conversation. I felt bad for days afterwards because of the wasted opportunity. What if I would have talked to her? High school lessons like this could be applied in life even fifteen years later. Just have the fucking guts to talk to somebody, just anybody and show your excellence and self-confidence! That's exactly the point of this kind of network events!

Right there in the middle was a guy with possibly the same threshold as me. I walked up to him and introduced myself.

"Hi, my name is Victor. Are you having a good time so far tonight?"

He looked up to me and introduced himself as well.

"My name is Luke. I am working in a professional relocation business." I nodded.

"So what is it you're exactly doing?"

"Well, in a nutshell, I'm a business development manager with responsibility for the sales, relocation and assignment of management solutions to multinational organisations here in Shanghai, but our business increasingly gains clients in the cities of Beijing, Guangzhou and Shenzhen as well."

He must be here to source potential clients.

"How about yourself? What brought you to Shanghai?"

"I did an internship here at Philips Lighting. Presented my thesis in June, graduated with an International Business and Management bachelor, and now I am back in Shanghai trying to give my career a shot."

"This is a good time to be here, Victor. The economy is growing with double percentage points where most of the world is heading towards a financial crisis."

"How will that affect your business?" I asked.

"I am responsible for leading business development efforts within large multinational accounts. The multinational companies are usually the first ones to cut costs and send expatriates back to their home countries. Even though a crisis is not good for an economy, we as relocation experts can benefit from this once the crisis started. We're usually busy up to the moment when the crisis hits the lowest point. Once the economy starts to show signs of recovery, companies will first be careful to send people overseas, but at the moment, relocation becomes a topic of discussion again. Luke all explained this making elaborate hand gestures to clarify the economic trends in his explanation. During this cycle, we design and implement a sales strategy that is aligned with our sales initiatives based on an overall growth plan."

"Seems your relocation industry is way more crisis-proof compared to the lighting industry," I answered.

"Homes and buildings always need light, but customers will try to save money on it. In professional projects where we usually make lower margins, the biggest part of the project budget is spent on interior decoration. Only at the very end lighting is considered. Most of the budget is then already spend so a cheaper lighting solution can only be afforded. And in times of crisis, a lot of projects are frozen or cancelled."

Luke laughed and gave me a path on the back.

"You're in the wrong industry, my friend!"

At that moment, a waitress passed by holding a platter with fresh fish snacks on slices of French baguettes. I realised that I needed to eat something. I glanced at my watch. It was nearly seven-thirty now, and I did not have anything for dinner yet. Just a glass of wine. Luke and I both took a fish snack.

"How long are you actually living in Shanghai?" I asked.

While he took a bite of the snack, he answered: "Nearly two years now."

"And what is your long term plan? How long are you planning to live in China?"

"As long as I feel happy here, I will work here. But if there are better opportunities elsewhere, I may follow my heart and leave China. Do you know? You can be sure of one thing. None of the expats you see here today will retire in China. Nobody is going to work here for thirty or forty years."

That's true, I thought. I once heard that working and living seven years in China is the tipping point for many expats to start asking questions about the future. They get tired of the lifestyle, crowded city, social services or like to escape environmental pollution. As well, starting a family could be reasons to move on and return to a home country. Would I ever feel tired of living in China?

"Well, I just arrived so in my case I still have six year left." I joked to Luke.

Meanwhile, more people walked in. One of the keynote speakers was preparing herself to start a presentation. From the opening slide, I could see that she is working for zhaopin.com, one of China's top job-hunting websites. This must be a perfect platform for her to show what her company can do for the job-seeking people in the room. Just for myself, online job hunting hasn't been successful. Out of nearly a hundred jobs that I applied for so far on a variety of websites like Zhaopin, I received zero reaction. Because of this, I doubt the effectiveness of job websites. There is one phenomenon in China that beat all the job application websites: guanxi, which means relationship in Mandarin. From that perspective, an FC Club could potentially be more effective as it allows you to talk and express yourself directly to people. It presents you with the opportunity to deliver a good first impression rather than being just another sheet of paper among fifteen short-listed candidates. Or perhaps applying for jobs online would be more applicable for locals.

I wished Luke a nice evening and moved myself to the bar for another glass of red wine. It would be good to talk to more people and if possible, some head-hunters before the end of the evening. The wine tonight was sponsored by Yellow Tail, an Australian wine. It's an easy to drink cabernet sauvignon considered in China as a medium end. In the rest of the world, it is just a bottle of ordinary table wine.

Meanwhile, the lady from Zhaopin finished her keynote session. The crowd gradually started new networking attempt conversations. I could feel that the ratio of people here looking for a new job or business opportunity versus the ones who could offer one must be ninety to ten per cent. I could imagine life as a head-hunter to be good. People are always looking for opportunities to improve their quality of life, salary or responsibilities. The challenge I could envision myself is to find the right candidate for the right job at the right time. But with candidates offering themselves during events like this is already a good start.

The host of the evening told us not to leave yet as there would be a lucky draw at the end of the evening. But I was never lucky during a lucky draw. Never did I come close to winning something during a lucky draw. Frankly speaking, I'm sure if a lucky draw were held with only two business cards in a bowl, providing me with a fifty per cent chance to win, I would still lose. When I turned around to grab a fish snack from the food platter, a lady was standing next to me. She looked up and said,

"Wow, you're so tall!" As a joke, I told her that I'm counting the number of times people said that to me and that she's the lucky one to be number one hundred thousand.

"I hear that all the time, eeehhh Joyce," I said while I looked at the name batch on her white shirt. On purpose or not, she stuck her nameplate right next to the two open top buttons of her blouse, making it very hard not to miss her gorgeous looking breasts smiling at me.

"So… what's your story?" asked Joyce with an expression on her face as if she expected me to give her my detailed story of life during the first fifteen seconds we just met.

"Well, where would you like me to start?" I asked.

"Where are you from? I mean, those big blue eyes are telling me you're not local. You're a long way from home."

"That's an easy guess, but I like your way of approaching people." I continued.

"I am from the Netherlands." Joyce interrupted me.

"And how did you end up here in Shanghai?" As if she couldn't wait to hear that.

"Just by plane." Joyce giggled.

"No, I am serious."

"Okay, I did my graduation internship for Philips earlier this year. I went back to the Netherlands and graduated with a degree in International Business and Management. After that, I travelled a month in Spain and France to make up my mind about what I wanted to do next." Joyce interrupted me.

"And here you are, back in Shanghai. Did it really take you one month to take this decision?" She giggled.

"Well, not really. Most of it was holidays. But travelling inspires me to do things. The Chinese economy is booming despite a looming crisis in the United States and Europe. I knew it would probably be easiest to pick up my life right there where I left it." Joyce nodded in agreement.

"So have you found a job yet?"

"Not yet. But I have some things running. I hope to get back into Philips."

"How about yourself?"

"You seem pretty settled here. Are you looking for new business opportunities or extending your network?"

"Naah, a bit of both." Joyce said and she took a sip of her wine.

"I am working as a consultant in an accounting firm. But the working hours are long, and I think I deserve to enjoy my time a bit more."

"I used to do an internship at PricewaterhouseCoopers just a year ago. I enjoyed working with clients in the hotel, car dealer and banking sector, but I missed the creativity I could put in my work." Joyce smiled.

"Yes, as an accountant, you'd better not be too creative in your work."

"Well, you'd be surprised how many accountants are still putting a lot of creativity in their work! But if you work by the rules, you can't indeed. That is why I pursued my career in marketing. I think I am better in marketing with a focus on strategic planning and leadership."

"Sounds interesting but you may need some more experience first to achieve that." Joyce said.

"I know. I am twenty-six now. I still have the time to gain experience." Joyce nodded in agreement.

"It's good for you to visit network events like these." While Joyce finished her sentence, the lucky draw was announced. One of the FC Club sponsors proudly linked their name to the draw and delivered a short brand introduction speech.

"Is your business card in there?" Joyce checked with me.

"Yes. But I never got lucky during a lucky draw." Joyce laughed.

"I did, in fact. I once won a spa treatment in Le Meridien on People Square."

"Well, by doing so, you're already luckier than me."

Tonight, the first price was an e-reader, the second and third prices were beauty and dinner coupons and a couple of free entrances to the next FC Club event. According to expectation, I ended up with empty hands once again.

"I see history continued for you," joked Joyce. I smiled at her.

"Well, being here is more important. I hope to meet friends and increase my network of people here in Shanghai."

Meanwhile and as if there was nothing more to gain, the first people started leaving the event. Joyce looked at her watch.

"I think it's time for me to go as well. I got an early morning again tomorrow. It was nice talking to you, Victor. Good luck in finding a job."

"Likewise Joyce," I answered. "We might see each other around. Shanghai is a big metropole but still a considerable small place on earth. Enjoy your evening!" I said when I shook Joyce's hand.

After Joyce turned around, I checked whether there were any fish snacks left on the snack plates. Nothing left. I checked my watch, and it was nearly nine o'clock by now. Maybe it was time to go for me as well. It did not make much sense to talk to headhunters this late in the evening anymore. Everybody seemed in a relaxed mood, with some acting like they had a bit too much wine.

10

Shanghai Ritz Carlton Hotel - 20:53

I decided to take the escalator down and see if there would be any taxi outside to drive me back to Putuo. Around my new apartment must still be a restaurant open where I can have dinner. Next to the high hotel entrance was a line of people waiting for a taxi. I did not feel like to wait twenty or so minutes while inhaling cigarette smoke of fellow FC Event club participants. Instead, I walked two blocks and stopped a taxi on the street. The yellow company on purpose as they are better to trust around this time of the day. Red and white are part of smaller companies and may give foreigners a city tour. The taxi stopped immediately, and I asked him to bring me to Wuning Road crossing Changshou Road. That would enable me to check the restaurants I passed by while walking to the supermarket earlier.

We first passed some designer shops. They were just closing. It was the end of a long working day in Shanghai. They often make twelve hours per day, and that for six days a week. A few blocks further, we passed Jingan Temple, being renovated but beautifully lighten up. The temple's original location was actually beside the Suzhou Creek, a bit up north compared to today's location. The temple was relocated to its current site almost eight hundred years ago during the Song Dynasty. The current temple was rebuilt in the Qing Dynasty but throughout the Cultural Revolution Chairman Mao and his government converted the temple into a plastic factory. After the cultural revolution ended, it was rebuilt and converted back to a temple. It's amazing to see this old but well-maintained temple among the nineteenth-century skyscrapers and shopping malls in Jingan District. It shows exactly the revolution Shanghai has been going through in the past fifteen years.

The taxi driver made a right turn onto Wanhangdu Road before driving in north direction of Wuning Road. This wide road is easy to recognise because of its two lanes in each direction separated with a low fence. On both sides is a lane for bicycles or electronic scooters to drive as well. Without saying anything, the driver stopped at the crossing with Changshou Road. I paid him eighteen RMB. When I got out of the taxi, red neon floated the street. The KTV located on the crossing of this street was still open. When I looked in the further distance most of the restaurants too. That's one of the advantages of Shanghai. You can get food anywhere at almost any time of the day. And at this time people still sit outside. Enjoying their evening with family or colleagues after a day of work. Celebrating a milestone or just to catch up. I could see big plates of food being shared by the people around the table. Most dishes looked tasty, or was it because I was just feeling hungry?

I walked into Yejiazai Road, a side street of Changshou Road where I remember seeing a nice-looking restaurant last time I walked by. The place has a traditional-looking wooden structure on the front facade with a place for three tables under a small roofing. From what I could see it looks like Sichuan style. People were still enjoying food both outside and inside the restaurant. That is usually a good sign. I decided to take an indoor table. As authentic the restaurant looked from the outside, as nice it looked from the inside. At the entrance was a small bar with four bottles of wines available for ordering and a pay cabinet. Further inside were about ten rectangular shaped tables. On each of the long sides was either a small bench or two seats.

As I was just by myself, I choose a table in the middle right next to the path leading to the bathroom area. After I sat down, the waitress placed a menu on the table and filled a cup with tea. The menu was easy to understand as all of the dishes contained pictures. From judging the picture, I almost misunderstood a cow stomach dish for chicken but everything else was clear. As this is a Sichuan

Restaurant, I should prepare myself for a spicy evening. I waved to the waitress and ordered Lazi Jiding, a spicy fried chicken dish with red chillies and peanuts, a broccoli dish and a bowl of rice. The waitress noted my order and not long after that, I heard the cooks in the small kitchen starting to prepare my order.

I looked around; most of the guests almost finished their meals. Three tables away from me sat a guy with two girls enjoying their meals. By looking the way they dressed, I could see they are colleagues enjoying an after-work dinner. As they continued to talk and laugh, I wondered about the topic of their conversation. They seemed happy. As I am planning to settle in Shanghai, I should make more efforts to learn Chinese. If I would speak a so-called survival level of Chinese would make my life already a little bit easier.

The three locals looked in my direction. Are they talking about me? One of the girls held her attention in my direction a bit longer. Out of politeness, I smiled at her. She smiled back at me while her colleagues continued talking. That moment was instantaneously blocked by the waitress arriving at my table with the broccoli dish. The good thing about these restaurants is that you never have to wait long for your dish to arrive. I asked the waitress for my bowl of rice as it usually is served as last. Chinese like to eat vegetables and meat dishes first, while the rice comes at last. Foreigners use rice more as a base and build the other dishes around it. The broccoli tasted nice together with the bacon.

While I was eating, I was thinking about a planning for the remaining part of this week. I hoped Gerald from Philips would come back to me with an answer on my email. Furthermore, it might not hurt to give the guy from Shanghai Jiao Tong University a call to ask whether the lecturer position is still available. Even by teaching three hours per week, I can do something useful, earn a bit of money and extend my network in Shanghai. I noticed the girl was looking in my direction again. Her eyes were twinkling when she smiled at me the moment our views crossed. This wasn't a coincidence anymore. As she was sitting at the head of the table, I noticed she was wearing a high waisted pencil skirt with a white slim-fit blouse, both fitting her body shape well. She dyed her long straight hair in a deep cherry brown colour.

She made a gesture to me whether my food tasted well. I gave her a thumbs-up, and she nodded yes in return. It seemed she was now less interested in her colleagues. It started to become a game. Sometimes and on purpose, I would not look at her for a minute, pretending to eat and enjoy the dish. But every time I looked at her, she comfortably looked in my direction. Or at least it was making my evening alone here a bit less boring. What would she think of me? A foreigner alone here for dinner at nearly ten o'clock at night? He must be lonely. On the moment her colleagues had gotten her attention, I grabbed a napkin from the table and wrote my telephone number on it. But I wouldn't have the guts to stand up and approach her while she is still together with her colleagues. What if they couldn't speak English? That would be embarrassing. The waitress walked towards my table with the Lazi Jiding dish in her hand. It was still sizzling when she put it in front of me. It was full of red peppers, so I prepared myself for a spicy first bite. And I saw the Sichuan peppers. They always give your tongue a tingle, so spicy as they are.

I noticed that the three colleagues were preparing to ask for the bill and pay. The girl looked at me with a dismayed expression on her face as if she did not want to leave yet. She giggled when she saw me struggling with the first rush of spices attacking my mouth. She stood up and where I thought they would leave, she walked towards my table presumably to pay a visit to the bathroom before leaving the restaurant. When she was nearing me, I pushed the folded napkin to her side of the table. She grabbed it from the table and followed her way behind me to the bathroom. I firmly hoped that she would be smart enough to open the napkin and read what could be written on it instead of wiping herself clean after the bathroom visit. I sniggered by the thought of this. I asked for the waitress for the rice to arrive as I needed it to quench the fire in my mouth caused by the Sichuan spices. Despite this, it tasted excellent. The colleagues continued their talk and were not aware of what just happened between her and me. Other people in the restaurant meanwhile had left. If my flirt and her colleagues would leave, I would be the only one occupying an indoor table.

Through the open window I could see that on the small terrace two tables were still occupied. But the persons occupying those tables finished their dinner and were now drinking beer instead. I could see their table full of empty bottles in between nearly or half-finished dishes. The poor and hungry surviving on the streets in Shanghai would still have a wonderful meal from the leftovers waiting on this table.

Meanwhile, my flirt returned from the bathroom, passing my table with her back towards me but not giving me any indication that she'd appreciate my napkin move. Was it perhaps just a game for her? Or did I come too close? I sipped my tea while I followed her towards the table where her colleagues were still waiting. She returned to her seat with a neutral expression on her face. Perhaps this wasn't going to work out. Within a minute or so, the waitress would return the change, and they would leave. While her colleagues were still talking to each other, she glanced at me again with a smile on her face. She kept the napkin a bit folded in the palm of her right hand so only I could see it. With her other hand, she gave me a thumb-up. I smiled back at her and felt released that she'd appreciate my commencing move.

Exactly at that moment, the waitress returned the change, and they were preparing to leave. It all worked out perfectly. While they walked out of the restaurant, the girl as third and last in line, she looked around one more time and waived to me. Now I could only hope she'd send me a text message in return. As they disappeared in the Shanghai night, I looked at the table in front of me. I nearly finished my dishes. Just from the Lazi Jiding only the red spices where left. I was told once that local Sichuan persons even eat fried red spices. I could only imagine that to be a disaster for my intestines. I finished the broccoli and rice. The people on the table outside seemed to have a mission to finish the entire beer stock in the restaurant. Their table was full of empty bottles. A good reason for the owner not to close his business yet. I asked for the bill as well, which was a moderate sixty RMB for three dishes. Not too bad for authentic Sichuan food.

On my way out, I handed the waitress the bill together with my cash, said thank you and walked upon the street on my way back home. I could see the top of my compound immediately, rising above the houses and restaurants located in this street. The end of this little road named Yejiazai Road leads to a bridge crossing the Suzhou river, which is only accessible for pedestrians and bikes. The end of the street was badly illuminated, and the bridge was based in complete darkness. On one side of the bridge, some street sellers were trying to sell me some clothes or electronics. The battery-led lights of their shops illuminated threw light over the small bridge, creating a bit more safety to cross it. I followed the uneven road towards the entrance of my compound, swiped the entrance card, and the door opened automatically. The security guy waved at me, either because he started to recognise me or just because it was part of his duties - and when I arrived back home Mr Lu just walked out of the kitchen, back to his room. He had prepared hot water for himself and wished me a good night. I walked back to my room, checked my mobile phone and saw a message from an unsaved number.

"Very nice to meet you. My name is Linda. This is my number."

I smiled while I read it and replied her with my name and wishing her good night. I went straight to bed after a shower. Tomorrow would be a new day.

11

Xinhu Riverside Apartments - 08:00

The worst are the weekday mornings when you wake up, and you have nothing to do. Nobody would notice whether I would wake up at 7 in the morning or stay in bed until 14:00 and waste my day. I have nowhere to go, no job with a demanding deadline is waiting for me. I feel pretty much useless, so to say. By now, I would have expected at least one invitation for an interview. How is it possible to send out a hundred applications and I literally received zero replies? With a resume mentioning study abroad at Texas State University, internships at PricewaterhouseCoopers and Philips? A major of International Business and Management studies? Isn't that worth anything? Or is it because of the economy that just turned shit?

I twirled around in bed. It was just after eight in the morning and the small beam of light entering the room through the middle of the curtains revealed another cloudy day. Mr Lu just left a couple of minutes ago, probably to have breakfast at his sister's home or to start some of the maintenance work he's entitled to do in one of the apartments she owns. I groaned. Raphael and Camilo had a job to go. Something I could only dream about right now.

I got up and walked with my bare feet over the cold concrete floor to the kitchen to prepare breakfast. The only bread I could find so far around my home was sweet factory-prepared bread. This neighbourhood is lacking decent bakeries selling fresh and crunchy bread as we eat in Europe. Access to good coffee at home is already considered a luxury. After I prepared a few slices with peanut butter I walked back to my bedroom, opened the curtains and as far as I could see into the Zhongshan Park direction from my balcony - a vast distance of two and a half kilometre - I could see a hazy sky.

Opening the laptop on my desk did not give me the satisfaction I was hoping for. No response to job applications and neither a reply on my email from Gerald. He must be busy or travelling now. I did not feel like to waste time on sending another ten or twenty job applications. What could be more effective is to contact the guy from Jiao Tong University I met last week at the Expat Show. With a bit of luck, the teaching position he offered is still open. It would give me some welcome distraction and challenge, and besides that, it would bring in some extra cash. Last but not least, I could see it adding value to my network in Shanghai. And perhaps I should start looking for a gym. Staying fit helps to create a positive mindset. I used to run outdoors as I lived close to the beach and forests in the Netherlands.

Fifteen kilometres three times per week. I never felt more fit compared to those days. But this habit soon disappeared after arriving in China. From June till October it is way too humid to run and not to mention the PM2.5 AQI air quality index - often dark red. I do not want to think about the small particles accessing my lungs and potentially causing severe health problems.

While I was eating my breakfast, I had to think about a couple of gym experiences during my internship here. When I first came to Shanghai as a student, and my budget wasn't so high, I joined a small gym in a residential compound nearby. For two obvious reasons: it was cheap and nearby. There wasn't much equipment but that didn't matter, I was happy to be out every once in a while. When the season changed from the cosy fall to the cold winter, I eventually figured out that this gym didn't have a heating system. Windows were always open, so the indoor temperature was basically the same as outdoor. The missing of a heat and air-conditioning system wasn't even what made me leave that gym. I once asked for a personal trainer to be better able to meet my personal goals. the only result I achieved after the first class was two excruciating nights without much sleep. He didn't have a systematic approach to start with lighter weights but instantly went for the heavy ones. That continued for an hour without any cooling down afterwards. That unpleasant experience made me want to change to a more professional gym. I visited a couple of brands and locations, and I ultimately joined Physics which is a well-known brand with multiple locations. I signed up with the Physics located in Metro City in Xujiahui not far away from where I used to live. It was reasonably cheap, but the disadvantage was that there were no windows. I had the constant feeling to be working out in a basement, even though it was on the 7th floor of a shopping mall. Another thing that turned me off was the fact that people smoked in the bathrooms. Avoiding the toilets wasn't such a big deal, and there was a comfortable sauna to use, which was perfect, especially during the cold Shanghai winters. Physics offered its members to make use of various locations. Convenient if you want to change scenery or when switching jobs or apartments.

I once happened to be around People's Square on a Saturday afternoon together with a colleague from Philips. He's British, but we studied at the same university in The Netherlands. As a result of having a Dutch girlfriend, he spoke basic Dutch. Saturday afternoons in the gym weren't usually that crowded as Chinese people prefer to spend time with their families. After finishing our workout, we returned to the dressing room area. While I was undressing, I recognised a guy looking at me from a near distance. He followed every move I made. I felt a bit uneasy about getting undressed and taking a shower. Instead, I asked, just to let him know I wasn't charmed by his offensive:

"What the fuck are you looking at me?"

It was like I crashed his dream because it took him two seconds to realise that I was talking to him. Without saying anything, he smiled at me and walked away. Weird. The individual showers didn't have any curtains or doors, so technically everybody was visible for everybody. I met my colleague nearby the showers, and we decided to enjoy a sauna session. A little corridor led to the sauna, where on each side a few local people were standing. We passed through and opened the sauna door. Nobody was inside, and there was hardly any light. Only one low-watt compact fluorescent lamp shined a dimmed light through the inside of the sauna, just enough to distinguish the bench and walking platform. Remembering my experience minutes before while undressing at the lockers, I wondered what would happen if this single light source would die. My colleague and I both took a seat inside the sauna, he on the long side and I on the short side. After a minute a Chinese guy walked in. We ignored him while he took place next to my colleague on the long side of the sauna. Seconds later, my colleague said with a panicking voice in Dutch: "Victor, this guy is sitting right next to me, and his legs are touching mine!" I looked up. "That's a bit odd, given the fact that the sauna offers a 4-meter bench for people to sit on. Why this guy decided to sit right next to you, or in fact against you?" I asked my colleague whether he was comfortable enough to stay or whether we should leave. Not surprisingly, he said:

"Let's go."

We left the sauna, with the same guys outside still hanging out. They didn't go anywhere during the time we spend in the sauna and stare at us while we passed by. Suddenly I realised what was going on at that moment. Did a group of guys proclaim the dressing room area of this gym as a casual meet-up location? Given the sexual attention we got by several guys, I would very much think so. Despite it not being accepted by many parents, family or friends, China certainly has a gay community. The stretches of it became visible that afternoon. I have nothing against gays or lesbians. Not at all. But I wish not to be involved in any of those activities unless I ask for it. Now I'm sure this experience must have been an incident. And while we did not go back to that particular gym, it did not happen in any of the other gyms afterwards. Maybe I should start to consider a hotel gym instead. Fewer people and a cleaner environment. But to afford this, I should find a job sooner than later.

I checked the time; it was nearly nine am now. I saw the business card from the Jiao Tong University employee laying on my desk. Would the position he mentioned to me last weekend still be available? Let's give him a call. It did not take long for him to answer the call.

"Wei Ni Hao?" I heard.

This is how the Chinese answer the phone. Not with their name and the company or institution they are working for.

"Eh,... is this James from Jiao Tong University?"

First, no answer. It sounded like as if he was figuring out how to reply to me through the telephone.

"James..? Hello..?" I tried it again. Now it seemed he heard me.

"Eeh yes, this is James from Jiao Tong University."

At least the second time he properly answered with his name.

"James, this is Victor. Remember the tall guy you met on the expat show last weekend? I was wondering whether the teaching position for the project management course is still open."

A silence followed for about five seconds. Just when I wanted to check whether the line was working, I heard

"Yes, it is, but you will have to talk to my boss."

"That's alright, how can I reach your boss?"

Apparently, his boss was sitting right next to him. After he handed over the phone, I heard:

"Yes, this is Johan speaking, I am the coordinator of the International Education Centre of Jiao Tong University."

I heard a fraction of a Dutch accent there. For sure he wasn't local. I continued.

"Good morning Johan, my name is Victor. I met James last weekend on the Expat Show where he told me that there is a position to teach the project management lecture in your Education Centre. I was wondering whether this opportunity is still open?"

Johan provided an immediate answer.

"Yes, it is. What is your background?"

"From January to June this year I did an internship here at Philips Lighting in Shanghai, where I wrote my graduation thesis on a market research of LED Lighting adaption in the hospitality sector in Shanghai, Hong Kong, Macao and Taipei. After I graduated with a bachelor's in International Business and Management, I decided to come back to Shanghai to search for a job. Johan interrupted me.

"Would it be possible to send me your resume now? I would like to have a look at it while we are on the phone."

Luckily, I had an updated version of my resume in my laptop for a consulting position I applied for - and of course heard nothing back from. I attached it in an email, send it to Johan's Hotmail address and we waited for about fifteen seconds.

"So how do you like Shanghai?" Johan informed.

"I think this is a great city to live and work in my current stage of life. There are excellent opportunities in the employment market, and as well to meet new people and increase my business network."

Meanwhile, I heard the sound of an email arriving on the other side of the line.

"Let me have a look." Johan said. "So I see your capabilities... You did an internship in PricewaterhouseCoopers?"

"Yes, that was a year ago. I provided support in business consultation for a couple of clients in the banking, hotel and car dealer sector on the Island of Aruba."

"And you studied in America?"

Finally, somebody who actually reads my resume in detail and seemed at least a bit impressed by it, or at least gave me that feeling. I continued:

"Yes, for an exchange semester. I followed a business program with finance, marketing management, business ethics, managerial economics and accounting."

"What kind of project management experience you have?" Johan informed.

"First of all, as a student, I had a very systematic approach to plan my work, executing it and controlling every step to make sure I meet the deadline. Later during my internship here in Philips, I was responsible for the timeline and deliverables of my thesis, which I had to plan together with stakeholders and some of the other tasks Philips asked me to do. Furthermore, I had a pretty good score for Project Management during my Batchelor at University."

This did not sound good, I thought. He must be looking for an experienced lecturer for his Education Centre and I am listing my experience in project management gained in an internship and a university course. How could this level of experience ever satisfy him? He must be looking for a candidate with throughout professional experience in teaching and project management. Not a newbie like me.

"You know what?" Johan suggested. "Could you prepare a course outline for me, with two whole classes and a lecture book you would like to use? Would you be able to pass by our office tomorrow end of the afternoon?"

Not really knowing what I committed myself to, I said yes. This was an opportunity I did not want to miss. How to make that course outline, two full lectures and to find a book I could worry about later.

"Good," Johan said. "Let's meet tomorrow at 5 o'clock in our office at Kai Xuan Road. You'll face it immediately after you enter the International Continuing Education Building."

"Thank you very much for offering me the opportunity to provide a course outline Johan," I said. "We'll meet tomorrow."

I placed my phone on the desk next to my laptop. A project management course outline, together with the two classes in one and a half-day. My hands went through my hair. Where to start? I remembered the project management course I followed in university, but I did not consider this an excellent and engaging course. I opened the files and presentation to have a look. Maybe I could use the base outline and revise according to my personal insights. But that wouldn't provide me with a matching book. The book I eventually choose should match the course outline I present. I considered it better to use a book structure as course outline, and add some aspects which I like or think should be added. I finished my breakfast and got dressed to go out to the Shanghai Foreign Language Book Store in Fuzhou Road. It usually opens at ten in the morning, so I would be perfectly on time to check for any useful project management literature I could use. When I left home, it was just after nine-thirty, providing me with enough time to take the subway down to People Square. From there I had to take exit fifteen and walk via Raffles City a bit up north to 390 Fuzhou Road near Shangxi Nan Road. I would probably meet the tale of rush hour, but most of the people would be at work now.

Walking on my way to the subway station, I could see the breakfast street sellers packing up their cooking equipment and loading it back onto their triangle bike. Some of them leaving food and eggshells behind for the street cleaners to deal with. I saw grandparents walking out of their homes, together with their grandchildren. Enjoying a casual walk or go to the nearby market to buy vegetables and meat for lunch. The little children often look at me as if I am an alien. With big eyes and no impression on their face, they can distinguish me as a non-Chinese, but because of their young age are not able to categorise me. The grandparents usually laugh because of the shocked reaction and explain them in Chinese that I am a foreigner. Most often, I understand that they tell their grandchild I am an American foreigner. Frankly, most foreigners in China are Americans through the eyes of Chinese people. The first thing they ask you after first meeting somebody is "Are you from America?" This is how conversations often start, followed by myself explaining that I am European and from a small country called the Netherlands. Most of the people can link the Netherlands with bridges, windmills or of course flowers. A few of them occasionally do so with the Red Light District in Amsterdam and our hard and soft drugs policy.

The subway station wasn't very crowded at this time of the day. Only a couple of passengers lined up in front of each door to go into People Square direction. While I was waiting for my train to arrive, the train on the other side of the platform following the outbound city direction was nearly empty when the doors opened. Only a few entered the subway for a drive up north. Sometimes during rush hour, the line in front of each door is so long that you have to wait for the second train to arrive. But trains usually come every three to five minutes. Meanwhile, the subway entered the station and slowed speed throughout the platform. Interesting to realise that all the people around me here have a different destination in mind. Some are off to work, others to school, possibly to see friends or family? And I am on my way to a bookstore, in an effort to successfully start the first chapter of my life after graduation in Shanghai.

Once the subway doors opened, the first people on the platform immediately rushed in, to guarantee themselves a seat rather than let people first leave. It still irritates me that some of the people have no patience to wait six seconds before entering the subway. I did not mind standing as it would only take a couple of stops for me to arrive in People Square. While the subway left Zhenping Road to Shanghai Railway Station, where I should transfer to line one, I remembered to send a message to Linda. After we met we did not have any contact except her reply on my napkin move, after which I wished her a good night. It might be a good moment to ask her how her morning is going. She must be in the office now. I pressed the send button and looked around.

Right before entering People's Square, I could see the crowd increasing. It is the heartbeat of Shanghai's subway system. It is the place where people go out to continue their way to one of the many offices around, or switch line in either north, south, west or east direction of the city. A digital clock in the main hall of the subway station is counting the months, days, hours and seconds down to the Shanghai Expo starting on the first day of May in 2010. Still, five hundred seventy-seven days left. While the construction in the city is already on full speed to make the city ready for this big event, people inside the station here seem to be not bothered with the countdown. The subway station looks like an average subway station in the last phase of the rush hour. Some people are dressed up for an office job, but most are just wearing casual clothes. You can't compare Shanghai with London, New York or Tokyo yet where the majority of people is wearing suits, ties, skirts and blouses. Other people were rushing to one of the exits, either to be on-time in office or to minimise the time they are already late. I followed the flow of people up to street level into Fuzhou Road. Restaurants are still closed, where an external company is cleaning some of them. Two other bookstores are just opening, and so are the few shops offering equipment for painters and other creative artists. From the outside, I can already see the huge brushes they sell, while I wonder for which occasion they are used. Perhaps for very rough paintings.

The Shanghai Foreign Bookstore is a heaven for book lovers. Separated over four floors you can find anything you need from novels, crime and business books, classics, and cookbooks to current bestsellers, IELTS or GMAT test preparation books, teen fiction, fashion and business magazines and school textbooks. The perfect place for me to gain some inspiration for a book on project management. At this reasonable early time of the day, there were not many people yet. I first browsed through the novels and bestsellers on the ground floor. Not because I expected to find a project management book in that section but just for my personal interest. Books like *The Black Swan* from Nassim Nicholas Taleb and Daniel Goleman's *Emotional Intelligence* where stacked up in hardcover versions for purchase. On the sides, I saw shelves with J.K Rowling's *Harry Potter* books and Stephen King's collection of books. It is interesting to see the real books all stacked up here in the bookstore. Less than five kilometres away there are street sellers in Donghu Road, a side street of HuaiHai Middle Road where you can buy the same books in illegal softcover copy and a fraction of the price here. Here the books are easily between one hundred and three hundred RMB. On the street? Just ten RMB.

But even in this bookstore, I should not fully trust what I see. The Writers' Publishing House who are involved with book piracy investigation in China, reported in a 2001 survey that as many as thirty to forty per cent of the books for sale in China could be illegal. The pirated copies are often not identifiable from real copies as they are scanned, re-printed and bundled by an underground publisher. They offer the books for a fraction of the price to sellers in China. They could either offer the book for less or take a bigger share of margin. As I did not see many interesting things among the new titles, I walked up the stairs to the fourth floor, where on the left side, the business and business school textbooks are shelved. On the same floor in the middle part, you can find cooking books, while on the right side I saw shelves filled with colourful children books. I wonder why children books are shelved on the highest floor. Luckily there is an elevator, so the mothers and children do not have to walk the stairs all the way up to see their favourite books. I looked around. I was the only person on the fourth floor together with the staff. They were unpacking books in the same location as I hoped to find a project management book. I browsed through a significant number of law and psychology titles until I found three project management books. Good to know that in case I get an offer to teach law and psychology there are here at least plenty course books to choose from.

What I am looking for in project management is a sort of handbook that guides the reader through the entire project management lifecycle. Something practical and if possible, with examples that I can use in class as well. And an easy to understand curriculum that I could divide over eight courses. I took the books with me and walked to a nearby table where I could read them. Meanwhile, some other people had found their way up the fourth floor. They were mostly university students occupying the walkways between the shelves. They must find it more comfortable sitting on the floor while reading books instead of finding a table. Once I sat down, I found the first project management book to be useless as it was missing the step by step approach through the project management lifecycle I was looking for. The second book was more focussed on case studies and questions to solve project management related issues and constraints. Useful but not something I could write an entire course about. Besides that, case studies are relatively easy to find online. This book provided me with the idea to add one case study to the end of each class, if possible related to the curriculum of that particular lecture. It would be interesting to solve the case study first individually per student and then followed by a group discussion. I started to feel a little bit nervous about not finding the right material for my class, and I opened the third book. If I could not find it here, where else could I? This is the only legitimate place for imported and English books here in Shanghai.

The third book was exactly what I was looking for. A comprehensive guide through all aspects of the project management lifecycle, written by an Australian writer and costing nearly three hundred RMB. For Chinese standards quite an expensive book but it seemed like a good investment to me. One I could earn back over the time of a couple of courses or maybe even a single course, depending on what the university pays. I walked back to the project management section and placed the other two books back. In a country like China, you would expect to find more literature about project management considering the enormous economic development that the country is currently going through. Chinese people must be eager to learn about project management. Perhaps the Chinese section might have more literature on this topic. Or in Chinese companies, people possibly care less about a clear project management framework. People do what they think is good and hope that a project will eventually be delivered. Different from Western culture, Chinese people are more expecting orders from their boss. There could be a clear process in place, but if the boss tells them to do something different compared to the written process, they follow the order without questioning the reason. In a Western business environment, we might question the reason why something has to be done differently.

   I walked towards the cash desk. To avoid people bringing books from one to another floor, one has to pay for the books on the same floor where you find them. On my way to the stairs, I almost stumbled over the legs of a student who was reading a schoolbook in the aisle. He politely apologised, even though it was actually my fault. I walked down the stairs and found my way out to the exit, meanwhile trying not to be distracted by the many books I passed. I can literally spend afternoons in bookstores, scanning the titles of hundreds of books to see if there is anything I like. But today I had another mission to accomplish; preparing a course outline for eight lectures and two complete test courses that could land me a job as a part-time lecturer in Shanghai Jiao Tong University. This could be the start of a successful Shanghai story and possibly opening doors to new opportunities. That day I locked myself in my bedroom behind my desk, only to go out to the kitchen for food, snacks and coffee whilst creating a clear course outline. With help from the book, a course outline from a project management course I ever followed and PMI test exams I found online. This was starting to look like something.

12

Shanghai Subway Line 2 - 09:30

It was just ten-thirty in the morning when the subway departed from Zhongshan Park station into the direction of Hongqiao Road and Yishan Road station. The interview would not start until eleven in the morning, providing me with enough time to depart the train in Hongqiao Road station and walk a couple of hundred meters to the university building in Kaixuan Road. I looked outside the window and saw multiple skyscrapers nearby and on the far horizon moving from right to left as in a puppet-show. Skyscrapers nearby blocked some of the others in the horizon, creating a great view from the bridge rail line. It was a sunny and clear day which helped me to be able to watch as far as Peoples Square with its iconic Tomorrow Square and Le Meridien buildings. When I checked the map this morning, it would not really matter whether I get out in Hongqiao Road or Yishan Road station. The university building is located in the middle of both subway stations. The only difference would be that Yishan Road takes a couple of minutes more to arrive.

After exiting the subway station, I walked into the south direction of Kaixuan Road. It is a busy street where everybody, and that includes cars, busses, bicycles, tricycles, scooters and electric bikes just give each other enough space to move forward. After crossing the traffic lights at Hongqiao Road, I continued to walk in the south direction. I looked at my watch. Still, ten minutes left and a couple of hundred meters to walk. The University building would be located on my left-hand side at the crossing of Kaixuan Road and Panyu Road. Whilst walking over the sideway I could look into the many small shops and some small restaurants that Kaixuan Road had to offer. An organised mess as well, as one shop offered wooden plates that could be used at construction sites, while others supplied signage logos. The wall had hard to distinguish from real logos from McDonald's, Dell, KFC, QQ and some Chinese brands I could not recognise. The restaurants seemed rather small, as most did not have more than five tables inside. The biggest restaurant was a junk food place offering a similar menu as you can find in KFC. In the same red colours. Fries, chicken and hamburgers but mostly fried chicken. Chinese love fried chicken. As big and mighty as they are, McDonald's had to adjust their menu to become more chicken focussed when entering the Chinese market. But this restaurant did not look like a chain restaurant.

Whilst I continue to walk, a building that could very well be the university building appeared on my left-hand side. A high fence led to a gate, from where I could see a glass door providing access to a big hall. I only had the building number as reference to make sure I was in the right place. I could not fully understand the Chinese characters above the entrance. I entered the hall and looked up. I could see five floors with a balcony ending up to the main hall. On my left hand, there were stairs up to the highest floor. Elevators were nowhere to be seen. A front door officer studied me from top to bottom while having a burning cigarette in his mouth. Smoking on the work floor must not be an issue here. I could imagine that sitting and smoking here all day meant that you arrived in life's final chapter before looking death in the face. Instead of windows you could close the main hall was designed with horizontal glass plates containing gaps in-between. All glass plates were installed with a one hundred twenty degrees angle to prevent birds from entering the building, but it must be a torture to work here both in summer and in winter.

Despite the significant breeze, I could smell the incense sticks burned in the toilets. The front door officer still looked at me with the same bored look on his face as before. The only thing that changed was the increased ash at the end of his cigarette. He did not really recognise the fact that it might be his task to lead me to the right office. Or he did not even bother to ask because of the high possibility of a linguistic problem that would follow. I glanced at my watch. Seven minutes before eleven, so I still have a bit of time to figure out which office I have to be. I remembered James's words, saying that the International Continuing Education Office was located right in front of the main door. So, I just had to walk straight. There were indeed four offices in front of me. All doors were closed as if they did not welcome any questions or inquiries. I tried the office right in front of the main entrance, while I saw the front door officer looking satisfactory in front of him as if he was pointing me to the right door. Another problem solved. A chain smoker as he was, he lit up another cigarette. That must be one of the only challenges he faces in a job like this.

Suddenly the door opened, which was indeed the office right in front of the main entrance. A Chinese guy walked out, and after I looked more carefully, I recognised him as James, the guy I talked to at the Shanghai Expat Show. He was quite easy to recognise, wearing Harry Potter look-a-like glasses and his hair pointing to one strange side as if he got up this morning without looking into the mirror. He was wearing a sadly knitted tie, but the smile on his face made up for that. With one hand behind my back and the other one pointing in the right direction, he both pushed and walked me into their office.

"It is good to see you again, James. How have you been?"

James seemed nervous even though I was the one that should feel nervous.

"Oh, fine, fine, thank you," was his quick response. He pointed at a small lounge area right after we entered the office.

"Please have a seat over there, Johan will be here soon. Would you like something to drink? Coffee, tea or water?"

I was dying for coffee, but when I noticed the instant coffee jar, I immediately changed my mind.

"Water please, thank you."

Nobody seemed to care about good coffee here. From my seat, I discovered the small rectangle-shaped office. Behind me was a cabinet with one silver trophy and several books. I couldn't recognise what the trophy exactly represented. It actually could have been purchased in one of the shops I just passed on the way to the university. There were six desks in this office, three on the left side and three on the right side. Only one was occupied by a Chinese lady who did not even look up since I walked in. A couple of plants delivered some well-needed oxygen in this fusty smelling office. James put a glass of water in front of me.

"It won't take long," he assured me.

He took a seat back behind his desk from where he continued working. Or pretended to do so. The reflection of his computer screen in the window behind him revealed that there wasn't any activity going on. The lady occupying the desk in front of him now talked over the phone in a dialect I could identify as Shanghainese. She still did not give me any look. As if I did not exist in that room. All out of nothing, a bell started ringing. James looked up from his screen. So far, I only noticed him right clicking his mouse and refreshing his empty computer screen. A snail would have been more productive in the minutes I was waiting here.

"That's the bell indicating…" and James looked on his watch while he continued:

"…indicating the end of the lecture."

I expected a big movement of students from one to the next lecture, probably the last one before lunch would start. That did not happen. As if James could read the expression on my face, he said:

"Most classes here start at night. This building is not located on the actual campus of Shanghai Jiao Tong University. Here is where the continuing education takes place, mostly for graduated students, young professionals or experienced industry experts who would like to follow classes on particular subjects and earn a degree with that."

I felt a bit more nervous. The students I will possibly teach project management to are way more experienced in business than I am? How could it ever make sense that I, a freshly graduated International Business and Management student, would teach project management to a possible general manager from a multinational company here in Shanghai? With such experience, he or she would probably be more suitable to teach me something. And what would they think? I mean, they sign up for a project management class in Shanghai Jiao Tong University, and all they get is a lecturer with nearly half their experience and possibly half their age in life? The best part in me decided to give it a shot, namely because I had nothing to lose.

While over-thinking this situation, the door swept open and a Western man with a briefcase in his hands rushed into the small office. He wore a bit oversized brown/golden suit, and his tie knotted slightly too low for the height of his shiny Gucci belt. He appeared in an after-retirement age, but that did not bother me. He noticed me instantly and said:

"Ah, you must be Victor! My name is professor Johan."

I stood up to shake his hand and formally introduce myself. His white hairs and oversized glasses surely provided him with the looks of a professor.

"Did my staff offer you something to drink?"

"Yes, they offered me a glass of water," I said to confirm.

"Only water? We have tea, coffee and by the way, whiskey too!"

I smiled.

"Water is good for now."

"Good," and Johan continued, assuming that I did not need an introduction for the institution he worked for.

"Let's go through your course outline and the two lectures you prepared."

I opened my laptop and handed him a paper with headings describing the main topic of each class. Sub-headings covered a break-down of project management theory classified under the main topic. The project management book I purchased yesterday provided a valuable source of information. Johan took his time to read through the course outline.

"This looks good and comprehensive."

"Thank you. I aim to take the students through the entire project management lifecycle in eight courses while finishing each of them with a related case study and group discussion."

"As you might have heard from James, most of our students are graduates and business professionals. They expect less theory, but practical examples used to explain the theory."

"Yes. Please have a look at the two classes I prepared. I believe I covered that well."

I opened the PowerPoint presentation, and Johan browsed through the slides.

"The opening class is focussed on the definition of project management and to emphasise the difference between projects and processes. It can easily be misunderstood."

"You have prepared yourself well," Johan concluded after seeing both classes. I was happy to hear that. If I compared the course outline and lectures with the lessons I once received in university, I considered mine much better.

"Let's talk a little bit about you." Johan continued.

"Do you have a hard-copy of your resume?"

"Sure," I said while opening my laptop bag, grabbed my resume and shove it in front of Johan.

"So, you are Dutch, right?"

"Correct."

"I am from the Netherlands too actually,"

"Oh really? I thought I recognised an accent but wasn't sure."

"Yes, but I left the Netherlands when I was nineteen years old and lived my life in Indonesia and New Zealand. I live in China since the nineteen-eighties."

"That is a long time; you must have seen the country changing a lot since then."

"Sure! You know how Pudong looks like now, right? A mass of skyscrapers. But when I arrived, Pudong was just a green field with a couple of homes built on it. Now they are aiming to make it the financial capital of the world." Johan continued to read my resume.

"I see that you enjoyed an education in both the Netherlands and the United States. And you did an internship here in Philips, good."

I nodded in agreement.

"After my internship, I came back to Shanghai so I could find a job here. I have sent out many resume's but was not lucky yet."

"Well, you'll be fine. It will take time, but you will get there."

"I hope so. This would be a good start." Johan smiled.

"Our course schedules are three hours per week, either on Tuesdays or Thursdays. That depends on when the students are available. And whether there are classrooms available in this building,"

Johan said while he looked at the Chinese lady occupying one of his desks.

"She is responsible for that. She works for the university. This International Continuing Education Centre is a department in Jiao Tong University that I run. I can use the name of the university to offer courses in adult education and pay commission to the university. But the Chinese Dean is a bit suspicious of how I run this department so basically most of the communication and approvals go via her to the Dean. A bit frustrating."

"Well, I guess every company or institution have their bottlenecks in processes and approvals."

"Oh, before I forgot, the minimum number of students we set to start a class is eight. This to break-even on the fixed expenses we have. One of those expenses is your salary. We pay lecturers five hundred RMB per hour, but this is only the time you are actually teaching. Preparation time is for your account."

Wow, roughly fifty Euro per hour. That is not bad at all. The first full lecture I will probably not make much money calculated in time per hour as the preparation time will be extensive. But after that, the preparation time goes down as the course structure is there. From the second or third course onwards, I could make nice money if we ever come to that point. Johan interrupted my reasoning.

"Now listen, would it be possible for you to start teaching next week Tuesday? I have enough students on the waiting list who cannot wait to start their project management course. But I have no lecturer."

I gave myself a couple of seconds to absorb his offer. I was convinced that my course outline and classes were pretty good, but did not expect an offer to start teaching five days later.

"Sure, I would love to take this opportunity!"

"Good to hear. Welcome to the International Continuing Education Centre! You have two courses ready now, so in week one you work on course three, week two you work on course four. In this way, you cannot get in any trouble throughout the lecture schedule. Just make sure you are here a bit earlier than six-thirty, so you have a bit of time to prepare yourself and get ready. Do you have some questions for now?"

I thought for a moment.

"How many students enrolled already for next week's course?"

"Right now, eight students paid already, so they are good to go. We are working to enrol two or three more. Now there is a lecturer it may be easier for them to make a final decision."

"Well, I will be there next Tuesday and make sure all students have an inspiring evening," I said confidently while I closed my laptop and handed Johan the papers with the comprehensive course outline for his reference.

"We will consider this first project management class your probation. Based on positive student feedback, we will start a second class under your leadership, and we have a China MBA program on Saturdays as well that could use a course like project management."

I nodded in excitement.

"But first make sure you handle this class well. The students have been waiting for a couple of weeks now, so their expectations must be high."

Johan offered his handshake as a symbol of our agreement.

"Thank you for offering this opportunity."

And while I looked at James, sitting in the back of the office, still in front of an empty desk screen, I said:

"Special thanks to you James, for talking to me at the Expat Show." James smiled because of this endorsement.

When I left the International Continuing Education building, I couldn't wait to call or send a message to my parents, brother and friends in the Netherlands. When I looked at my watch, I noticed that it was only five-thirty in the morning in Europe, so they are still sleeping. It would have to wait a little while. For sure and to celebrate this first milestone, I will treat myself a nice Vanilla Latte and cheesecake in Starbucks. After that, a couple of days is enough to optimise the first lecture where necessary and to work in advance on future classes. While I walked back to the subway station to take a metro back to Zhongshan Park, the sun came out, feeling very comfortable on this October afternoon. This could very well be the start of something beautiful in Shanghai.

13

Yejiazhai Road, Sichuan Restaurant - 18:49

It was Friday evening, just before seven o'clock. From inside the restaurant, I could see people leaving office towards the nearby located subway station. Ready to start the weekend. Even though I had quite a successful week when it comes to Jiao Tong University, I lost a bit track of the weekends. Since arriving here every day felt like weekend. The next two days I would be finalising my lecture for Tuesday. The reason for me sitting in the same Sichuan restaurant as four days ago is the napkin with the telephone number I handed to Linda. After sending a couple of texts throughout the week, we agreed to meet for dinner. Linda mentioned she would bring a colleague, perhaps not to let it instantly look like a date. Chinese girls do that. I agreed if it would make her more comfortable to meet again. It's interesting how those things can go.

Linda just sent me a text message that they were leaving office and would be arriving soon. As far as I knew her office was on walking distance from the restaurant. Meanwhile, the waitress came with the menu. The smile on her face made me feel like she recognised me from earlier that week. I told her that there would be two more persons arriving, so she left me with three sets of crockery on the table. In many restaurants, this comes tightly pre-packed together in plastic to ensure hygiene. This is a system where the restaurant owns the crockery, but the dishwashing is outsourced. At the end of the night, all the used crockery ends up in a plastic basket and picked up by a company that'll take care of washing the dishes. The next morning everything will be delivered back to each restaurant packed in plastic. But to ensure ninety-nine per cent hygiene, you can still ask the restaurant staff to bring you hot water and a bowl so you can sterilise your pottery. For now, I would wait to do this until Linda and her friend arrived.

I felt my phone buzzing in my pocket. A text message from Linda. She told me that they just left the office and were walking to the restaurant. It would only be a couple of minutes before they would arrive. I browsed a bit through the menu to get some inspiration on what we could eat. The restaurant slowly filled with guests. Some of them were waiting for their friends to arrive, just like me. I was the only foreigner sitting there, and that earned me glances from everybody who walked in. As if an alien after travelling a million kilometre in space just landed on earth and decided to have dinner in the nearest Sichuan restaurant. Suddenly Linda and her friend walked in. From the expression on their face, I could see that they might have run all the way from the office to the restaurant. They both looked sweaty. Linda pulled her hair away from her face and talked something to the waitress. The waitress nodded and pointed in my direction, after which waived to them. Linda smiled and waved back. Once they arrived at the table, I offered them a napkin to dry their face a bit.

"Did you really have to run?" I asked Linda with a smile.

"We were afraid to be late, as my boss did not let us go earlier." Linda explained.

"You have risked your life to be here on time, Linda!" I said while I looked down at her high heels.

"Can you actually run on those?" Linda laughed.

"Pretty good yes. They're good quality." I poured two glasses of tea for them.

"Oh, by the way, this is Cheryl, my colleague." Cheryl first looked at me as if she was forced to join Linda for dinner tonight but calmed down after we shook hands. I could imagine Cheryl never had dinner with an alien-like-me before.

"So nice of you to be here, Linda and Cheryl. I bet you must feel hungry. What would you like to eat?"

"You choose for us," Linda said. I smiled.

"So, you are trusting a foreigner living in China for less than a year to pick your food tonight?" I joked. Linda and Cheryl both giggled.

"Alright," I said while I waived at the waitress who was taking an order at a nearby table.

"Let's choose three dishes with meat and fish, two veggies and three bowls of rice."

I browsed through the menu again. The first picture catching my attention was a dish where slices of beef were bathing in oil, green and red bell peppers and garlic. It looked very spicy but tasteful. As well a plate of Sichuan string beans would be nice, cooked in garlic. As the meat was a boiled dish, I decided to go with a spicy Chong Qing grilled fish. The entire fish including the head is grilled with sauces, garlic, chilli peppers, coriander, ginger and onion. I decided to have another dish that looked like chicken and last but not lease Huigou Rou, which is double-cooked pork belly with leeks and a hint of chillies. The Huigou Rou is not spicy, which will balance the level of spiciness a bit. The waitress arrived back at our table, so I started ordering while pointing at the dishes while I said "Zhege," meaning this one in Chinese Mandarin. And I added three bowls with rice. Linda seemed amused by this.

"Your Mandarin is so good, Victor!" I immediately responded with:

"Oh, please don't get impressed Linda, it's just on a survival level."

Both Linda and Cheryl laughed. Chinese people are easy to impress with only a few words of Mandarin.

"So, tell me something about yourself, Linda" I started.

"Are you originally from Shanghai?" Her gesture already told me she was not, but I kept my role as a foreigner who did not live in China for too long.

"No, I am from Sichuan province."

"Oh! So, this restaurant must feel like home to you?"

"Yes," Linda concluded. "The food is very authentic here."

"And how about you, Cheryl?"

I did not want her to feel like she's the fifth wheel on the car tonight.

"I'm from Zhejiang province."

"That's much closer to Shanghai compared to Linda's hometown."

Linda returned the question, so I explained to them my Dutch origin and that I was living in Shanghai till June for an internship.

"What made you come to China?" Linda asked.

"It was my curiosity that led me to Asia, fuelled by many stories about Shanghai from a Chinese friend in college. And from an economic point of view, China made most sense to relocate to for an internship. After graduating, I considered China a good place to return and start a career. So that's how I ended up sitting right here in front of you."

Both girls seemed impressed.

"So how long is the flight from China to the Netherlands?" Cheryl asked.

"It depends in which direction you're flying, but from Shanghai to Amsterdam is nearly twelve hours. On the way back it will be slightly shorter, roughly eleven hours.

"That's so long..."

"Now tell me, how did you two ended up in Shanghai?"

"We both studied in Shanghai and found a job afterwards. Our family is in our hometown. We both grew up in smaller cities, where development and social security is not as good as in Shanghai. Many Chinese would kill to be able to live and work in big cities like Shanghai and Beijing. Over the longer term, a hukou gives them all the social benefits as well, significantly better compared to any other city in China."

"So that's your plan as well?" I asked. Linda looked serious.

"Not per se," She said. "Once my parents are growing older, somebody will need to take care of them. They do not like to live in a big city, so I can't imagine them moving to Shanghai."

Cheryl nodded as if she faced the same situation, although Zhejiang province is significantly closer to Shanghai compared to Sichuan province. To show the contrast; Zhejiang Province is a two-hour drive, where Sichuan province is a roughly three hours flight. I continued:

"I've never been to Sichuan province, Linda. But it is on my list. I have been reading about places to visit if I ever end up in Chengdu."

"Such as?" Linda informed curiously.

"I would love to visit the districts of Jin Li and Kuan Xiangzi for lunch or dinner, because of the many restaurants." Linda looked surprised.

"That's just like Xintiandi here in Shanghai. Why do you mention that as first, while there are so many historical places to visit? You foreigners always like to visit these fancy places. We locals prefer to spend our time in different locations."

"So where would you bring me instead then?"

I knew I should not start talking about temples now. Locals do rarely visit temples unless they follow a religion. Tourists visit temples as they are listed as historic sites in every Lonely Planet or on travel websites, but I found that after you've seen a couple of them, they all start to look the same.

"I love to walk down the riverside of the Jin River." Linda answered. If I have more time and the weather is good, I go on a day trip to Mount Emei Shan to go hiking and enjoy nature."

"And do you go and watch the pandas?"

"Yes, sometimes I go to the research base of the pandas in the north eastern suburbs of Chengdu."

Meanwhile, the Huigou Rou dish arrived, probably the easiest one to prepare as it is only made by pork belly, leeks and some spices. Sometimes when dining in Chinese restaurants, the dishes arrive so quickly that it makes you wonder how fresh they actually are.

"You try first," I said to Cheryl.

"I know you people from Zhejiang like fresh and soft flavoured dishes, not the spicy stuff Linda had to suffer when she was a child." Linda giggled.

"But actually, the Huigou Rou is the least spicy dish among everything I have ordered. Go for it!"

Cheryl took her chopsticks and tried some of the pork belly slices. While she was chewing, she looked at Linda in search of the right description of the taste.

"Very delicious," She confirmed.

Meanwhile, the waitress placed the second dish on the table. Both Linda and Cheryl looked at it, followed by a smile.

"Did you order this?" Linda giggled even more.

"I am impressed Victor,"

The dish did not exactly look like the one I ordered.

"I think this must be a misunderstanding," I said while I grabbed the menu to confirm.

"I have ordered this one," I said while I pointed to the dish.

"This is chicken, right? At least from the picture it looks like that?!"

The confused expression on my face made both Linda and Cheryl laugh even more.

"Don't let yourself guide by the pictures in the menu, Victor. This is not chicken."

I was getting curious now to what I had ordered instead. Linda continued:

"This dish is prepared with stomach." I looked a bit disgusted. What looks like white chicken in the picture on the menu is actually cow stomach.

"Now since you have ordered it and I am sure you don't usually eat this in the Netherlands... why don't you try this dish first and tell us how it tastes?"

Linda had an entertaining expression on her face. I could see that Cheryl amused herself too. I could not refuse this and better play this game along. It was a cold dish prepared in slices swimming in a spicy red sauce with scallion on top. I took my chopsticks and grabbed a slice of the clean and white stomach. I could feel Linda's eyes following my hands, absorbing every move I made.

"It is okay, Victor, it's not going to kill you. I promise." Linda tried.

"Hmm, I hope so."

I took a bite of the slice. At first, no taste. It actually just tasted like chicken. Two seconds later, the spices hit my tong.

"You see? It's not as disgusting as the expression you just had on your face," Linda concluded.

"A lot of foreigners have preconceptions about Chinese food when they are in China.

"Yes," I added. "And as well without visiting China. Do you know how that is possible? The kitchen of an average Chinese restaurant in Europe is not comparable with authentic Chinese food."

"Oh?" Both Linda and Cheryl seemed surprised.

But how could they know? They never set a foot outside of China's far-stretching borders. I continued:

"The food served by a Chinese restaurant in for example the Netherlands has Indonesian influences if you ask me. Have you ever heard of a dish called babi panggang in China?" Linda nodded no.

"It doesn't even sound like Chinese."

"What is it made of?" Cheryl asked.

"It is made of grilled pork in a sweet sauce with ginger."

"We have grilled pork dishes too," Linda confirmed.

"I bet you have, but not this one. I love babi panggang by the way."

I tried another slice of the cow stomach.

"It seems you love it," Linda said.

"No, I'm actually just hungry. But I have to say it tastes better than I expected."

"Welcome to China," Cheryl said while I welcomed one of the other dishes to arrive. We still had the fish and beef to come. Compared to cow stomach that is more worth waiting for. And rice. I looked around. The restaurant was now full of guests. As usual, I was the only foreigner among locals, however locals may not be a correct definition. Almost sixty per cent of Shanghai's population owns an ancient Chinese originated Shanghai hukou. That doesn't mean that all those people are actually born in Shanghai. As a student, you can earn a Shanghai hukou by earning your educational degrees in Shanghai. As a matter of fact, only the best students with the highest scores in and outside of Shanghai can apply for high school or university in Shanghai. As an employee, your company may apply a hukou for you and your family. This can only happen after a couple of months, and a base requirement is that you've paid healthcare and taxes from the moment you started your job.

There is generally speaking a high demand for hukou's in cities as Shanghai and Beijing due to the fact that the living standards, education, social and healthcare systems are among the best in the country. The structuring hukou system avoids that hundreds of millions of people will move to the big cities with hopes for a better life. I looked around. The majority of people here are certainly migrants enjoying the better side of life. When walking through the malodorous tunnels of Shanghai North Railway Station, you often see struggling immigrants. They make the railway station their home through cold winters and hot summers after leaving their hometown to make it in the big city without any money and often constrained by low education. Coming back to the hometown is seen by family and friends as a failure so immigrants try to avoid this by all means so they won't lose their face. In the big city where nobody knows them, they can save a great amount of money by sleeping on the street or in railway station tunnels. To their home-front, they tell that they are still in prospect of building their business. But the tough reality is different.

I looked at Linda. She was surely a part of the educated group of immigrants. She would survive if she decided to stay in Shanghai. But Shanghai is as flat as a pancake. I could not imagine a Sichuan girl would easily feel like home after growing up between the world's most stunning mountains. Now her eyes almost pierced me.

"You don't eat." Linda pointed to me.

I first looked at her, and in expectation of the other two dishes to arrive at the kitchen. Nothing yet. I took a bit more of the Huigou Rou. The waitress had passed our table a couple of times with sizzling plates, leaving a wonderful smell of spicy prepared fish behind but none of them was ours. The volume of people having conversations with each other always increased throughout the evening, fuelled by the consumption of beer and baijiu. The more people drink, the more excited they become and the louder they talk. Other tables are reacting to this too. It is especially obvious when you are sober while others are drinking. Actually, I love to drink beer when eating spicy food. Just to extinguish the fire in my mouth as a result of the Sichuan spices. But tonight, I do not want to appear as an alcoholic to Linda. I just stick with green tea, complimentary served at the table.

All out of nothing two sizzling dishes were served to our table. The Chong Qing grilled fish and boiled beef arrived. The look of food like this is already a piece of art. Mostly red art, caused by the many spices included.

"Wow!" Said Cheryl.

"You have good taste in ordering food!"

"Yes, I like a balanced meal. In this way, we have vegetables, meat and fish."

"And stomach. You forgot the stomach!" Linda added.

Both girls laughed. I grinned. This must be Chinese humour.

Meanwhile and always as last, the rice was served. Perfectly normal for Chinese people, but Westerners see rice more as a fundamental part of their dinner. We eat potatoes, veggies and meat in even quantities. All are contributing like thirty per cent of the complete meal. We do not first fill ourselves with veggies and meat and serve the potato at the very end. All of it comes in one go. But the quantity of rice Chinese people eat is probably contributing only ten per cent of their entire meal. They first eat a variety of dishes on the table. Once a small bowl of rice is served, they combine it with some sauce, meat or vegetables. Some don't even touch the rice. It is less of an integral part of their dinner. I could see both Linda and Cheryl loved the fish dish. They carefully picked the fish meat out, slowly leaving a visible skeleton behind.

"This is a river fish." Linda noticed.

I could taste that as well. There is a distinctive difference in taste between the two. Sea fish could be even healthier to consume. I was fishing the meat from the bowl, sometimes accidentally catching a red spice too. I could really use an ice-cold beer now, right at the moment that the spices started to explode in my mouth.

"Once you eat Sichuan food more often, you'll get used to the spices." Linda told me. I suspected she could see me having trouble with the level of spiciness of tonight's food. Cheryl, who came from Zhejiang province and not raised with this food, seemed to have fewer problems eating the tingling Sichuan spices. But she might have lunch with Linda on a regular basis. They are colleagues, after all. Nevertheless, Sichuan spices are different compared to Thai or Cajun spices. The effect of Sichuan spices is not as torturing. Sichuan spices give you a tingling feeling in your mouth.

I remember once in America while having lunch in a Thai restaurant that my friends asked me whether I was doing fine after I was sweating like crazy and my head looked red like a tomato. Or the other time when I was a student and worked part-time cook in a New Orleans restaurant. The first time I ate the locally famous shrimp pasta before starting work, I literally had tears in my eyes. That doesn't happen with Sichuan spices.

"Did you always eat spicy food when you were young, Linda?" I asked. She pointed with her chopsticks to her mouth while she was chewing. Her table manners were good, that's for sure.

"Yes," Linda said when she swallowed her bite of food.

"My mom used to cook three times per day for me. But among the daily breakfast, lunch and dinner's dishes, less spicy dishes were served too. So, it's not all like very spicy."

"You must have had a nice variety of food when you were young." "Yes. And besides that, our food is prepared with seven basic flavours: sour, pungent, hot, sweet, bitter, aromatic and salty."

"So, you can have one flavour every day," I joked.

"Next time when we have dinner together, we should have hotpot!" Linda said with a very excited tone. Even Cheryl got a smile on her face.

"We eat spicy hotpot in the winter to warm ourselves up."

"I like hotpot," I answered.

"When I did my internship, I used to have a hotpot restaurant right across the street from where I lived. Together with my flatmates, we went there about every other week, but the problem I have with hotpot is that I always feel hungry afterwards."

Linda looked surprised.

"You never have that?" I asked in return.

"No. But we usually eat the entire night. For two or three hours."

"I think the reason for me is that there are so many vegetables involved. It's too easy to digest. At some point, I feel as if I had enough food. But two hours later, I am hungry again."

"You must have a different digestion system," Cheryl added. I smiled.

"Probably yes. More build on heavy food. So, would you like to order more food?"

We almost finished the dishes on the table. Or at least the eatable parts of it. Whatever left of it were bones, oil and spices.

"No, I am nearly full," Linda answered. Cheryl nodded as well.

"How about yourself?" Linda returned the question.

"I'm good too." And before I could add anything to that, Linda said:

"But you might be hungry again in one hour from now!"

She actually had a certain level of humour. Dry humour that is, not as sarcastically as my jokes usually are.

"There is a twenty-four-hour McDonald's restaurant around the corner here, ready to supply me with Big Mac's once I start to feel hungry again."

I fished the final slices of fish from the bowl filled with oil, veggies and spices. The fish leftover was just the skeleton and on top the head. None of both ladies dared to eat the fish head in front of me. For many Chinese, the fish head is actually the cherry on the pie - a delicacy you can't miss. I wonder how Linda and Cheryl would react if I simultaneously start to suck on the fish head. Chinese people actually think that any organ you eat from an animal will be good for your own organs too. So for example, if you eat the fish eyes, it will be good for your own eyes. Luckily my eyes are perfect. No need for me to absorb fisheyes tonight. Around us, other people started to leave already while the restaurant staff prepared tables in hope for a second seating. My mouth was still on fire.

"How long will these spices usually last?" I asked Linda.

"About twenty minutes?" She answered.

"But you might have some problems tomorrow morning." Linda laughed. Her jokes somehow started to get to me.

"It's quite fun having dinner with you, Linda."

I waved to the waitress to ask for the bill. She was just standing at the cash desk, so it arrived almost immediately. Linda made an attempt to grab the bill, but I was quicker.

"It's my treat, tonight ladies," I said.

"It is nice to have two new friends here in this beautiful city."

I gave the waitress two red one hundred renminbi bills with Chairman Mao on the front. I received the change back immediately as the waitress prepared herself with a few bills to provide as change. With a smile and a thank you from the waitress, we walked out of the restaurant and from the corner of my eye I saw Linda inspecting the table to make sure that we did not leave anything behind.

When we entered the street, we discovered that it rained while we had dinner. The reflections of the buildings around us were visible on the street, even though this small street was not well illuminated. By looking at the trash laying around on the side of the street, dumped by restaurants, I assumed the street cleaners would be busy tomorrow. People passed by, either on their bikes or slowly walking into the Shanghai night. I looked at Linda and Cheryl. It must be around eight-thirty now.

"What is next?" I asked them.

"Do you have any other plans for tonight? If not, we can go to KTV if you like?" Linda and Cheryl looked at each other and had a short conversation in Chinese. At some point, I felt a conclusion was made and Linda said:

"Cheryl will go home because she feels tired."

As if there was no time to waste Cheryl offered her hand, said thanks for dinner and disappeared into the tenebrous Shanghai Friday night. I looked at Linda while she witnessed Cheryl leaving. It was still early.

"She is the nicest colleague I have," Linda concluded.

"We are more friends than colleagues."

She was indeed a nice person. She understood her role tonight, present at the table but not claiming too much attention. She let the conversation go as to how Linda and I initiated. The fact that she left after dinner indicates that I passed the test, or at least I succeeded in making Linda comfortable enough to spend the rest of the evening together.

"What do you feel like doing next?" I asked Linda.

"Hmm," she said while she got a considerable look on her face.

"How about we go to see a movie?"

"Sure, is there any movie you still like to see?"

"Yes, but it is a Chinese movie. I'm not sure whether you will like it."

She got a point. I do not like Chinese movies. The acting deliverables of actors in traditional Chinese movies are terrible. Newer movies are better, but I usually do not make it till the end as the storyline is either predictable or boring. In order to show my best intentions, I said:

"I have seen a couple of Chinese movies I liked." But that was my first lie to Linda already. I did not.

"The problem is that the movies might not have English subtitles. Most of them only have Chinese subtitles while they are Mandarin spoken."

Time for me to propose a plan B. We had to be quick as it started to rain again. The reflections of millions of city lights were now united in the low passing clouds, making it look like a grey blanket covering the city.

"I do have a couple of new Western movies at home. They have both Chinese and English subtitles. I live just right across the Suzhou River,"

I said while I pointed towards the three towers of Xinhu Riverside Apartments, towering high above the houses and restaurants of the street we enjoyed our dinner. Suddenly the feeling grabbed me that it may be too soon to ask her to my apartment. She might not feel comfortable with this offer. Linda overlooked the skyline in the direction of the Xinhu Riverside apartment compound.

"That will be nice too," She concluded. People driving bikes and tricycles passed by. They suddenly appeared in the already dark street. This little street is actually a dead-end street for cars. But the small bridge between Yejiazai Road and Guangfu West Road is an important connection for pedestrians and bicycle drivers. Once we got closer to the bridge, the street sellers were taking measures to hide from the rain by covering the clothes or electrical gadgets they were selling. Once on the other side of the bridge, it would only be a couple of hundred meters until the entrance of the compound. From there we could walk through the underground parking garage in order to avoid the rain. These days it is always recommendable to carry a small umbrella as rain appears out of nothing. But I always forget. Linda had a bit of difficulty keeping my pace as the structure of Guangfu West Road was highly uneven, and she wore high heels. Every other five or so steps complete tiles were missing. The Putuo district government would do good to spend a part of their budget on constructing this street.

After arrival at the gate, we took the stairs down to the parking garage. I navigated Linda and myself in the right direction.

"Wow, look at the cars here," Linda said with an open mouth while we passed by along a couple of Mercedes models, BMW's, Porsches and a Maserati.

"The people living here must be rich," Linda concluded. I nodded.

"But I am only renting."

I did not want to give her the wrong impression. Linda seemed impressed by the cars. I decided to minimise her expectations a bit.

"What you see here is only the outside, Linda. We see a nice home and a nice car. But what we don't see is how much money these people owe the bank in order to achieve this. Sure, they still need enough cash flow to be able to pay the monthly mortgages and car loans but don't stare blind on what you see."

Linda looked at me with a questionable expression on her face.

"But don't let this stand in your way to work hard, earn success and one day be able to afford yourself a home and car like you see here," I advised Linda.

The sound of her high heels echoed through the parking garage. One of the neighbours passed by but did not say a thing. We followed the signs to the right building number and arrived at the elevator from where we could go directly to the tenth floor. I still considered it a bit strange or possibly unusual to stand here in this elevator with Linda. She had a bit of a tensed expression on her face, or that is at least how it appeared to me. She stood silently next to me and looked at herself in the mirror with an expression on her face as if we would face a big crowd after leaving this elevator. What makes this girl following a guy home after she just barely know him for four days? Trust probably? And a bit of curiosity? Suddenly Linda looked me in the eyes via the mirror and asked me with an excited tone:

"Which movies do you have?" I took a moment to think. I had quite a few DVDs at home.

"Ehm, among some others I have *Transporter 3*, a movie called *Australia* with Nicole Kidman, *Hancock,* and *Yes Man* with Jim Carrey. And *Californication*, but that's a series." Linda looked confused. None of those names seemed to make any sense to her.

"Let's see after we arrive," Linda concluded while the elevator doors opened up.

The lights in the hallway automatically turned on as a result of the sound sensors in the wall. While we walked to the front door, I took the keys out of my pocket, and the fact that there was no light showing underneath the door meant that Mr Lu was not at home. I opened the door and turned on the lights in the living room.

"Welcome," I said to Linda. "This is where I live."

"It looks nice and spacious," was her first reaction. Linda walked around in the living room as if she was viewing it with an aim to rent or purchase the place.

"You live here so nice Victor," I nodded.

"How do you live?"

"I share a small apartment with Cheryl. We have two small bedrooms and a small corridor ending up in a kitchen. Not even a living room. We just spend most of the time in our rooms."

"So do I. The only time I am out here in the living room is to watch a movie. Or to have dinner. But I mostly eat outside." Linda sat down on the couch.

"Do you have a pair of flip-flops so I can take off my high heels?" She asked.

I walked to my bedroom where I remembered to have slippers I took from a hotel. When I came back, Linda found the DVD's and was carefully checking each of them. I looked outside. Right in front of our apartment tower was an exact same tower. I remember myself once while entering the compound in deep thoughts ending up in the wrong building after taking the wrong path. As the walkway towards the tower and the entire interior looks identical, I only figured it out once I was in front of the apartment number D on the tenth floor and noticed a rack with shoes that could impossibly be mine or Mr Lu's. And when I turned around and looked through the window, I saw my laundry hanging on the balcony of the building where I live. When I confessed this embarrassing moment later to Mr Lu, he told me he had the same experience before. The distance between the buildings was created by a small natural lake and two paths. Close enough to see people hanging laundry outside, sitting on their couch and watch TV, arguing to each other in the living room or peacefully smoking a cigarette on the balcony.

Downstairs I saw people walking towards the main entrance of the tower, probably just arriving home from dinner or work. It had stopped raining now. But the sky above us seems filled with clouds as if it could rain anytime soon again. I decided not to close the curtains somehow to make Linda feel safer.

"I will make some tea for us. Let me know which movie you would like to see,"

I told Linda while I walked to the kitchen. The spicy food made me feel thirsty. I felt like I could drink a gallon of water. While the water was boiling, I walked back to the living room.

"I would like to see this one," Linda said while she handed me one DVD.

Out of all movies she chooses *Californication*.

"That's not a movie. Those are episodes. I'm not sure whether we can finish season one tonight." I said jokingly.

"Never mind, we can watch just one or a few episodes depending on how we feel." I heard the whistling sound of the boiling water and walked back to the kitchen.

"Oh, by the way, I live with the brother of my landlord," I said with a louder voice while I was in the kitchen. Just to make sure that Linda would not feel threatened when all out of nothing, a strange man walks into the apartment.

"I noticed there is a second bedroom yes," Linda answered.

"He might come home later tonight, usually around nine o'clock."

"That is all right," Linda answered. When I walked back into the living room, she managed to turn on both the TV and DVD player and browsed through the menu of *Californication*.

"Are you somewhere in the middle of the season or shall we start with episode one?"

"Let's start with episode one,"

That will save me a lot of explanation of background information for her to understand the series. Suddenly I remembered that the first scene of episode one starts when Hank, played by David Duchovny, walks into a church and asks Jesus to help him get his life back on track. While asking this, he is approached by a pretty blonde nun offering him a blowjob on the spot. I wonder how Linda will take this season opener. Well, she can't blame me. She was the one choosing to watch *Californication*. While I took a sip of tea, Linda was focussed on the screen while Hank drove his black Porsche to the church, guided by a choral version of the Rolling Stone's *You can't always get what you want*. He walks into the church while dropping his cigarette into a bowl with holy water and starts to talk to a crucified Jesus. This must be totally new to Linda. A new level of comedy. She actually laughed when the nun offered Hank the blowjob, and Hank repeats "a blowjob from you?" where the nun looks at zip height of his pants and answers "well, something tells me it's not going to suck itself, Hank." Within the first minute of the episode, the tone was set. *Californication* would not have been my first choice out of all movies because of the high degree of sex, but again, Linda chose it.

While *Californication* continued, I looked at her, positioned on the couch next to me. We both sat in the corner, leaving a small unused space between us. The living room was poorly illuminated by the table light. What was missing here is a light source with dimming function right next to the couch to create a bit of atmosphere. The interior of this apartment was a mix of IKEA and other unknown branded furniture. Not a collection fitting together according to my taste, but it had a touch of designer styled interior, especially for a Shanghai apartment. It probably helped that the landlord and her husband have a designer background, but I seriously questioned myself whether that experience could have shown them the need for a light source in the far-end of the living room. Next time when I go to IKEA, I might purchase a nice floor lamp in case I feel like to spend more time in the living room. So far, both Mr Lu and I spend most of our time in the bedroom. The living room and the kitchen happened to be more of a non-official space separating the two bedrooms. A wide corridor leading to the front door when we were on our way out. Or to say hi when our paths coincidentally crossed.

Inspired by Hank Moody and while *Californication* resumed, Linda asked me whether I wanted to become a writer. Did she fear that all writers are like this and I would ultimately end up like a drunk-writing-sex-addict too?

"I have thought about publishing a book about project management in China," I answered. "As a guideline for project managers to make them aware of the cultural differences in the Western and Chinese project environment. But I need more experience to be able to write an interesting story." Linda nodded in agreement.

"If you could choose your dream job right now, what would that be?"

"Working for a multinational company and if possible, in the lighting industry. As a result of a lighting research I conducted in Shanghai, Hong Kong, Macau and Taipei I have learned a lot during my internship earlier this year, which was a real source of inspiration for me. But it is not easy to re-join Philips at this moment. The economic crisis in the US and Europe is threatening new hires globally."

Linda had no eye for *Californication* anymore and turned herself to me.

"Or you can start your own company."

"I feel like I need more experience for that and a network. I'm just starting here. How long are you working now?"

Linda thought for a second while pointing her eyes to the wall.

"Just six months if you count my internship as well. I first joined this company as an intern."

"So you're fresh to the workforce as well. In fact, I will start teaching the course of project management from next week onwards at Jiao Tong University. Just for three hours a week, but I hope it gives me an opportunity to further expand my career in Shanghai."

"That sounds great Victor," Linda said now with an excited smile on her face.

"Jiao Tong University is a famous university in China."

"In fact, I just had the interview today."

"You have something to celebrate then!" Linda said. "Where is the champagne?" She laughed. "I'm just kidding. But I am happy for you." In her happy flow, she continued:

"Have you visited Yiwu?"

"Yes, I went there for a weekend earlier this year."

"How did you like it?"

"Well, if you plan to start your own company, it's worth paying a visit. The interesting thing is that there are four districts now, and I walked around for three days, and I haven't even seen half of the exhibition floor. There are more than forty-thousand individual shops where you can buy literally everything in mass quantities. District five is in the planning, extending the total shops to more than seventy thousand. Exporters and business owners go there to bulk-buy their goods."

Linda listened and seemed impressed that I knew so much in detail about Yiwu.

"I sometimes go there as the logistic company I work for ship goods from Yiwu to the Middle East or Africa." I nodded.

"But I learned that it makes not much sense to plan a trip to Yiwu if you don't have a clear business plan in mind. If you have a product you'd like to sell, for example, cups, you can specifically visit the shops that sell cups to check their prices, options and quality. I went there with an open mind, more like to get inspiration. With seventy-thousand shops, it is easy to wander around and lose focus."

Linda turned a bit closer to me while *Californication* was still playing. She missed the last two sex scenes as a result of our conversation. Better anyway, it wouldn't be good to just sit silently on the couch and watch a movie. It's so interesting to meet new people and learn about new things.

"Next time I'm going there I will let you know. It might be good for you to meet some of the people I know there." I liked Linda's proposal. Without asking for it, she offered to introduce me to her network in Yiwu.

"But let me first have a business plan,"

With California playing further, I had to think about the two guys from India I met while I visited Yiwu. They offered a service in quality checks for goods before they leave from China to India or the Middle East, so exporters did not have to travel to China to inspect every single delivery on any possible issues. Two friendly guys. We first met in a bar, where they approached me with the question of what business I was in. When I answered that it was more of an orientating trip for me, they explained Yiwu more in detail and the service they offered. As they recognised the need to establish a business relationship, they ordered a bottle of vodka, which we enjoyed together with some other most likely new friends. From that first bar, they showed me around in Yiwu on a small motor, none of us wearing helmets. When you look back on it seems dangerous, but its China. In a city like Yiwu, nobody really cares. Despite the vodka, we consumed none of us seemed drunk. While carrying the bottle of vodka with us, we drove to another two bars. At the end of the evening, they asked me whether I was in for some fun, as they knew the best place in town for massages and more. The Ramada hotel seemed to have a hidden floor - as many hotels in China have - where excellent service was offered for a good price: enjoy a shower together with one of the model girls inside, followed by a blowjob, thereafter a naked body soap massage and last but not least sex. It seemed like they experienced it before, as I listened to the high level of detail in which they introduced me to this hotel. They may even earn a commission on my visit! But it was around 3 in the morning at that time I excused myself and went back to my own hotel.

    The second night was less fun, though. I went out for dinner in an Indian restaurant, leaving me with a food poison that kept me almost all night in the bathroom. I suspect it was the tofu in one of the other dishes must have been expired. The next morning, I felt so incredibly weak and empty that I asked the hotel whether they knew a pharmacy where I could buy some medicines. They actually send one of their staff with me to a local hospital, where I was given a cocktail of seven Chinese medicines that must have made Michael Jackson jealous. But it worked. I never recovered from a food poison so quick, and at night I had a normal dinner again.

    I looked back to Linda. The changing colours from the television were reflected on her face. She'd taken her shoes off and comfortably sat with raised legs on the couch, holding one pillow to cover her belly. We were heading towards nine o'clock, and I started to wonder what would be next. Make her some more tea and watch another episode of *Californication*? Go out for a drink? Barbarossa, a Moroccan styled lounge right in the middle of People Square would call for a night like this. Nice cocktails, beers in an Arabian styled environment with dimmed lights would add a touch of romance to our newly established friendship. Or Linda would simply decide to go home around ten o'clock.

"Will you work tomorrow?" I asked.

Not an odd question to ask anybody in Shanghai or China. Many companies still apply a sixth day to their working week. Or ask their employees to show up two Saturdays per month. They still have the traditional mindset that efficiency is higher when employees work six days per week, while many employees take it easy on Saturdays.

"No, I just work five days per week," Linda answered. "All of our clients work from Monday till Friday, so there is no need for us to be in the office on Saturday. What's your plan for tomorrow?"

I considered what to answer. Actually, not that much.

"I have to work on my project management class," I answered. "The first three classes and the course outline are there. But I still have some points I would like to improve. As well do some reading on project management."

Linda nodded as if she agreed and approved my plan. The first episode of *Californication* finished, and the DVD was back at the main menu selection, repeating a short theme song every fifteen-seconds. If we started another episode, it would finish around ten pm, which would be good timing to decide on what to do next. Or possibly the moment for Linda to tell me that she feels tired after a long working week and prefer to go home. Fine too. I browsed through the menu to search for episode two and pressed OK for it to start playing.

"How did you like the first episode?" I asked to check her opinion.

"Funny and smartly written," Linda instantly answered.

Despite our talks, she did manage to catch some parts of the episode. She did not seem to bother Hank's character heavily affected by sex, drugs and alcohol. I'm sure some Chinese girls would be scared off by that, fearing that they would end up sitting in front of a similar womaniser as Hank Moody. But Linda seemed perfectly able to separate fact from fiction.

"Would you like some more tea?" I offered Linda.

I still had a big thirst as a result of our spicy dinner. Linda must be better capable of dealing with it.

"Yes, please."

While I walked to the kitchen, I heard the key moving in the front doors lock.

"That must be my flatmate," I said from the kitchen.

"All right," Linda said but did not look up while she was browsing through an interior design magazine left by the landlord.

When the door opened, it was indeed Mr Lu, arriving back from his sister's home. He said politely "Ni Hao" which is nothing more than "Hello," and walked directly into his room. This is a normal way for the Chinese to introduce themselves to strangers. If we Westerners would find a welcome stranger in our home, we would probably be a bit more open by introducing ourselves with a handshake and our name. Chinese may not want to be involved too much in a friendship between a flatmate and a stranger.

I walked with two cups of tea in my hand back to the living room. Linda looked up when I approached the couch.

"Here, a nice cup of black tea. But be careful, it is too hot to drink right now."

I walked to the window. The fact that more lights in the building in front of us were switched on indicated that more people were home now. Our room was just illuminated by one ceiling light, and even in dimming mode. Most of the light came from the television. I pressed the enter button so episode two could start.

"What fascinates you most about Shanghai?" Linda interrupted.

"You came a long way. There must be something here that you don't have in the Netherlands." I thought for a second.

"Well, it's not just something. Firstly because of the job opportunity right now. In the Netherlands, and as a result of the financial crisis, it is difficult to find a job as a graduate. Shanghai with twenty-four million people is bigger as the Netherlands, and the economy is still growing. What's helping is of course life convenience. Shanghai has everything to offer what you need when it comes to food, restaurants, shopping and dining. I never feel bored. It offers more options than you actually need in entertainment. The only thing I miss here in Shanghai is a beautiful beach," I concluded.

"If you want to experience nice beaches, you'll have to travel to Sanya. Chinese people call it the Thailand of China. But you have to understand that Chinese people are not so fond of the sun. We rather stay outside the sun in order to avoid getting tanned."

"I noticed that yes. People here are carrying umbrella's all the time. No matter whether the forecast mentions rain or sunshine." Chinese people like to stay as white as possible," Linda added.

"Why?"

"Very simple. If you are tanned, people tend to think that you are a farmer. Your skin must be tanned as a result of the work you do on a farm."

I looked at Linda. She had a white face indeed. We, Westerners, like to get a bit tanned, otherwise people may think you're sick or unhealthy by the way you look so white. Linda must always carry an umbrella too, no matter what the weather will be.

"Sichuan people do naturally have better and whiter skin compared to other provinces." Linda said.

"Why is that?" I asked.

"Because you see less sunshine compared to other parts of the country?" I smiled when I said this, just so it was clear that I was joking.

"It actually depends on where you live in Sichuan," Linda ensured me.

"There are many differences in heights and terrain, so that comes with a highly variable climate."

That was true. Sichuan is a mountain area. Linda continued:

"As a result, we usually have long, hot and very humid summers. They are followed by short, dry and cloudy winters. I believe we have the lowest sunshine rate in China."

So there is no need for me to move to Sichuan province. From June till September, Shanghai is already too hot and humid for me.

"People joke that you can walk into a shopping mall on the first floor and get out on the other side of the mall on the same floor, but you leave the mall on the sixth floor."

"You build shopping malls against mountains. You know, the biggest part of Holland is as flat as a pancake. Just in the south, we have a couple of hills. But not steep enough to build malls against it."

"I would love to travel to Europe once and experience the difference in cultures it has to offer in such a small place."

That's true, I thought. France has roughly the same size as Sichuan province. Such a different contrast.

"Did you know when I drive from my hometown to London, I cross four countries in five hours?" Linda looked amazed.

"I start driving in the Netherlands, cross through Belgium to the north of France and take the train under the canal from Calais to Dover. We actually bring our car onto the train and continue to drive in England."

"Wow, that sounds amazing. We can drive for twelve or twenty-four hours, and chances are big you are still in China."

"Yes. But even though you are in the same country, there are differences in cultures. This is probably most noticeable in food. In Zhejiang province, people like to eat seafood prepared with light and sweet flavours. This taste is shared with almost the entire East coast, in the Guangdong, Fujian and Jiangsu provinces. Only when you move up a bit North-East to Shandong province, you will recognise a saltier taste to generally seafood dishes. Moving a bit to the West, Anhui province has the characteristic to add wild plants as ingredients, preferably stewed and using more oil for cooking. For spicy food, you have to be in Hunan province and where you grew up Linda, in Sichuan province."

Linda nodded in agreement.

"But despite knowing that both Hunan and Sichuan favoured spicy food, is there a clear difference between the taste? I know for example, that New Orleans' Cajun spices are significantly different compared to the spices used in Thai food. That is geographically understandable. Hunan and Sichuan province are much closer. I figured you must be the perfect person to ask this question."

Linda laughed.

"Yes. Our food is considered spicy and bold, prepared with more garlic, ginger, chilli and peanuts. One distinguished flavour is the Sichuan peppercorn. It is hardly used in other regional dishes."

I suddenly remembered the power of that peppercorn. I used to have a numbing, tingling taste in my mouth for thirty minutes afterwards. It completely paralysed the taste buds in my mouth. I had to flush two big bottles of Tsingtao beer through my mouth until I only felt a little bit better.

"Then how about Hunan spices?"

"Hunan food is prepared while stir-fried, steaming and smoking, which… how to explain, add a more sautéed, hot and sour taste to the food."

"Is it therefore even spicier compared to Sichuan food?"

"I do not like to admit this, but Chinese people often say that Hunan cuisine is tastier compared to Sichuan's cuisine."

"Why is that?"

"Because the Sichuan peppercorn isn't used in Hunan cuisine." So at least Hunan food won't paralyse my taste buds. I should check it out next time I am in search of food.

I looked at Linda. This is why I like meeting new people. The conversations you have with these people often bring new perspectives. But this conversation wasn't finished.

"It is not just cuisines which are creating cultural differences in China, Linda." Linda turned her face from the TV screen to me.

"What do you as foreigner consider another cultural difference in China?" As a native Chinese, she would surely be able to tell me, but instead, she was interested to hear it from my mouth.

"Despite the fact that there are right now one point three billion Chinese people, there are multiple ethnic groups. You are part of the biggest group if I am correct, the Han people." Linda nodded in agreement.

"Han people are contributing a bit more than ninety per cent to the Chinese population. But there are fifty-six ethnic groups in China recognised by the government." Linda interrupted me.

"Did you learn that in school?" But I continued, ignoring her question. "In Yunnan, the Han population contributes sixty-seven per cent to the ethnic composition. The Yi people are second, living as well in Vietnam and Thailand, but in China primarily in the rural areas of Yunnan, Guizhou, Guangxi and Sichuan."

Linda seemed impressed by my knowledge in this field.

"How do you know all this?"

"Well, it is part of the interest in a country and region when you travel somewhere." Linda yawned and stretched her arms in the air. I started to feel sleepy too. I am not an evening person, so usually from ten o'clock onwards I am pretty useless. By just sitting on the couch, I could easily fall asleep. But frankly speaking, this does not appeal to a Saturday night in a nightclub. As long as I am walking around, it is fine.

The second episode of *Californication* reached its end. On the background, I could hear Mr Lu taking a shower. He would be sleeping soon. Linda looked at me as if she was waiting for an invitation to stay overnight. I would not mind but did not have the guts to directly ask that. What if my assumption on her looks is wrong? That would be embarrassing. Linda looked at her watch.

"It is just after ten o'clock now," she concluded.

"It may be a little bit too late to go home. The subway will stop driving soon."

As far as I knew, most subway lines in Shanghai do not stop driving until at least eleven or eleven thirty at night, but I accepted this as a reason for her to stay overnight. Safety would not really be a constraint either; Shanghai is globally one of the safest cities to walk around at night. I did not question her. If she for any reason would not feel comfortable to go out at this point of the evening, why would I push her?

"You can stay here if you want?"

Linda smiled.

"Can I shower before we sleep?"

"Sure, no problem. I will give you a towel and a t-shirt to sleep in."

I walked to the closet in the bedroom, where I selected my most comfortable and soft towel. As well a gold yellow t-shirt with big scarlet red Texas State letters that I purchased in memory of my semester abroad. My XL size would fit her like a short dress. I left both the towel and t-shirt piled up on the marble countertop in the bathroom.

"All is ready, and the bathroom is yours." I said while I walked back into the living room.

Linda was staring through the window, with her back towards me. Her long black straight hair covered more than half of her back.

"This is such a nice place to live, Victor." I walked up to her, stood next to her and nodded yes.

"You can watch all the way to Zhongshan Park,"

"Yes, but I heard that they are planning a phase B of Xinhu Riverside Apartments right next to this tower, downstairs where you see all those old homes."

I pointed to the neighbourhood besides us. It consisted of very old Shanghai homes with narrow streets so small that cars couldn't enter. Even with a bicycle would be difficult. I would be curious to walk into this little neighbourhood and see what is actually going on in there. But foreigners don't live there, so I would be strange for me to walk around. I did not want to be a lookie-loo.

Some of the homeowners were building extra rooms on their roof as if they knew that time would come when a rich property developer would buy the ground and build a new residential compound. A house with five or six rooms sells for more than just two rooms.

"I wonder how it is to live there," Linda said.

"Some of those homes don't even have front doors or windows."

"Really?"

"Yes, when you follow the path to the Carrefour, there is a hotel. It must be the smallest hotel in town, with only two or so rooms and the front door is missing. There is no reception area at all. You can watch straight inside the place, where the guest's privacy is only created by a curtain hanging in front of their door."

"That must be terrible in the winter!"

"And how about summer?" Linda joked.

"In the summer you have a constant thirty-degree temperature, a lot of cockroaches and other bugs that can enter the hotel and your room without any problem. There is almost no difference between sleeping on the street and in this hotel. Except that you are surrounded by four walls and a roof that's leaking."

Linda turned to me.

"Hey, you can go and shower first if you want,"

"Either way, whatever makes you feel comfortable. I can have a quick shower first."

I walked to the bedroom, took some clean underwear and followed my way to the bathroom. While I was undressing, I could see Linda walking into the bedroom, her body appearing like a vague gesture through the diffused glass door. I opened the shower tab and soon felt warm water streaming from top to toe. In order not to delay Linda too much, I quickly washed my hair and applied soap on my skin. After that, I brushed my teeth, reminding me that I had to arrange a toothbrush for Linda as well. For a second, I considered whether it would be a good idea to walk into the bedroom while only wearing my underwear. I didn't have anything else to wear here except for the clothes that I wore today. I looked into the mirror. Never mind, I am in my own home, and if Linda did not want to see me like this, she should not be in my bedroom right now. Or even staying over at all. I opened the bathroom door leading to the bedroom where Linda lay on my bed, reading one of the designer magazines from the living room. She looked up.

"Ah, you are ready." She said as if she saw me like this a thousand times already. There were no embarrassing or shocking elements in her voice.

"All you need is already selected in the bathroom. A t-shirt, towel and a toothbrush."

"Thank you, Victor." Linda walked through the open door into the bathroom and closed it. I established myself on the side of the bed, spread the cover and pulled it all over me. I could feel the warmth left by Linda, who just laid here for ten minutes while I took my shower.

"Let me know if you need anything else," Since she was in there, I did not hear any movements. As if she was looking at herself in the mirror. The silence was broken by a short but conclusive

"Okay."

The diffused glass door exposed a vague gesture and movements, providing enough privacy as it intended to do. I could hear her unzipping her dress, after which she bent a little bit to get her legs out of it. Should I play some music as a distraction, giving us both a bit more privacy?

I got out of bed and walked to the laptop on my desk. Maybe Keane with *Bedshaped* would be a good choice for now since we both will be bed shaped soon. Through a small gap between the glass door and the wall, I saw Linda standing in front of the mirror, naked now and exposing just enough for me to see her body curves from her hip up to her breast. She then turned away from the door, walking into the shower and opening the tap.

"Screw the music," I whispered to myself and went back to bed. Linda minimised the time in the shower as well. Chinese people living in the northern parts of China are known for their providence with water. Inner Mongolia for example, know short water supplies, but I could not remember that this water consideration is embedded in Sichuan province as well. In mountain villages probably so as they depend on rainwater. Linda dried herself fairly quick, and with her leaving the bathroom, a flow of steam followed her into the bedroom.

"How was your shower?"

"Nice, I liked the rain forest shower head."

Linda looked cute in my oversized Texas State t-shirt. It just covered her body enough.

"What do you think?" Linda asked while she was standing next to the bed.

"What do I think about what?" I asked just to clarify.

"About me, like this." Is she looking for confidence or encouragement for a possible next step? One more step will bring her into this bed, closer to me than she ever was.

"You are looking gorgeous Linda." This was simply the best possible answer I could think about for this moment. And it is true. In my opinion, outer beauty is best reflected when a girl is still stunning without wearing make-up. Linda ticks that box.

"I see you have a nipple piercing?" Linda giggled while she pulled the cover and step into bed.

"Yes, since I was eighteen years old."

"How did you come up with the idea?"

"I saw guys wearing nipple piercings on French beaches during the holidays I spend there with my family. After we came back to the Netherlands, it a good time to visit the tattoo shop for a piercing. So I called my parents to tell them my idea."

"And your parents agreed to that?" Linda looked surprised. "Chinese parents would freak out over such a thing."

"Pretty much. My mum was okay with it, while my dad said that perhaps I had to overthink it a bit more. But I thought it over for a long time already, so the decision was made. Do you have any hidden piercings or tattoos?"

Linda laughed.

"No. My parents would never agree with something like this."

Linda was laying on her left side now, her head supported by her arm and looking in my direction. I lay on my back, looking Linda in the eyes and felt the difference of two bodies now warming up the bed instead of just myself. We looked at each other without saying a word. This is the moment that either Linda or I could reach out for a kiss. But nothing happened.

The silence was overwhelming for a moment. It's never silent in cities like this. There is always noise. People are talking, emergency sirens, Mr Lu taking a shower or nearby firework because of a wedding. I slowly moved my hand under the bed cover towards Linda. Despite the silence she did not notice until my fingertips touched her belly. Her look seemed more intense now. I could feel my heartbeat increasing. I moved a little bit closer to Linda, which she answered with a shy smile on her face. With that, I could see a hard nipple pressing through the gold yellow cotton of my t-shirt. Considering the temperature here, that wasn't because she was feeling cold. I moved on my side as well and put my hand on Linda's hip. Still, no objection, which increased my confidence to reach out for a kiss in her neck. I could smell the left-over of a sweet and seducing perfume right before my lips touched her skin. Linda slowly released her breath as a reaction of excitement, and I moved my hand from her hip to her leg so I could feel her soft and warm skin. I continued to kiss her while I slowly moved up to her cheek. Linda enjoyed every move so far with her eyes closed. I pulled my hand from her leg up to her butt and noticed that she did not wear any underwear. She opened her eyes and laughed naughty while my hand was touching her bare-naked skin. I pulled my hand further under her t-shirt and massaged her firm breasts. Now Linda took the initiative and kissed me full on my mouth. What a feeling, as if we are the only two persons on earth. Or the entire universe.

I surrendered myself to Linda, while I undid myself from my underwear. I was laying bare-naked next to her now, and while she continued to kiss me, I could feel her hand moving from my shoulder down to my back, butt and ultimately moved to the front where she curled her fingers around my cock and massaged it slowly. I twitched her t-shirt up, while Linda pulled her arms, so it smoothly went over her head and on the ground next to the bed. We were both naked now with our skin touching each other, embraced in each other's arms. The kissing continued until Linda climbed up on me, giving me a nice view of her round breasts. I cupped them in my hands, and while she reached down for another kiss, I could feel them both pressed against my chest. She got back up and blindly pressed her fingers around my cock from behind her back while she looked me seducingly in the eyes.

"Do you keep some protection around here in your apartment, Sir?" She said with a hoarse voice and a naughty smile while she bit her lip. I looked up.

"Oh, yes, of course."

She is clearly the wise one among us. I reached to the bedside table, where I kept a couple of Durex. I pulled myself up with the support of my elbows and tore the Durex packaging open. While keeping the top of the condom between my left pointing finger and thump, I rolled it down with my right hand. Linda kept the fire between us burning with soft kisses in my neck. Essential on a moment like this. Even though condoms have the advantage to provide an increased level of security, it is usually a mood killer on the moment you actually have to wear one. Once the condom was settled, Linda grabbed my cock again and guided me to the entrance of her wet pussy. She slowly leaned backwards, leading me deeper and deeper inside of her. Her body shuddered with pleasure.

"This feels so good…"

She reached down to me for more kisses while she slowly moved up and down. My hands went from her breasts down over her hips to her butt, pulling her a bit quicker. Linda moaned softly in my ear, making me feel even hornier. Can we just continue doing this all night long? It feels so good. I am melting inside! We ultimately turned around, so I ended up back on top. Linda's breasts, I estimated a small C size, moved along with the rhythm. She pulled me towards her and started to French kiss me. The pure passion increased to the moment I felt my heart stuttering and reached an intense orgasm. I wanted to pull out, but Linda gave a little whimper of protest. She pressed me against her with my cock fully inside her.

"This was so good Victor…" She whispered while she looked me deeply in my eyes, expecting me to confirm.

"It was indeed…" I slowly eased out of her, yanked the condom off me and ended up on my side right next to Linda with our skins still touching each other. Her eyes were blinking and staring at one point of the white ceiling. I pulled the duvet cover over our bodies to keep us warm. Linda, whilst still staring at the same point on the ceiling, said:

"It is interesting how things can go. Who could have foreseen this to happen a couple of days ago when we had dinner in the same restaurant?" I nodded.

"It was a good move to visit the bathroom right before you left. Otherwise, I am pretty sure I would not have the chance to give you my number. I am not the kind of guy with enough confidence to walk up to your table and start a conversation." Linda giggled.

"That was exactly the reason for me going to the toilet. I was actually hoping to talk with you."

The white IKEA clock on the wall showed it was just after eleven. I dimmed the light, making the room completely dark. I pressed Linda firmly against me and kissed her on her cheek.

"Good night Linda," I whispered.

"Good night."

14

Xinhu Riverside Apartments - 08:20

I opened my eyes. Bright sunlight was entering the room from behind the edges of the curtains. It took a few seconds to realise what happened last night. Linda was still asleep laying with her face towards me, partly covered with hair. She was naked, providing me with a glance of her body. I didn't wear much more. What time would it be? I turned around to look at the clock on the wall. Twenty minutes past eight. Time to get up. With my best efforts not to wake up Linda, I got out of bed, quietly leaving the bedroom to prepare myself a coffee. Mr Lu already left to have breakfast in his sister's home. I was lucky to rent a place like this. No other situation where you would share an apartment with another person would give you as much as privacy as I have here. He is out pretty much all of the time. And, Mr Lu won't judge me in a situation where I bring different girls home. And being the brother of my landlord, I consider it his responsibility to be on my side. In return, I provide a peaceful living environment without regular parties or dinners at home. And I pay my rent on-time.

    Meanwhile, the kitchen was filled with a smell of fresh coffee. I filled one cup and walked back to the bedroom. I noticed that Linda changed her position. She was now diagonally claiming the entire bed but still in dreamland. She looked as comfortably as a girl could be on a Saturday morning. I took place behind my desk and started my laptop. It has been a week since I send an email to Gerald, but I did not receive any response yet. Would he be travelling? Or just as busy as always. The soft breathing of Linda on the background confirmed that she was still in a deep sleep. Even the smell of fresh coffee didn't seem to wake her up. I logged into my inbox. Maybe I could find a response to some of the jobs I applied for during the past weeks. The inbox showed a couple of spam emails and to my surprise a reply on my email to Gerald:

From: Gerald van Tatenhof
To: Victor de Lange
Send: 10/07/2008

Victor,

It has been too busy and too hectic, apologies. I will be in Shanghai until Friday, then out for two weeks. We are in the midst of a big turmoil, AOP/budgets etc. But still interviewing people... The fact that you do not speak Mandarin may be the biggest issue to get you back on board.

Are you still in town next week? I am leaving on Tuesday.

Regards, Gerald van Tatenhof

That's a welcome start of this Saturday morning. When browsing through the website of *The Wall Street Journal*, I noticed stories covering the fear of a financial crisis in America and Europe is spreading, and is affecting MCN's in Asia as well. Yesterday's financial markets sharply fell as investor confidence declined. It was reported that Singapore's market ended down seven per cent and therefore became the second Asian country to enter a recession this year after New Zealand. Closer to Shanghai, Hong Kong's Hang Seng index fell seven point per cent as well. Further to this China's domestic product growth slowed to ten per cent during the first nine months of this year from ten point four per cent in the first half of the year. In a reaction, the Chinese government said it would decrease the control of the exchange of land among the local farmers with hope to boost the rural economy. The recent global developments would not be doing my job search any good. Even though China is still expecting to deliver economic growth, multinational companies will be cautious in hiring new employees. Especially recent graduates who require a special employment visa. As Linda was still asleep, I decided to reply to Gerald's email first.

From: Victor de Lange
To: Gerald van Tatenhof
Send: 10/07/2008

Dear Gerald,

Thank you for your reply, I know your situation so didn't expect an answer the other day. I am in Shanghai at least until December 23 since I want to focus on the start of my career here in Shanghai. I know the fact that I don't speak Mandarin is a weakness now, but I am still working on that. It takes a couple of months to be able to make conversations, but it even means that I can practice in a working environment while learning. Let me know if you have time this week, or next Monday or Tuesday. Any day and/or time convenient for you is fine with me.

Kind regards,

Victor

Send. It was nearly nine o'clock now. After having my morning coffee, I started to feel a bit hungry too. The problem was that I did not really have breakfast at home besides three days old bread and peanut butter. That's not a way to treat Linda on her first morning here. I could either order breakfast or take her out for a bite outside. I walked back to the bed and slowly lay next to Linda. She was half covered. I lay on top of the bed next to her. I whispered slowly
  "Linda..." but even this did not seem to wake her up.
  I touched her cheek and called her name again. She opened her eyes. It took her a second to realise where she was, in this for her strange bedroom.

"How was your sleep?"

She rubbed her hand through her eyes while she made an effort to sit straight up in bed. The sleepy look and her messy hair, the naked upper part of her body and her legs entangled in the bed cover made her look like a mermaid.

"My sleep was excellent, how long are you awake for?"

"I only got up about thirty minutes ago, made myself a coffee and sent a couple of emails. Do you drink coffee? Or can I make you happy with tea?"

"I would like to have a cup of tea," Linda answered while she lay back in bed.

"I must have slept so deep," she continued. "I did not notice you getting up at all."

"Yes... It took me a while to get you awake."

"Let me get you your tea."

I walked out of the bedroom to the kitchen. Mr Lu's water boiler in the kitchen only required me to tap some pre-cooked water in a cup and add a tea bag to it. Easier compared to making coffee unless I would like instant coffee. Linda sat up again when I entered the bedroom. I left the tea on the nightstand next to the bed.

"Be careful; it's scalding."

"Thank you, Victor,"

"What kind of emailing you were doing if I may ask? It's Saturday morning."

"This is for a job I would really like to have in the company I did my graduation internship. I have sent an email to one of the directors and I saw he replied to my email."

Linda nodded and sipped her tea.

"I can check in my company whether they are hiring? It's only a small company, though."

I smiled.

"And then we would become colleagues? Thank you for the initiative Linda, does your company have any open positions? Usually, smaller companies do not hire foreigners. Most of them are hired in multinational companies."

"In that case, I can ask my friends as well."

I looked at her. She was waiting for me to react. I realised she had a good heart. We only knew each other for less than a week, but she was trying to help me out.

"That would be nice, let's see if they have an opportunity."

I knew the chance for success would be small. But it is nice that she is trying to help me. I took a sip of coffee.

"Are you hungry?" I asked.

"We can either go out for breakfast or order some at home. There is a nice lunchroom nearby we can go if you like."

"Can I have a shower first?" Linda asked.

"Then you decide what we do for breakfast."

She pulled the cover away from her, disclosing her entire naked body to me. As if she had the purpose of seducing me once again. While she stepped out of bed and walked towards the bathroom, I looked at her from the back. Once she approached the matt glass bathroom door, she turned around, smiled at me and told me

"I'll be back soon, unless you want to join me..?" She kept silent for a few seconds to finish her sentence.

"By showering together, we can save water."

"That's a very legitimate reason!" And I heard a new email coming in.

"I'll be there in a minute, let me check first whether it is Gerald replying on my email." I opened my mailbox and yes:

From: Gerald van Tatenhof
To: Victor de Lange
Send 10/08/2008

This week is impossible, next week Monday & Tuesday are not better. As I will probably stay in Shanghai the week after next week, suggest we take Wednesday at eleven in the morning for thirty minutes or so.

Please confirm

Regards,

Gerald van Tatenhof

It's Saturday morning, and he is working. Or at least almost instantly replying my email. On the background, I heard Linda opening the shower tap, while in the kitchen boiler started working for the hot water supply. I replied Gerald's email instantly to lock the time in his agenda. This would create an excellent opportunity to discuss any employment opportunities in Philips.

From: Victor de Lange
To: Gerald van Tatenhof
Send 10/08/2008

Dear Gerald,

That's perfect, thank you for the time you made available in your busy schedule. I'll be there on Wednesday October 22 at 11:00.

Kind regards,

Victor

In a good mood as a result of the fixed meeting with Gerald, I walked to the bathroom. I could hear Linda already showering. I opened the door, where the steam of the hot water instantly welcomed me. Even though Shanghai felt like summer now, she apparently liked to take hot showers. I undressed and pushed the shower curtain aside. This shower had a rainforest showerhead and an overall rectangular shape. If necessary, I could shower here with at least four people. Linda was washing her hair and stood with her back towards me. She turned around.

"Would you like to help me soaping my body while the shampoo is working in?"

That's a question she did not have to ask me twice. I poured some of the Dove body wash on my hands and started massaging her shoulders while she faced me. From her shoulders, I went to her upper arms, lower arms and moved to her hip. I needed a bit more shampoo for her hips and belly. I could feel myself getting excited again, especially when I went up from her belly, touching the underside of each breast. She pulled me towards her, resulting in our wet bodies firmly touching each other, and she started to kiss me. She was obviously in for more than just a shower. The feeling of our wet skins and her firm breasts against my belly turned me on. As she just transferred the body soap from her body to mine, she started to move her hands over my belly, not ignoring my hard cock.

"Are you in for a second round...?" She asked with a shy smile on her face.

There was actually no need to ask rhetorical questions on a moment like this. In fact, it made me want her even more. She knew exactly how to play this game.

"Do whatever you want to do with me... I'm all yours."

Instructed as she was, she slowly kneeled, while on her way down softly kissing and licking my skin. Some of the soap leftover on my skin didn't taste so well and made her rinse her mouth with the hot water pouring down. It both made us laugh.

"Your body soap tastes like it's full of chemicals Victor, I can recommend you a biological one. It's much better for your skin. And my mouth right now."

I laughed.

"Okay, once we're done here let me know which recommendation you have. I would love to hear that."

Linda continued her mission. She softly kissed the scrotal and mid shaft of my cock before she gently took it in her mouth and started slowly sucking it. She moved her hand firmly around the middle part. Linda stopped.

"Do you like it?" She asked in a seducing tone. This was another rhetorical question.

"Liking is an understatement Linda," I answered. "I love it. Please continue..."

It gave Linda more drive, and she continued. The bathroom meanwhile had the look of an original Turkish steam bath. If she continued like this, it wouldn't take long for me to come to an orgasm. "Would you like me to let you know before I come...?" I tried to make clear before doing so. Not all girls like the idea of a guy coming in their mouth. Especially not if they just know you for less than a week. Linda made her mouth available so she could answer but continued to massage me.

"You just let it come, Victor…"

She took my cock back into her mouth and surrounded it with a sweet invasion. This view, a beautiful lady in front of me, naked and kneeling in the shower while litres of water are pouring down over both of us was quite rare for me. Is this what is called love in China? Or be loved? The moment Linda touched my scrotal again, I could feel there was no way back any more towards a mind-blowing orgasm.

"Please continue like this, Linda."

Seconds later I saw twinkling stars on the horizon of a bathroom full of steam, and where I expected her to finish me off with her hand only, she kept me in her mouth until after ejaculation. It seemed Linda had absolutely no reservations towards me.

"You have a fresh taste." Linda said with a seducing smile on her face while I helped her up standing on her feet again.

"After having soap in your mouth, everything tastes fresh." I was still a bit of sex drunk as a result of the orgasm I went through.

"That was just… marvellous Linda," I said. I pressed her firmly against me.

"Let's have breakfast," Linda proposed. I had to confess that I felt hungry after this exciting morning shower.

"Let's go to Element Fresh," I proposed.

"They have a perfect breakfast selection that'll give us a protein boost. Both in Asian and in Western style. I think we could both use that." Linda agreed and left the shower as first.

"Let's get ready and go," she said while she wiped away the condense on the shower window so she could look me in the eyes.

"We should have showers like this more often, don't you agree?"

15

Shanghai Jiao Tong University ICEC Building - 17:56

It was a couple of minutes before six when I entered the International Continuing Education building of Shanghai Jiao Tong University. Right now, there was clearly more activity going on compared to last week Thursday during my interview. The majority of people are taking courses directly after they finish work. People entered the building carrying white plastic doggy bags with dinner. That must create a pleasant environment when everybody enjoys their dinner right before or during class. Imagine the smell of curry, tofu, Sichuan fish, reheated veggies and suddenly you understand why this building does not have any closed windows in the main lobby.

Until now, I did not see any foreigners. I walked up to the office where I had my interview just five days ago. The door was closed, and the small window on the left was blocked with a white curtain. I knocked three times. No answer. I knocked another three times. Suddenly the door opened. It was the lady occupying the second desk during the interview, the one not giving me any glance back then. I doubt she would recognise me at all. To my surprise, she smiled and made a welcoming gesture for me to enter the office.

"You must be Victor, right? Our new project management lecturer."

She looked at me through matt-glass, as if she did not wipe her glasses for ages. I wondered how she could actually recognise me at all.

"That's correct. My course will start in just a little more than thirty minutes."

"My name is Jilly, and I am working as the course coordinator."

That sounded already friendlier compared to the description of operational burden Johan had given her during the interview.

"I have planned your classes in room four hundred which is located on the fourth floor of the building on your left hand after you take the stairs.

"All right, I will find my way up."

"Oh, and here are the prints you asked me to prepare."

I reached out and accepted them.

"That's correct; the case studies for discussion at the end of the course. Thank you for preparing those." I walked up the stairs, carrying a bundle of papers in my right hand and an office bag in my left hand. I wore a suit and a tie as if that was supposed to make me look more like an expert. I was on the stairs making my way up to the second floor when a girl asked me:

"Are you teaching here?" I nodded yes while ignoring the fact that my first minutes as a lecturer were just about to start.

"What are you teaching?" She continued asking.

"Project management, in room four hundred. Feel free to enrol and join if you like!" She giggled.

"I have English class. But once this class is finished, I may consider it."

She smiled and waved while she took a right turn on the second floor. The busloads of students walking stairs on the ground floor in the lobby gradually decreased every floor I walked up. I counted the floors in this building. Six in total, even though the sixth floor seemed pretty much closed. When I arrived on the fourth floor, looking identical to the three floors I just passed, I took a left turn and counted the even classroom numbers on my left-hand side. The door of room four hundred was open and white lights were switched on. None of my eight or so students arrived yet. The room looked exactly like a traditional teaching room in American movies. The projection screen was at least ten square meters in size. I put my papers and bag on an old oversized wooden desk with a microphone stand and looked into the auditorium. There were about twenty rows of fixed desks with upholstered seats divided into three sections, with two paths in the middle. A full room could easily accommodate two hundred students. For my lecture, only the first row of desks would do, and there was no need for me to use the microphone. The stand was mounted inconveniently in such a way that it could only be used if you sat behind the desk. And that was not how I pictured myself teaching project management. Just as I plugged my laptop to the connector cable of the projector, a gentleman appeared in the door opening. He was hesitating to walk in as he was not sure whether he found the right classroom.

"This is the project management course, right?" He said. I nodded.

"You're in the right room, please find a seat. We have more than enough space as you can see."

Instead of taking a seat behind one of the desks, he first walked up to me and introduced himself to me with a handshake.

"My name is Timo, nice to meet you."

"My name is Victor, nice to meet you too."

"Where are you from Victor?"

"I am from the Netherlands, yourself?"

"From the States, Michigan to be precise."

That was no surprise, judging his accent.

"I have been to Amsterdam once," Timo said.

"Just for a couple of days but I loved it."

As I had to represent a professional attitude, I decided not to continue asking what exactly Timo loved about Amsterdam. In a bar over a couple of beers, this would be an appropriate question to ask. But not in this authentic, dusty smelling classroom right before the start of a project management course. Timo smiled and followed his way to the first empty desk he found. While the projector showed the opening slide of the presentation, two other students walked in. Same as Timon, they introduced themselves before finding a seat. The noise on the corridor continued, and most classrooms were now filled with students. I took a seat behind the oversized desk. In an effort to screen Timon and the other two students, I tried to gain a first impression on whether they would be difficult students or not. The thought that any of the students here tonight would leave the classroom without a good feeling caused an uneasy feeling inside of me. They pay quite a significant amount of tuition to follow this course. Only that already raises expectation. Meanwhile, more students entered the room, saying hi before following their way to an available desk. I counted. There are seven students now, with nine minutes to go till six-thirty. Johan told me that there would be at least eight students, possibly a few more. No matter what, I aimed to start at six-thirty straight. As if he could hear me think, Johan entered the classroom.

"You're all settled, I see?" he started.

"Yes. Presentation is ready, projector works, and Jilly took well care of the prints. How many students do we still expect?"

"There will be eight plus three, so eleven students in total. Not bad for this course."

"Oh, yes? How many students you have on average for his class?"

"The size of this class is usually around ten students. But China MBA's are more popular."

I nodded, even though this was all new to me.

"Would you mind if I sit-in the first part of your class?" Johan asked.

"Sure, I have no problem with that."

Strangely I felt more confident regarding the quality of my course towards Johan instead of other students. I checked my watch again. There was only a couple of minutes left until six-thirty. Right at that moment, a Chinese gentleman stepped in. I would estimate him in his fifties. He was well dressed in a brown plaid suit with a dark red tie and carrying a notebook. His hair was neatly combed to the right. He appeared different to anybody else in the room. Different but in a professional way. As if he represents a higher class. Who is this guy? He wished me a good evening and entered the room at a slow pace. He took a seat right in front of me and slowly opened his notebook as if we were now ready to start. I looked at my watch again. It was Six-thirty straight. Indeed, time to stand up and get the students attention. Sounding as confidently as possible I started:

"Thank you for signing up for this project management course, my name is Victor, and I will be your lecturer for the next eight weeks. During this period, I will guide you step by step through the project management lifecycle, where theory will be combined with real-life examples and case studies."

Some of the students nodded in expectation. Others started already making notes. I continued while I lifted the book in front of my chest:

"The book we use is this handbook of project management. The university will provide you with a copy but will need to be paid additionally on top of your tuition. But with 70RMB this is quite reasonable. After every class, I send you a copy of the PowerPoint presentation as well, but it is recommended to purchase the book for extra reading."

As an introduction to myself, I had one slide devoted to my experience. I told them about my time at HZ University, Texas State University, PricewaterhouseCoopers and Philips. As the next step, I offered the students time to introduce themselves. It would be interesting for me to understand in which industry they are working so I could use industry-related examples to explain the theory. Between students, it would be nice as well to understand for whom they are working as it could increase network opportunities. The introduction for both sides took half an hour to complete. That meant one and a half hour for the presentation, where I planned to cover roughly twenty-five slides. This minus a forty-five minute case study, discussion and a ten-minute break somewhere in the middle. Three hours seemed like a long time to fill, but you have to calculate the time for questions, explanation and discussion as well during the presentation. The first slides covered the introduction of project management, the difference between projects and operations, characteristics of projects and operations, corporate project management, a history of project management and an explanation of the project management process. Together with some real-life examples of Starbucks and Hewlett Packard, I felt I amused the students well as they were listening with full attention. The presentation and discussion moved on until the nine-thirty bell marked the end of the class. While I was disconnecting the laptop from the projector, one of the students had come forward. It was the Chinese gentleman.

"Thank you for this very interesting course, Mr Victor." He started. "My name is Wang."

"Nice to meet you, Mr Wang, and I am glad to hear you liked the course today."

"Where are you from?" Wang continued.

"I am from the Netherlands, but I live in Shanghai now for about one year."

Wang smiled as if we now had a common topic to discuss.

"I have been to the Netherlands a few times, where I visited Doetinchem."

His pronunciation of Doetinchem was surprisingly good.

"I visited a customer there for my business."

I remembered Wang explained during the start of the class that he was president of a big high-end suit brand in China.

"I am travelling to Europe quite often. Great Britain, Italy, Switzerland…"

While he continued talking, I noticed he carried an English copy of the Chinese newspaper the People's Daily. I watched him reading it before the class and during the break as if he did not require any time to relax.

"I need to understand project management better to implement it in my company," Wang continued.

"And I need to improve my English."

Meanwhile, I finished packing. Now I understood why he brought an English newspaper into the classroom. Not very usual to do so for Chinese people. My laptop, the project management book and some left-over case studies that Jilly printed were all in my bag.

"Let's walk downstairs together so the cleaning team can do their work."

They were patiently waiting for us to leave.

"So you are working in the garment industry?"

I asked while we walked into the corridor towards the stairs. As most classes finished already at nine o'clock, the building appeared empty now. It was such a difference compared to a couple of hours ago.

"Yes, Mr Victor, I am the President of a high-end suit brand named Baromon in China. We have a flagship store in East Nanjing

Road. You may have seen it when you walked there." In fact, I did not see it. There are so many shops on East Nanjing Road that I actually only pay attention to the brands I am interested in. And with all respect, those are usually not the Chinese brands. But I said:

"I have not noticed the shop but will definitely look for it next time I am on East Nanjing Road. It would be interesting to see the kind of business you are in."

While we walked into the entrance hall, I could see that the lights in Johan' office were already switched off.

"It is very nice to meet you, Mr Victor,"

Wang said while a big black car drove up in front of the building.

"I am looking forward to next week's class. And I will study the materials you provided today."

A driver stepped out of the car to open the passenger door on the right side of the vehicle. Wang stepped in, waved to me with a smile on his face, and the driver closed the door. Without looking up, the driver walked back to the front of the car, opened the door and jumped onto the driver seat. The left direction light flickered, and the car drove away with low speed into the Shanghai night. And there I stood, alone in the entrance hall of the International Continuing Education Building of Shanghai Jiao Tong University. The bright red signage describing the name of the institution was switched off now, and the security officer right next to the door had his eyes on me while smoking a cigarette. Or he could as well be looking straight through me. He might still be facing a night shift, on a mission to protect this building from burglars and thieves through the night. Not that I could think of anything interesting to steal here though. I felt both exhausted and excited. Parts of the course continued to flash through my mind. Questions students asked, answers I provided, explanations given and discussions we held. Furthermore, some action points for next week, and as well some improvements I already had to implement for next week's lecture. Now I know my students I have a better understanding of their responsiveness. From a time point of view, everything was well planned today.

I watched over the street in the distance. Even though it was nearly ten o'clock now, traffic continued to flow on Kai Xuan Road as if it was like three o'clock in the afternoon. One part in me felt like taking a taxi, which would cost me about thirty RMB to get back home. By metro, it would only be three RMB. And it would provide me with a nice walk to clear my mind. By the time I arrive at home, it would be ten-thirty. Anyway, I did not have to work tomorrow morning. I could spend all morning in bed if I wanted to. I started walking towards the subway station and had to think about Linda. We only had sporadically contact between Sunday afternoon and now. She knew I was working on my class, teaching tonight, and she was busy with her work as well. While I walked, I sent her a text message, to tell her about the class and that it just finished. A simple message like this is better than nothing, even though she might be already asleep.

16

Xinhu Riverside Apartments - 09:36

It was just after nine-thirty in the morning, and today was a big day: I was invited for a talk in the Philips office. Not for an interview, just more as a basis for orientation. While I was shaving, I glanced at myself in the mirror. I felt relaxed. I walked back to the bedroom to turn on some music to increase my mood even more. Keane's *Somewhere Only We Know* usually worked well. While I searched for the song on my laptop, I heard the front door close. This meant that Mr Lu left home to go to his sister. Including the apartment she lives with her family, she owns five properties in Shanghai, so there is often something to be fixed, cleaned or looked after. His departure was a reason for me to turn up the volume a little bit more. Since the release four years ago, I must have heard this Keane song a thousand times by now, but it still sounds as impressive as it was the first time I heard it on the radio. The first time I saw a live show was not long after that after winning concert at a Dutch national radio station for their second ever show in the Melkweg in Amsterdam.

I stopped in front of my closet, and I looked at my suits. Which colour combination of suit and shirt would I wear? And should I combine it with a tie? Better not, it is just a casual talk, no interview. Just a suit will do. A black suit and a Philips blue shirt. I finished off shaving quickly, got dressed and packed a notebook with a pen into my black Samsonite backpack. *Everybody's Changing* was playing now, meaning that it was almost fifteen minutes ago since I started listening to music. I know the playlist of the Hopes and Fears album by hard. I remember the lyrics better than anything. Sometimes I wish I could remember the content of my Chinese language classes as good as the Keane lyrics.

As it was nearly ten in the morning, I had to go out soon to catch a subway towards Yishan Road. There I had to switch lines to line nine and then it would only be three stops to Hechuan Road. This is the nearest metro stop from the Philips office. When I entered the elevator, I looked at myself in the mirror. Not bad. My hair looked streamlined, and the black suit made me look beyond a part-time project management lecturer looking for a full-time job. Downstairs and on street level, the road to the subway station was still quite busy as a result of the morning rush hour. Retired Shanghainese people sat on a self carried chair on the side of the road while they looked at people passing by. Some of them sat in groups of three or four, and I could imagine them gossiping about things happening in the neighbourhood while looking at people passing by. It must be comfortable sitting out there now the sun is coming out with a nice twenty-three degrees temperature.

A little bit closer to the subway station a man in his sixties spanned a cable between two trees to which he attached nine wooden cages with birds. They were chirping when I passed by, giving this part of the street a happy character while their wrinkled owner kept an eye on them with a satisfying look on his face. They appeared quite special to me. Three different species peacefully shared a cage, some with tropical colours. Not the usual blackbirds you see on the street. While I paid attention to this, other Chinese pedestrians rushed by without paying attention to what was hanging above their heads. A hundred meter after the birds, I smelled the strong smell of sweet potato's produced by one of the street sellers near the main entrance of the subway station. Not my favourite smell, but some people must like it for breakfast. I walked through the entrance gates and started to walk faster as I could hear the subway above me entering the platform. If I could run up the stairs, I would still be able to catch it, but this would only be possible if people would not block the escalator on the way up. Lucky for me, not many people did so, and as a result, I could just get through the peeping doors before they closed. I could feel my heartbeat going quicker than normal as a result of this exertion. I probably had to stand for the next few stations as all seats were occupied. Never mind, it would only be a few stops until Yishan Road, from where I would switch to line 9. Standing wouldn't kill me. While passing the stations towards Yishan Road station, more people got in than out. I moved slightly towards one of the exit doors, to make sure that I had time enough to get out of the subway. When we entered Yishan Road station, I followed the flow of people to exit the subway. It can be hard sometimes to get out on time. Whilst entering the platform, I followed the directions towards line nine. This is a brand-new line, so the platforms are not properly connected yet. To access the line nine section of the station, I walked through a small construction area in the open air. Once I entered the line nine section of the station, I noticed the difference in design, materials and style between the old station built-in 1993 and the new one in 2008. A blinking tunnel welcomed me towards line nine. From the monitors, I could see it would only be a few minutes until the next subway would arrive. I increased my walking speed and glanced at my watch to see what time it was. Ten thirty, still enough time to reach the Philips office. If I missed this train, I would have to wait about nine minutes for the next one to arrive. More people started to walk faster.

Once I arrived at the platform, a significant group of people was waiting already. A warm breeze showed up through the platform, while the noise out of the tunnel increased. People gathered between the marked areas on the platform. Given the position I was standing, I had no way to get a seat this time. The train came to a stop, and the doors opened. I managed to get a standing position in the middle while I held one of the horizontal bars to keep myself balanced. The subway took off, and I looked around. So many people and we all have a different location to go to. Nobody was talking to each other. We were all individuals on our way to the next destination. Meeting family, heading to work, going back home... And I was hopefully heading to my next chapter in life. At least I was closer to it than ever before. I've been waiting for this moment for months now. This is just an orientation talk, but hopefully a step in the right direction. We passed the first station. Not many people left or got in as the next stop will be the Technology Centre. That's where usually most people leave to go to work. I can remember that during my internship, this subway line did not exist yet, and I drove my bike every day to the office over Yishan Road. No matter how low the temperature or how bad the weather.

I looked right of me. A cute girl was standing next to me, holding the rail too. She was reading a small book. I couldn't see what it was about, but it seemed like a business book to me. She wasn't paying attention to anything happening around her. She was dressed quite well, combining a black skirt with a white blouse and high heels, but they did not help her to be much taller. She could just reach my shoulder. Her hair was loose and falling just over her shoulders. I would guess her around the age of twenty-one, but could that be possible as she was dressed like she was heading to work? The woman sitting on the seat right in front of me was attempting to stand up. She took her bag and moved towards the doors. Her seat was now free. I looked around, but nobody seemed eager to take this seat. For me, it would not make much difference as I had to get out at the next stop in Hechuan Road. I looked at the girl next to me.

"Please take the seat," I started, "Before anybody else will take it."

She looked up to me.

"Oh, no, thank you. My stop is next." And she put her attention back to her book.

I looked at her. Her hairs shined as she washed them just this morning.

"Are you working in Hechuan Road?" I asked.

"I'm going to Hechuan Road too." Now she turned her neck and put her book down. The make-up on her face looked natural.

"No, I am going for an internship interview." That explains why she dressed up so nice. Her book was still at hips height; this could be an indication that she was interested in talking.

"Which company do you have an interview with?" I continued.

"Philips," she instantly replied. This was such a coincidence. Meeting somebody in the same subway, at the same time on our way to the same location.

"Actually, I am heading to the Philips office too," I said. "I'm having a meeting there at eleven." She smiled.

"Do you know the way to the office? Because I have no idea where to go after getting out of the station."

"Yes, I know. You can follow me if you want."

"Sure," she said. "By the way, my name is Serena."

To formally introduce herself, she offered her right hand she wasn't holding her book with.

"I'm Victor. Nice to meet you!" Meanwhile, the subway had stopped already for Technology Centre and was heading into Hechuan Road. People around us were preparing to leave the subway. Luckily, we now stood close to the exit door.

"Where are you from?" Serena asked.

"I am from the Netherlands, and you originally?"

"I am from Beijing, but I study in Shanghai."

"Ah, which major?"

"Marketing, but I am interested in consultancy." I nodded.

"When will you graduate?"

"At the end of this year, I just have an internship to do."

Meanwhile, the subway doors opened, and at the same moment that people were leaving the train, other people attempted to enter.

"I seriously can't get used to his," I said to Serena.

"Can't people just let us walk out first?"

Serena laughed.

"Not in China," She said.

"I used to study in Europe, so I know how people behave where you are coming from."

"Well, in Europe we have our problems too," I added.

With pushing, we ultimately ended up on the platform and walked towards the stairs.

"Which exit should we take?" Serena asked while we entered an intersection.

I confirmed exit one. From there, it was only a few hundred meter walk to the office.

"Which business unit do you have an interview with? Because there are two buildings. I will go to the lighting division in the right building. The left building is where healthcare and consumer electronics are based."

"I need to be in consumer electronics," Serena confirmed.

So that's the other building. Whilst the escalator brought us up to the street level; the Philips office became immediately visible. Two grey square-shaped buildings, each with five floors. The environment looked instantly different here. More industrial. We passed a small street on the side of the business park. It would not take long until the old, gutted homes here will be destroyed by rich commercial property developers, most likely paying only a little to obtain the ground. A line with children clothes hung out over the street.

"So, there is a coffee shop in the left building. I will meet there with one of the Philips directors. What time is your interview?"

"At one o'clock."

"That's still two hours and fifteen minutes! What are you doing already here?"

"Well, let's say it in this way. I treat interviews like catching a flight. I check in at least two hours in advance."

"You surely do. An international flight in this case."

Serena giggled. We now walked between the two Philips buildings. One red and yellow Volkswagen taxi drove in and out to drop people off. It was my ultimate dream, working for this company. Representing the Philips blue, building the trend of LED Lighting and working hard to achieve a successful career within the company. I felt so close now but yet so far away. We crossed the street and entered the consumer electronics building. From the lobby, we continued walking left into a corridor towards the cafe. I noticed a small line with Philips employees waiting for coffee. I looked at my watch. Ten minutes early for my meeting.

"I'll get you a cup of coffee if you like so you can prepare for your interview here. What would you like?" Serena grinned and nodded thankfully.

"A latte please." I told the barista our order and turned back to Serena.

"Where did you study in Europe?"

"In Rome."

"I've been to Rome once, it is a beautiful city!"
"Have you been to the Netherlands too?"
"Yes," Serena confirmed. "Where did you go?"
"Amsterdam." Serena answered. I giggled.
"That is a standard answer when asking somebody about their trip to the Netherlands. Did you smoke weed or tried some of the other stuff?"

I thought I asked a rhetorical question as Serena looked so pure and innocent to me.

"Actually I did yes, I was with a friend and we tried marihuana and space cake." When looking at her face, I did not expect this answer.

"We stayed in a hostel, based in a houseboat. I ended up getting so sick from the space cake that I spend one and a half day in bed recovering and getting that stuff out of my body." I giggled.

"The ultimate Amsterdam experience. I am sure there are busloads of tourists who ended up feeling worse than you did." Serena laughed.

"Have you travelled to other countries in Europe too?"
"Yes, quite a bit. I travelled to Eastern Europe for a road trip, and within Western Europe too as all countries are so close."
"Have you been to the United Kingdom?" I asked.
"Yes, we stayed a few days in London."
"Nice, I have been a few times to London too. Last time was for a Keane concert."
"Ah, you like Keane?"
"Yes! Have you heard of them?"

That is a reasonable question to ask in China. Not so many Chinese people are familiar with Western music or artists.

"I like their song *Somewhere Only We Know*," Serena said.
"But I am not so familiar with their other songs. I like Brit-pop overall speaking."
"Yes, like Placebo, Coldplay, Manic Street Preachers, Oasis... Just to name a few."

At that moment, our coffees were ready and I handed Serena her coffee.

"A freshly brewed latte for you."

"Thank you, Victor," Serena said with a smile on her face.

I could sense the appreciation.

Right at that moment, I heard a familiar voice coming closer. It was Gerald, exactly on time for our meeting. He was still talking to a colleague, so I said bye to Serena, wished her good luck for her interview and took a seat at a table in the corner. Gerald was talking in Dutch, but I could not clearly understand what about. There was too much noise from the coffee machine and the people around me talking. Gerald shook the hand of the gentlemen and looked around in the coffee shop. I lifted my arm to wave and catch his attention. That did not take long.

"Hey Victor!" He said with an enthusiastic smile on his face.

"How are you? It has been a while!"

"Yes, it is! I'm fine Gerald, happy to be back in Shanghai. How are you?"

"Oh, I am well but currently on an exhausting travel schedule. I am travelling for three weeks per month. One consecutive week in the United States, Europe, Asia, and the last week of every month in Shanghai. Good that you could meet today."

I was not going to tell him that I had all the time in the world to meet at any day in any week. During my internship, Gerald was R&D director. Now he worked as global marketing director, taking the position from Michael who left the company and initially hired me as a trainee in Philips. Gerald pointed to the coffee machine.

"Have you had a coffee yet?" I shook no.

"What would you like? I will order one for myself too."

"A cappuccino please, thank you."

I looked at Gerald. He was wearing jeans and a dark blue polo. He looked slightly slimmer than six months ago. The demanding travel schedule certainly paid his toll. From what I know is that he only needs three to four hours of sleep per night. That resulted in the fact that he sometimes would send you an email at three-thirty in the morning but would enter office with a smile on his face by eight-thirty. Gerald handed me my coffee while he took a sip of his own.

"Let's go back to my office," He said.

"We can have a quiet conversation there." While we walked away, I looked over my shoulder to Serena. She lifted her hand and waved to me with a smile on her face. I smiled back and followed Gerald on his way out to the exit.

The corridor walls were decorated with historical Philips pictures. From an old factory in 1930 to a new television system.

"How have you been?" Gerald asked.

"I am doing well, thanks. I'm back now in Shanghai since early September. It's good to be back, and I have been looking for jobs since then. But it is actually more difficult than I initially expected. I presumed that PricewaterhouseCoopers and Philips on your resume would open doors."

"For locals, it would probably have a better effect yes," Gerald stated.

"To hire foreigners, many companies are looking for experience in a particular field." Gerald was right. Why would a Chinese or multinational company hire a foreigner in China if a local person can do the same job? After crossing the street, we walked into the lighting building. It was still the same as before during my internship. The reception area, the gates towards the elevators and corridor… Working here again would be my ultimate dream. Gerald walked to the elevator and pressed the button to bring us to the fifth floor. "I moved to a new office since I changed position," Gerald laughed. He seemed so relaxed. When we reached the elevator, the door opened almost immediately, and five Philips employees walked out. Gerald greeted them all. By looking at the other employees and Gerald, I felt slightly overdressed. From my internship, I knew that Gerald only wear suits when the higher management pays a visit to Shanghai. After we got up to the fifth floor, we continued our walk through the office towards Gerald's office. His office was on the left side of the building, providing him with a nice view over Minhang district.

"Please take a seat," Gerald said while he closed the door.

"Tell me briefly about your first months in Shanghai, and why did you feel like to come back?"

"Well, after my internship, I went back to the Netherlands to graduate. I spent a month in Spain and France to figure out what I actually wanted with my life. Stay in Europe, go back to America, or perhaps return to Shanghai? As I had the sweet taste of travelling in my mouth, I decided that abroad it would be. With the global financial crisis, it would be increasingly difficult to find a good job in Europe and America as a university graduate. So I decided to come back to Shanghai. Just myself and one piece of luggage and try to find a decent job."

"That makes sense," Gerald interrupted me.

"So what have you been doing since arriving in Shanghai? Have you had any interviews yet?"

"I am having a part-time job now. I am teaching project management in Shanghai's Jiao Tong University for about three hours per week. It's in their International Continuing Education Centre, so my students are mostly graduates who are working already."

"You're off to a good start!"

"Yes, but between three and six hours of paid work per week is not enough to cover my rent. Even though they are paying five hundred RMB per hour."

"Well, you can use that class to extend your network in Shanghai, and that may ultimately open more doors for you in the future."

I nodded in agreement and sipped my coffee. The gatekeeper towards my dream job was sitting right in front of me.

"How are things in Philips?" I asked to switch to topic back to what hopefully would be my future.

"Really busy. We're launching a new family of LED lamps in March next year, and there is a lot of developing and testing going on." I smiled. Gerald continued:

"We used your research to educate our team and new team members on how LED bulbs are used in the Asian hospitality market." I smiled even more. It was good to hear that my thesis was anticipated so well.

"Towards the launch of the new product family, we are considering to hire somebody who can fly around in Asia to promote these products to the sales team in each country. We're considering to hire a foreigner for this position, as a Western face may help to sell the products in front of Asian customers. And another advantage is that this person ideally does not need a visa for each country they visit too. It could be something for you."

Suddenly I felt my heartbeat increasing as if I just completed a run towards the subway to catch it.

"We're still in discussion with HR to create a budget for it. This is quite a difficult topic as headcounts are frozen for the time being. But towards the beginning of next year, things may look more positive."

"That would be really nice Gerald; I am surely interested in a position like this if it becomes available."

"You can become our Flying Dutchman!"

Gerald laughed. It was a major step forward that Gerald was considering how to fit me into the organisation.

"Which visa are you on now?" Gerald asked.

"On a business visa. It was the easiest way to get back. But it will expire early next year."

"Alright. Let's keep this in mind."

Meanwhile, Isabella, Gerald's secretary, was knocking on the door. I could see her through the blinds of the window that separated Gerald's office from the main office floor.

"Oh, that must be my next meeting," Gerald said.

"That's alright; I am happy we could catch up."

"It's good to see you back in Shanghai, Victor!"

Gerald opened the door for Isabella.

"Oh hi!" She said surprised when she saw me sitting. "Are you back in Shanghai? Nice to see you again!"

She was still acting with the same enthusiasm as during my internship. I never saw her angry or stressed.

"I do not want to disturb you Gerald, but your next meeting will start in a few minutes. The meeting room is ready, and the team is waiting for you."

"They are all so punctual," Gerald laughed while he looked at his watch.

"I gotta go, but let's stay in touch and let me know if anything changes on your side. I will try my best for you." I stood up and shook Gerald's hand.

"You still know your way out?" Gerald smiled and left his office.

I looked again at the view. The sky seemed hazy now in the further distance. All I could see were lower apartment buildings, three floors high and divided into even grids. Towards the horizon, I saw construction cranes and taller buildings, presumably apartment towers too. Minhang is an industrial area but mixed with a lot of residential neighbourhoods. I turned around and walked out of Gerald's office. The first people started preparing for lunch. Lunch for the locals started around half past eleven. Some would go at noon. While I walked towards the elevator, I saw some colleagues looking up and smiling to me. Nice to see they recognised me. I saw some new faces too. The office cubicles were still the same. Separated into two groups of four desks followed by an aisle. Some of them looked neat and clean, while others had a lot of boxes stored underneath. Some desks were still free, so at least there would be space to hire a few people more. I followed my way towards the elevators, passing the coffee machine I'd had so many coffees from. I made a quick calculation. About a hundred per month times five. That's a lot. I took the elevator down towards the reception area, and suddenly I heard

"Hey Victor!" It was Divit. Originally from India and working as an expat in Shanghai.

"Good to see you here again! How have you been?"

"I am fine, thanks, and you? Are you still travelling a lot?"

I remembered him as the one travelling all around Asia in a business development role.

"Yes I am," Divit confirmed.

"But this week in Shanghai. How about you? Since when are you back in town?"

"Just since the beginning of September," I answered.

"I'm back with high hopes to find a good job and start my career in this wonderful city."

"Ah, that's why you are here... Will we see you back any time soon?"

"I've had an orientation talk with Gerald just now. He was interested to know how and what I am currently doing. It was the first time to catch up after my return to Shanghai."

"That's good to hear. We can always use good people like yourself." I smiled.

If everybody in Philips thought about me in this way, it wouldn't be too hard to find a job here.

"Well, it was good running into you, Victor. I hope to see you soon."

"Likewise, Divit!" and I continued my way out.

The haziness I saw from Gerald's office was falling as a humid cover over my body when I walked onto the street. It was suddenly warm. I looked at my watch; it was nearly a quarter before noon now. Serena must still be in the coffee shop. She still has a bit more than an hour to go until the start of her internship. I probably shouldn't disturb her now, let her prepare for her interview in style and send her a text message around two-thirty this afternoon to ask her how the interview went. I took off my coat, as I felt the sweat running down from my back. The way to the subway was short. Feeling very satisfied with this morning, I thought about the afternoon. I had to work on my project management classes, to make sure that from a material point of view, I am at least two classes ahead of what I am teaching. That seemed like a pleasant outlook. Let's take it from here.

17

Xinhu Riverside Apartments - 20:36

The elevator arrived on the tenth floor, and I invited Linda to walk out first. Predominantly because it is polite to let a lady walk out before you, but let's be honest: it would even provide me with a glance of her attractive body. She was wearing white ankle slim mid-rise skinny pants, while she was walking on black high heels. I noticed that she always wears high heels when we meet, probably to minimise the difference in length between the two of us. It surely was not because of convenience. She wore a black top with open shoulders, and her back was covered with her loose hanging deep cherry brown dyed hair. I loved the look of it. Linda turned around and said with a smile:

"Come, will you get out of the elevator too?"

She reached out for my hand, which I offered her. I giggled and followed her towards the dark corridor. The sound detector noticed our talking and the lights switched on. During daytime the corridor windows provide a nice view on Dongxin Road, but now after sunset, the bright downlights above us are creating a mirror effect. While we passed the windows, we both looked at each other in the mirror. Linda smiled at us.

"It's nice to see you again," said Linda. I smiled at her.

"I think so too." I softly pinched her hand.

After I opened the front door, a dark living room welcomed us. I switched the lights on while Linda immediately switched her high heels for the more comfortable hotel slippers. The apartment seemed perfectly clean after my return. The living room was back in order after I - not on purpose - left all the DVD's and magazines disorganised on the floor in front of the TV. When I walked into my bedroom, I noticed that the bedsheets were washed, and my bed was made up exactly as in a hotel. Just a welcome message and a chocolate heart were missing. The bathroom was blinking as if I moved in for the first time. My clothes were washed and folded and placed in the closet.

"Did you leave your apartment so clean?" I giggled.

"Yes, I think it is important to leave your home in a good state before going anywhere."

Linda moved with her finger over one of the book boards on the wall above my desk.

"No dust at all, very clean," she confirmed.

"Did you seriously do this yourself?!"

Knowing me reasonably well, her voice sounded now less convinced.

"No, my landlord arranged a cleaner to maintain each of the six apartments she owns. Our cleaner comes to clean the apartment twice a week."

Linda poked me and said with a funny face:

"I knew you did not clean your apartment by yourself. Or at least not as carefully and clean as it looks today."

I tried to defend myself.

"Well, in that case, you do not know me well, Linda! I am actually an immaculate person."

Ignoring my defence statement, Linda asked:

"Do you know in Mandarin Chinese a cleaner called is an Ayi?"

"Yes, that's one of the first things you learn in Chinese class after Ni Hao and

Wo Hen Hao. I know that translated to English it means aunt, but everybody in China knows when you talk about an Ayi you don't talk about your auntie but a cleaning lady. Or just an older lady in general, aged thirty till fifty or so. After that, the name changes to Lao Nai Nai. But don't worry. You are still my Piao Liang."

Linda giggled, and I continued:

"Actually, among my foreign friends it's clear too. If you ask another foreigner on whether they have an Ayi, they will most likely tell you yes but not meaning any family members in general."

Linda looked at me with an understanding expression on her face.

"But how much do you have to pay for an Ayi?"

"Generally speaking, Ayi's are quite cheap. For twenty-five RMB per hour, you can hire a reasonably good one."

"And how many hours do you need them?"

"Well, they work for about six hours per week, or at least that is enough for me. As I told you, I am quite clean by myself."

I smiled and poked Linda back.

"But if you wish her to speak English and even cook for you is possible too, but you will have to pay more. And she will eat with you, as she is the one who cooked dinner. If you really trust her, you can choose to give her the key to your apartment."

"But you better give her a background check and keep a copy of her ID." Linda said.

"Chinese are trusting each other less compared to Westerners."

"Yes, indeed. I did so with most Ayi's. Like for example today almost nothing is better than coming home after a holiday or long working day and find your home completely neat and clean. You know, the odd thing is, paying her just happens in cash at the end of every month."

"That means they do not have any worker insurance," Linda said.

"That's correct. I sometimes asked myself who would be liable in case Ayi would break her leg after slipping on a wet bathroom floor. But fortunately, this never happened." Linda walked towards the bed and let herself fall on the flat duvet surface. I opened my laptop and selected a random pop music playlist. I moved from my desk chair to the bed as well and stretched myself out, so I ended up facing Linda.

"You know, one of the Ayi's I previously had I will never forget. She was hired because my actual Ayi offered her as a replacement during a holiday. I figured out that the replacement was actually much better in her work and I had already a few complaints about my current Ayi's performance, so I asked her replacement to work for me from that moment. I particularly remember two moments where she really stood out from an average Ayi; the first time was when I locked myself out from my apartment at eleven o'clock. I was lucky to carry my phone with me when I walked the trash out to the shared trashcan in the stair house. To not let the cat walk out, I left the door open with a little gap. Of course, when I was just on the corridor, the incoming breeze closed the door with a smash and leaving me without a key outside the apartment."

"Oh really?" Linda disrupted me. "That's so bad!"

"Yes. For a second, I feared that I had to wait until the next morning until I could contact a lock opener. But I was lucky that I had my phone so I could call Ayi with the question whether she felt like to pass by and open my front door." Linda giggled.

"And? Did she come?"

"Well, she lived on the other side of the city, so it takes her about thirty minutes to drive her bike. For safety and time reasons, I offered her to take a taxi. I still remember the smile on her face when she stepped out of the elevator and how much fun she was making about the fact that I locked myself out."

Linda started to laugh, as well.

"I can totally picture that moment, yes. And I would be making fun of you too." "But I was so happy she passed by! I paid her the taxi fee and one hundred RMB extra for the fact that she came out so late to save me from sleeping on the street."

"That's very nice of you. You're a good guy." I nodded in agreement.

"Yes, I try to be as good as I can. But it was my own unfortunate mistake, and Ayi had to make up for it. I think it is not more than normal that I compensate her?"

"Was she always that nice?" Linda asked. "Yes, I remember another time. You know, she usually drove her bike to my apartment so she could save on subway or bus fees. On one day earlier this year in June, I remember there was a typhoon raging over Shanghai with massive showers and gusts of wind."

"Yes, I remember that day," Linda said. "My boss ordered us to stay inside."

"Yes, correct. It was the first time after I arrived in Shanghai that the local government announced code orange, which means schools are closed, and offices are advised to be closed. Going out on the street is just on your own risk." Linda nodded.

"I remember one person died because of a glass panel that fell off a building."

"Exactly. Better just to work from home and be safe. But this happened on a Tuesday, which was the day that Ayi would usually come to clean my home. Therefore, I expected her to read the news too and understood if instead, she would come to clean my home on Wednesday or Thursday. In addition to my expectations, exactly at ten in the morning, I heard a key turning around in my front door, and there she was, rained completely wet despite the poncho she was wearing."

Linda got an impressed expression on her face.

"Really? She is very loyal to you."

"Yes, I told her I didn't expect her to come because of the weather. But in the middle of a typhoon, she drove her bike from the other side of the city to come and clean my apartment. That was the day she really gained recognition from me."

"Yes, I can understand that! If I need an Ayi in the future, I will ask her name and number for reference."

We sat there silent for a short while when *Nine Million Bicycles* from Katie Melua started playing.

"Are there really so many bicycles in Beijing?" Linda asked.

"I have read that researchers estimate the registered bicycle riders in Beijing on seven million. So she might over-estimated the total a bit"

"I know that Shanghai counts six and a half million bicycle drivers. And it is a common understanding that only the poor drive a bike in China, but in a city with 20 million people a bike can actually be quite convenient to own." I nodded in agreement.

"I have a bike too. I mean for smaller distances you don't want to take a taxi, right? And they are too long to walk. Or locations without subway location. I bought a bike because there was no subway connection from where I lived in Xujiahui to my internship in Hechuan Road. And during the weekend I sometimes used the bike to discover the city. Did you know you'll find places you never knew they existed? Places you certainly won't see while taking an underground subway. Or in a taxi, you'll miss them likely too. You just see much more while riding a bike."

"I can't ride a bike." Linda confessed with a sad expression on her face.

"You can buy a cheap one first to learn. Try it here in the compound as there is no traffic. The worst thing that can happen here is that you drive yourself into the fountain."

Linda giggled.

"But I can't swim too!"

"No problem, I watch you from the balcony on the 10th floor and throw you a life vest if you end up in the fountain."

"You're so bad," Linda said with a smile on her face and pushed me flat onto the bed as well. She gave me a quick kiss.

"You know, during my internship here I lived with an Irish guy named Dominic and one day he asked me whether I was in for a bike tour. The only problem was that he didn't have a bike. So, I brought him to Carrefour. There are plenty of bikes to choose from. We drove together on my bike to the nearest Carrefour, which was five minutes from our apartment in Nandan road. When we entered the bicycle department, and Dominic was impressed by the number of bikes available at such a low price. Remember that back in Europe, bikes start with a couple of hundred euro, here you have a reasonable one for a couple of hundred RMB."

"What?" Linda punctuated me. "Yes, bikes are expensive in the Netherlands. And we all own two or three bikes!" Linda stared wonderingly in front of her.

"If I buy a bike, how much should I spend?"

"That depends on how frequently you plan to drive it."

"Unlike you, I won't plan on driving the bike very often."

"Then go for something cheap. That's exactly what I recommended Dominic. I spent roughly five hundred RMB for my bike in Carrefour. Not a top line but definitely a good value for money bike. It was a red bike, and it looked quite strong with mountain bike wheels. Although the bike did not have any additional gears, it had a platform at the back for passengers to sit on."

Linda seemed excited now.

"Do you still have that bike?"

"Ha ha no. It got stolen twice."

"Twice?" "Yes. I purchased the bike twice within a year or so."

"How did that happen?"

"The first one got stolen after I parked and locked it at Caoyang Road subway station. You know, in one of those bicycle parking areas where you pay a guard one RMB actually to keep an eye on your bike. But after I came back, the bike was gone and so was the guard.

"Nooooooo!" Linda said.

"I will never trust those security guards anymore!"

"Not that I directly suspect him from stealing my bike, but I am sure he had a share in the missing of it. He might just have told his henchman that a nice red bike arrived, and he should come to pick it up. If this is the case, I'm sure he is financially involved in this business because I can't imagine those guards are paid a fair salary. The second version of the same bike I bought got stolen at the exact same subway station."

Linda had now an expression on her face as if it couldn't get any worse anymore.

"I even do not understand why I parked my bike again at the same subway station. Anyway, Dominic decided that he wouldn't use his bike very often so only a minimum investment would do. There was a basic model for one hundred RMB, at that time, roughly ten EUR. For that price, the Carrefour employee even helped us making the bike drivable. Ten minutes later, we were back on the street. Without any route or destination in mind, we drove up slightly north over Huashan road, and at some point, we took a right turn over Zhaojiabang Road as it offered a bicycle lane. After driving for about thirty minutes, Dominic felt that his front tire looked slightly flat. You know there are countless little shops on the sideway of the street with people who can fix your bike for five RMB. We ended up having one of the bicycle experts on Taikang road looking at Dominic's bike."

"Taikang Road! I really like that place." Linda said.

"Yes, that was the moment that we actually figured out that Taikang Road had a few little restaurants and shops. That was in the early days."

Today Taikang Road offers a Shanghai authentic neighbourhood with little shops, restaurants and art galleries.

"Did you know that a Chinese millionaire bought the entire neighbourhood and decided to commercialise the area and renting out the spaces to local entrepreneurs?" Linda asked.

"Yes, imagine being the owner of that... but to continue my story, we parked our bikes at one of the entrances, explored the narrow historical streets of Taikang Road and had a beer together in one of the restaurants before we continued our trip to in Xijiahui direction. After driving a couple of minutes, I noticed that Dominic's position on his bike changed compared with earlier that afternoon. It was the result of his seat leaning backwards, it wasn't able to hold his weight anymore. But he said we would be fine as he could still sit on the front part of his seat. Dominic was an interesting guy. He worked as a business development manager for a local company. I remember he spent his weekends basically between the bar and bed - or the other way around. As a stereotype Irish guy, he could drink all night. Sometimes he would come back home around four in the morning. If he really had a tough night, he would arrive home the next afternoon, remembering not much of what happened the evening before. In one of his drunken adventures, he put Steven, my other Swiss roommate, his own and my life at risk after he forgot - or simply didn't realise to turn off the gas stove's fire. He attempted to make himself a midnight snack but probably gave up halfway leaving an empty pan on the fire."

Linda looked shocked.

"I was the first one to enter the kitchen the next morning where I found the fire was still on. Although most of his weekends were drenched in alcohol, he was a responsible guy. After I confronted him with his latest achievement, I could read the realisation from his face that he went too far. Overall speaking, he was a nice guy. If he recognised either Steven or I would spend a Friday or Saturday night alone, he would always invite us to join the party of his friends. We regularly went out with the three of us, often picking up Steven in Element Fresh in Grand Gateway where he was restaurant manager. At around eleven o'clock the night was still young, and we would end up in Velvet Lounge or Muse, co-owned by famous Hong Kong actress Carina Lau. We would have a good time, but at some point in the evening we would lose each other, or the group would just split-up and go their own way."

"You were such a party animal." Linda said with a concerned expression on her face.

"In fact I was usually the one to arrive home first, followed by Steven roughly two hours later and last but not least, Dominic. I am generally not an evening person."

"Yes I know. You always sleep earlier than me." I giggled.

"Anyway, meanwhile we drove onto Hengshan Road, back to Xujiahui into the Grand Gateway direction. We increased our speed intending to catch a green light of a nearing traffic light. Once we almost made it, the light went from green to orange and ultimately red. We both stopped last minute in front of the red light, and I saw Dominic staring at the road. He said look, and he pointed to the street. There are the brake-blocks of my bike! I just lost them! I couldn't stop laughing when thinking about Dominic's face while I repeated this story to Linda. She started to laugh too.

"You know, I didn't think this bike would live forever. But a life expectancy of only two hours is not what you expect when you purchase a bike. Luckily for Dominic, the distance back to the apartment was only a couple of miles. As he couldn't use his breaks anymore, we had to slow down our speed a little bit. Meanwhile and as well his back tire started to bend. We both concluded that this bike wouldn't make it much longer. A flat front tire, a broken seat, the brake-blocks spontaneously dropping and a bending back tire - within 3 hours of usage.

"What happened with the bike? Did you go back to Carrefour to complain?"

"No, Dominic did not care. The bike ended up in the garbage. So you see, one hundred RMB for a bike doesn't seem much at first. But you may be only able to drive it once." Linda nodded in agreement.

"I would rather choose the bike you had. But with a better lock." I laughed.

"Your bike is nowhere safe here in Shanghai."

I am almost certain there must be an organised crime team running it. Both my bikes probably started a comfortable second life in Hangzhou or Suzhou."

18

Xijiao State Guest Hotel, Changning District - 18:57

The taxi dropped me off in front of an immense entrance. An entrance that made you feel substantially tiny. I was here because Mr Wang, one of my project management students, invited me for dinner. After witnessing him leaving class in a luxury car with driver, I understood he probably does not belong to the traditional Chinese middle class. Inviting me for dinner in a palace like this did not change that presumption. I handed the taxi driver sixty-five RMB while the staff from the hotel opened the back-door of the taxi. The time to drive from the main gate, secured with security guards to where I stood now took about ten minutes. In between, we crossed beautifully maintained gardens, small rivers and traditional arch bridges in Chinese architecture. This was not just a hotel; this was a five-star resort. Built in the middle of nowhere. Wang had just texted me the address with a note saying to show it to the taxi driver. He should know the location.

    I had no idea where I was going to end up. Technically he could have sent me to the countryside where a Chinese gang would be waiting to kidnap me and ultimately sell as a slave. I felt relieved when it turned out to be a more positive scenario. When I entered the brightly illuminated hotel lobby with an immense high ceiling, glistering marble floor and big paints on the wall for decoration, a Chinese lady walked up to me and asked me

    "Are you Mr Victor?" I nodded yes, and she answered politely with:

"Please follow me."

She walked to the elevators and after one opened up, pressed the button which would bring us to the second floor. She looked at me without saying anything. I scented the moisturiser of the elevator. Could this be Wang's assistant? She actually looked a bit aged to be an assistant. This lady was probably in her late forties for as far as I could guess. I could be wrong. In fact, I am often wrong because Chinese women appear much younger than they look like.

When the elevator doors opened, we immediately entered the restaurant. This place looked more than just luxe. There was a small check-in desk on the right side, but the Chinese lady seemed to know the waitress, and without any questions, she guided me through the seating area with perfectly dressed-up tables. It was completely empty, though. Anyone hosting a high-end dinner or wedding could just walk in and start their party. On the right side of the banquet hall, there were a few doors, leading to what I assumed separate dining rooms. The lady opened one of the doors and let me walk in first. The first thing I saw was Mr Wang sitting at a big round table, reading his English copy of the China Daily. As if he wasn't aware of my entry, he turned a page. The Chinese lady attempted to get his attention by raising her hand and kindly said Ni Hao. As if he just woke up from a dream, Wang looked up.

"Ah, Mr Victor, you're here!" He remained seated and said:

"You see? I am just reading my newspaper. Did you know that China made an operating profit of over one billion yuan from the 2008 Summer Olympics?"

"Ehm no, but that's a lot of money, isn't it?"

Wang looked at me and nodded in agreement.

"Thank you for inviting me for dinner," I continued.

Wang had a serious expression on his face as if I was not allowed to say thank you for a dinner we still had to start.

"You're welcome, Mr Victor, please take a seat."

He told the Chinese lady to leave the room. Now it was only Wang, me and a waitress who just walked in. Wang reached for the menu and started browsing. Assuming that I liked everything listed on the menu, he started to point to dishes while the waitress patiently wrote his choices down. When he was finished, she asked in Chinese whether he still wished to order something to drink. He said no, and reached beside his seat, where he grabbed a wooden box with the size only a wine bottle could fit in. He opened the box and took out a Great Wall wine with the year 1970 on it. Would he bring a nearly forty-year-old wine to this dinner? From what I could remember, The Great Wall Wine brand was only founded in 1983. If this is true, they might have purchased old barrels with quality wine and put their name on it?

Meanwhile, one of the other staff walked up to the table with two glasses, took the bottle with care and soon I heard the plopping sound of a cork leaving a wine bottle. She poured a sip of wine in one of the glasses so Wang could taste the wine. He nodded as a sign of acceptance. Soon after that, the glass in front of me was filled with the red substance. The wine did not look dark red but came with similar transparency of a Bordeaux or Pinot Noir.

"Thank you, Mr Victor," Wang started,

"Thank you for sharing dinner with me tonight."

I did not expect to enjoy such an exclusive dinner tonight. Remembering the empty restaurant just now, I realised that from the moment of stepping outside the taxi I did not see any guests but just staff in this hotel. They must make their money from weddings and rich guests staying over. This place looks like a dream location to celebrate a wedding.

"I really enjoy your class, Mr Victor. As I said before, Project Management is critical for companies to apply in their daily business."

"Thank you, Mr Wang, I am happy to hear that you like the class."

I did not exactly know how to react, as this was my first semester only. Personally, I did not feel the class was outstanding.

"As I told you, I am the Vice President of a well-known Chinese suit company, and I think we do not adapt project management well into our business. Your course is very practical, so I can apply what I learn directly back into my business."

I nodded with a smile on my face.

"I try to make my class as practically as possible, so it is easier to understand the theory."

"I like it very much, especially the case study at the end of every class."

This was the first compliment I received regarding my project management class. Meanwhile, Wang grabbed his China Daily newspaper and started browsing through it. In order to do something, I took a sip of wine.

"The wine is very nice, Mr Wang," I said.

But Mr Wang did not react. He was whisper reading an article. I listened but could not hear what it was about exactly. I felt a bit uneasy. It was just me and Mr Wang in this empty hotel occupying in a spacious room where each of us had a seat on one end of a big round table. The distance between us would not even allow us to cheer our glasses formally. We would have to walk to cheer. And this same distance made me not understanding the whisper read of Mr Wang. On the left side of the room, three staff members were waiting for the moment that the first dish would arrive, or for either Mr Wang or myself to finish our glass of wine so they could give us a refill. While Wang was still quiet, the look of the waitresses made me feel more insecure. What would they think of this? They must think I am the most boring person in the world to hang out with for dinner. Within twenty minutes, my only dining partner is already reading a newspaper. A little bit more uneasy, I took another sip of wine. From the corner of my eye, I saw one of the waitresses walking towards our table. She took the bottle of wine and refilled my glass even though it was not empty yet. While she pulled the bottle back, she looked me in the eye and smiled.

"Thank you," I said with a gentle smile on my face.

She poured a little bit into Mr Wang's glass too, but he did not notice it. He was too busy getting into the second article of this newspaper. If he planned to read the entire newspaper for me throughout the evening, I estimate that we leave here quite late. All out of nothing and in the middle of an article, Mr Wang put his newspaper aside.

"Have you heard about the National People's Congress?"

I thought for a second. Heard about yes. But I am not an expert in Chinese politics.

"Yes, that's the congress held annually in Beijing, isn't it?" I answered.

"Correct, Mr Victor. Every year, three thousand delegates from every province in China travel to Beijing to listen to the planning of our Chinese government. I am there as well every year. In fact, I came back from Beijing only last week."

"Oh really? That sounds interesting. Now you mention it, I had read about it in the Dutch newspapers. This year's Congress was followed closely by foreign media because of the possible impact any policy changes would have on the Chinese and world economy." Wang nodded with a satisfied expression on his face.

"Yes, Mr Victor, very good." Without any questions from my side, he continued:

"This year the agenda was focussed on the global financial crisis, Chinese industrial revitalisation, social welfare and unemployment. This was all discussed between March five and March thirteen."

"And what was the conclusion?" I asked.

"The main conclusion was that the Chinese economy would continue to grow at a rate of eight per cent in 2009."

"That is actually pretty good. Everywhere else economies are shrinking with the same digits or even higher." Mr Wang nodded.

"China can supply the world with cheaper goods, which will be in higher demand from now onwards. The capitalism of the West has opened the door for China to become a world power in the future."

"Yes, the ingredients are there. If China plays it right, I am sure they can do so. Especially in the field of technology, which is already a source for heavy investments. Industries like clothing, toys and other easy to produce industries may soon be taken over by low wage countries as Bangladesh, Thailand, the Philippines or Indonesia."

Mr Wang looked up. I suddenly realised that this might not be the best thing to say during dinner to a vice president of a Chinese garment company.

"But I am sure that the companies and brands that are focussed on high quality will survive," I added.

"Just the commodity clothing for brands such as Uniqlo, H&M or possibly Zara in the future will move at some point production to other countries because of wage constraints. Brands like yours deal with customers with a bigger wallet. They can afford more, so you don't have to worry."

Right at that moment, the first dishes arrived on the table. We both got a plate in front of us with as how it looked like a steamed Mouse Grouper Fish bathing in Soy Sauce, Ginger, Scallion and Cilantro. The fish had black spots all over his body, and its head was still there. It looked me straight in the eye. Another plate with steamed broccoli with garlic in soy sauce arrived as well. Mr Wang looked satisfied to the Mouse Grouper Fish in front of him.

"Enjoy, Mr Victor."

Wang said and waited for me to pick up my chopsticks first. I started with a piece of broccoli. It was interesting that in this Chinese restaurant we did not share dishes as in most restaurants. Here we have our separate dishes. Mr Wang raised his glass and said:

"Thank you, my friend."

I raised my glass as well.

"This looks like really nice food, thank you again for inviting me." Mr Wang smiled.

"Do you know East Nanjing Road?"

"Yes, I have been there a couple of times."

East Nanjing Road is one of the most famous shopping streets in China and one of the busiest shopping streets in the world. East Nanjing Road is part of Nanjing Road, which is the world's longest shopping street of about five and a half kilometre long and attracting over one million visitors on a daily basis. That is even one of the reasons I usually try to avoid East Nanjing Road. And of course, the street sellers approaching you every twenty meters with whether you are interested in a massage or sex with a beautiful girl.

"Do you know the building on the crossing of Henan Road and East Nanjing Road? It's under construction now. It's located on the block before you walk onto the Bund."

I remember an authentic-looking building under construction when walking there a while ago.

"The only thing what's open now in the entire building is a Starbucks, on East Nanjing Road."

Starbucks. Mr Wang used a familiar location for me to locate the building.

"That building..."

Mr Wang started while he looked for his glass of wine, grabbed it and took a sip.

"That building is my property. I purchased it earlier last year together with two investors from Hong Kong."

I looked impressed. That's a seven-story department building located on the hottest shopping location in China - if not the world. When purchasing a building like that you're not talking in millions, but billions of RMB. Mr Wang continued:

"I will have shops and restaurants opened in the property later this year, and my office will be there too. There is more office space on the top floor of the building. They are perfect for conferences or training. I'd like to start a training and consultancy company there. You can be a lecturer and business partner."

Before Mr Wang said that I just put another piece of broccoli in my mouth. It took me five seconds to process this nice offer, and seemingly a great opportunity.

"You can choose whether you have fifty-one per cent or forty-nine per cent of the company shares," Mr Wang added. "Furthermore, you write the business plan, and I come in with money."

On the one hand, I felt impressed, on the other one a bit uncomfortable. If he is really attending the Chinese Communist Parties National People Congress and owns that building on East Nanjing Road, he must be powerful. This man can make or break my career in China. I felt a bit overwhelmed by this offer. Mr Wang looked me in the eyes as if he expected an instant answer.

"What do you think?" He continued to ask.

"It sounds like a good opportunity," was my first reaction while I still thought about the offer.

"But there are so many training and consulting companies in Shanghai. It will be difficult to start a business in this field."

Mr Wang did not seem to agree.

"We won't start it and see who is interested in our services. We first make sure we have a network and some opportunities in the pipeline. That's the moment where the business will be registered."

Your experience in providing training will benefit the business, and you have an existing network within the university."

"But how will we work out the visa arrangement?" I asked.

"Don't worry too much about that. My company can sort that out for you. What kind of visa are you on now?"

"I'm currently on a business visa. It will expire in a few months."

Mr Wang looked serious.

"That's alright, that will give us more than enough time to do all the necessary paperwork. But before that and if you like the offer, we have to work out a business plan."

"Yes."

But I felt that this is not the kind of offer I should instantly agree on. Professionally speaking, I should consider it and come back to him in a week or so. Mr Wang stared with satisfaction to his plate. He had excellent table manners. While I noticed this, the soup was served. As I never had dinner with a Chinese who did not slurp his or her soup, it would be an ultimate test to see how he would deal with this. When the soup was in front of us, Mr Wang lifted his spoon and let it sink into the soup. The soup looked transparent, filled with chicken, roots, ginger and red berries.

"This soup is delicious and healthy, Mr Victor." said Mr Wang when he took a sip of his soup without making any sound.

I took a sip too, and to my surprise, it tasted quite sweet. Meanwhile, watermelon was served. This is the desert and an indication that there are no more dishes to come anymore. I felt quite satisfied after the six dishes we ate tonight. It did not look like a lot, but enough to make you feel satisfied. And the good thing compared to having dinner in another Chinese restaurant is that there wasn't any food waste here. I finished my soup and reached for a slice of watermelon. On the other side of the table, I saw Mr Wang waving to one of the waitresses and making a sign that he was aiming to pay the bill. She must have been prepared the bill beforehand because she instantly could provide him with a copy. I just sat there and saw everything happen. I looked around, absorbing the luxury interior of the room around us. This could be the start of a glamorous career in China if at least I could trust him. His offer seemed at least promising. I just have to write a business plan. And that is actually the hardest part. Writing a business plan takes time and requires careful consideration of many factors. As well, I have to make myself familiar with the training and consulting market in Shanghai. There is a lot of competition. While I took another slice of watermelon, I saw Mr Wang paying for the dinner. He looked satisfied in my direction.

"Did you enjoy the dinner, Mr Victor?"

"Yes. This venue and the dinner we had is the best I have had so far since arriving in China."

"That's good to hear."

Judging his reaction, dinners in locations like this for him must happen in a fairly high volume. From the beginning onwards it seemed he knew the restaurant staff well. Mr Wang reached for his newspaper, which looked already a bit worn-out at the end of the day. It looked like the kind of newspaper you find abandoned in a train, read throughout the day by whoever sat nearby and was interested.

I stood up as well, and before I could reach for my coat which hung over my seat behind me, the waitress already had my coat in her hands and helped me get into it. When we left the room, they all lined up towards the door and made a low bow. I felt a little bit overvalued. Given the fact that I enjoyed a dinner with Mr Wang in this location, they must think I am a successful businessman. Not a just graduated foreigner with a part-time teaching job looking to launch his professional career in Shanghai. Anyway, they can think what they want to think. Tonight, I felt special and valued. Even though I knew that that was Mr Wang's intention.

The beautiful elevator opened, and we walked into the lobby. A man wearing a black pantaloon and pullover stood up from the lounge area in the lobby once he saw Mr Wang. I could recognise him as the same man who came to pick up Mr Wang after the project management class.

"My driver already arrived, Mr Victor," Mr Wang said while we walked out and stood in front of the entrance.

It was quiet outside beside classical music coming out of the outdoor speakers high above our heads. A soft, warm breeze came up from the south. When we stood beside his car, Mr Wang said:

"Think about my offer."

The driver opened the backdoor of the car. While Mr Wang stepped in, he pointed to a villa on the left side of the hotel entrance.

"That building there," he started, "That is the villa where the British prime minister stayed during his last visit in China."

I looked to my left and saw a big villa, covered in darkness. As empty as the hotel seemed, so did this villa. I wondered how often a place like this would be occupied. Probably just a few times per year when high levelled government officials are visiting Shanghai.

Mr Wang reached his hand out and said:

"Let's stay in touch. I'd like to hear from you soon."

With a serious look on his face, he stepped into the car, after his driver opened the door. The car door closed, and through the window I could see him opening his newspaper. The driver nodded something in Chinese to me, opened the front door and jumped behind the wheel. Once the engine started, it only took seconds for them to drive away, leaving me behind at a luxury hotel resort on about forty-five minutes from downtown Shanghai. While I was standing there, one of the hotel staff walked up to me and asked me in English whether I needed a taxi. A reasonable question at that moment.

"Yes please,"

The gentlemen ordered a taxi for me.

"It should only be a few minutes, Sir."

"Thank you. I will wait here."

This was the first night in Shanghai where I enjoyed absolute luxury. Having dinner with what looks like a Chinese billionaire with a sincere interest in starting a consulting company with me. I've had worse nights. A car drove up to the hotel entry, which looked like a taxi. I entered the taxi with enough food for thought to spend thinking about tonight, until I would arrive at the gate of my compound.

19

Xinhu Riverside Apartments - 20:23

It is the start of December, and Shanghai is getting colder. Streets are covered with yellow and red leaves from the many London Planetrees. People dress in warm clothes when leaving their homes, and days become shorter with sunsets already starting before five o'clock. Christmas lights appear in the street view and shopping malls. With a bit of luck, the first snow of the season becomes a reality soon. During the evenings, I start using the heating in my room as the temperature outside goes well below ten degrees. Compared to the Netherlands, the December climate in Shanghai is mild. For Shanghainese, it is just cold.

I was laying on my bed while I stared into the distance. The only thing I could hear was the buzzing sound of the heating system and the ticking IKEA clock on the wall. It made me realise time was running out literally and at a higher speed than I hoped. I arrived here three months ago intending to find a job by Christmas. So far, I only succeeded half. I only settled a part-time job as a project management lecturer at Jiao Tong University. Nice, but not enough to fully cover my living expenses. It was a part-time job with potential due to the students I have in my class with the majority of them working for multinational companies in a management role. As long as I keep on delivering good and inspiring project management classes, the opportunity to grow my network and job opportunities will be there. Until that moment I'll have to ask my parents for financial aid each month. But for how long are they willing to do this? I presume not until the end of times.

What are my other opportunities and possible threats? Mr Wang is definitely an opportunity. Starting a company at this age is probably too early, I'd rather gain a few more years' experience in a multinational company and take that experience into my own enterprise. I heard some movement in the living room. It must be Mr Lu walking to the kitchen to refill his cup of tea. I was quite lucky to live like this. The situation I have here is shared living, but I have the place basically for my own. If Mr Lu is at home, he is behind the laptop in his room. The kitchen and the living room are basically for me, and I have my own bathroom. I looked at the matt glass IKEA lamp in my room. When I moved in, it came with a white light bulb, like many of the light in Chinese apartments. Just a few understand that you can create a comfortable atmosphere with warm light. I replaced the CFL lamp in matt glass IKEA luminaire with one of the warm white Philips bulbs I kept from my internship. If only Philips would confirm my return... that would make things a lot easier.

The situation I am facing now is that a return could become a reality within a few months, a year, or possibly even more? I can't wait for that. It could even be just never. At this point, it's most wise to keep all options open. If I would fly back to the Netherlands during Christmas to stay there and pick up my life, I would never get what I aimed for. I would end up as just another Dutch guy working in a Dutch company, living in a Dutch home, earning a Dutch salary, and hanging out with my Dutch family and friends during weekends while complaining about the bad weather. I want something different. Don't get me wrong, I miss my family and friends, but I feel this journey is not over yet. I'm only half of where I want to be. I'm in the city where I see my future. This is where I hope to find my future wife and who knows ever walk the Shanghai streets with a little child walking by my side.

Then not to mention the economic situation in Europe. The Netherlands is already officially in a recession, and the European Commission forecasts that Germany, Spain and the United Kingdom will all enter a recession by the end of the year, which will be soon. France and Italy are expected to have flat growth in the third quarter following second quarter contractions. Also, China does not know any recession so far. Earlier this year, industrial output in the Netherlands fell by six per cent, while here industrial output rose twelve point nine per cent year-on-year in 2008. Under these disappointing economic influences, companies will be more careful with hiring. Finding a job would, therefore be difficult.

Or I could perhaps go back to study. Do a master with a marketing or strategy related background. I got up from the bed and opened the long heavy curtain. I slide the balcony door to the left, and immediately felt the cold wind on my face. On the fifth floor of the building in front of me, people were still doing laundry. The white balcony light was switched on. Just in a tub, washing their clothes piece by piece. Rubbing everything to a wooden plate. It was an example of village people moving to the city. They live in a brand-new building, but some of their habits would not change. I walked to the balcony railing. When I looked up again and watched into the far distance on my right side, I could see the contours of the Renaissance hotel in Zhongshan Park, illuminated by Philips blue tubes on the edges of the building. Despite the cold air, which often leads to increased pollution, it was clear tonight. Beyond Zhongshan Park, I saw the flickering lights of aeroplanes landing and arriving at Hongqiao airport.

When I looked downstairs, I could see the old Shanghainese homes. Similar homes must have been on the place of this compound too, until two years ago. And I am afraid the people still living in those dark old, and cold homes may need to move soon as well, once the housing developer reached an agreement with the government on the price he has to pay to get these people out of their homes. I felt a bit chilly, so I decided to move back indoors on the bed. Except for Linda, I did not have anybody to stay for. I have good friends in Camilo and Raphael, but there comes a day that they will leave Shanghai. My family would support me to stay longer in Shanghai if I wanted too. I could continue to work at Jiao Tong University, earn about five thousand RMB per month and whatever I needed more, I could ask as a loan from my parents. It was clear, the benefits of my doubt pointed to Shanghai. I had to put everything on everything to get that job in Philips and start right from there. It is a gamble, but I would be in a higher chance of winning it when staying in Shanghai.

I rolled myself from the bed, walked to the desk where my laptop was recharging. I opened the web browser and logged with my name and reference code into the website of British Airways. I could choose to postpone or cancel my flight. I pushed the pointer on the screen first to postpone, but this could cost me nearly two hundred Euro. Imagine I postponed it to let's say May and I had no opportunity to fly back? That would waste my money. I pressed on cancel. The system asked me to confirm, and a few seconds later, I received the confirmation that the flight was cancelled. A relieving feeling felt over my shoulders. I did not have to look at a deadline anymore. Now I could stay here for another month or three months or even a year without worrying about flights. I felt free. From now onwards, I would book a return flight once I needed one, either for visiting family and friends in the Netherlands or when I had to leave the country for my visa extension. A return flight, from Shanghai to somewhere and back. This was the plan.

20

318 Fuzhou Rd, Huangpu, Shanghai - 20:30

And so, it was Friday again. I worked all day on my project management class. That's why I really feel about going out, have a drink and enjoy the evening. Once per year, it's time for the Shanghai International Film Festival (SIFF). Together with the Tokyo International Film Festival, the SIFF is actually one of the biggest film festivals in Asia. Chinese actors, actresses, movie directors and screenwriters can win awards in a variety of categories such as the Golden Globe Awards (which is the most prestigious award), International Student Shorts Awards, China Movie Channel Media Awards and Jackie Chan Action Movie Awards.

You can imagine it's hard to get access to the film festival if you are not representing something important in the Chinese movie industry. So, for outsiders as myself, there is an annual SIFF afterparty in M1NT, an exclusive Shanghai night club in Huangpu's district on Fuzhou Road. This happens at the very end of the SIFF, which usually takes up to a week. I called Raphael whether he was into joining me, and thankfully he said yes. It's important to get yourself on the guestlist; otherwise you risk not to be granted access, but that is the case for any given evening in M1NT. I met with Raphael downstairs in the building lobby, and we walked towards the elevator as M1NT is perched on the twenty-fourth floor of the office building. Big Western bodyguards were looking at us in a judging way. We did not explicitly look like movie stars, big ass producers or anything else related to the movie industry. To make sure I dressed up well wearing a suit, while Raphael chose for jeans and a polo. At least we did not show up there as Dumb and Dumber. I mentioned my name as the reservation name, and after taking the elevator up, we first passed the garderobe to leave our coats. We passed the impressive twenty-seven-meter long shark tank with real sharks and continued our walk into the luxuriously decorated nightclub.

"Have you been here before?" I asked Raphael.

"Yes, with some colleagues after work."

"I have been here a few times, usually do not go here that often."

We passed a small red carpet where all the famous guests halted for pictures. You can imagine the amount of attention for this Dutch and Brazilian guy, so we quickly walked through to the bar.

"Do you know? Usually, alcoholic beverages such as wine or mixes are starting from twelve EUR onwards," I said to Raphael. He laughed.

"So M1NT is usually not the place you want to get drunk unless you don't mind spending a lot of money."

"Exactly. People usually drink a few beers downstairs from the convenience shop before heading up to M1NT."

I looked at the bar. Tonight, a selected number of beers, wines and cocktails were on the SIFF tab, enabling everybody to access a free flow of drinks. Tens of glasses filled with wine and cocktails were positioned on the bar, providing us with the ultimate opportunity to get wasted if we had the intention.

"Let's stand here for a while," I said to Raphael.

This was a comfortable spot at the bar with an open view on the red carpet where guests entered M1NT. More important from a hydration point of view; a dozen glasses filled with red wine stood next to us within arm's length. With other guests eagerly consuming wine and cocktails, the bar was frequently re-supplied with new glasses by M1NT employees. Suddenly a familiar face walked around the corner.

"Do you see her? That is the American actress Heather Graham. She participated as International Jury member of the Golden Goblet Award."

"I think I know her, but help me with a few movies she played in?"

Raphael said while he took a sip of his wine.

"She's playing in *The Hangover* movie. That must have been the only one I have seen she's starring in. Or at least the only one that came to mind instantly."

While she made her way into M1NT, it was clear she was one of the special guests tonight. She was surrounded by three circles of people, making it impossible to get close to or have a short talk. We looked at her from a distance.

"She looks pretty." I nodded.

This was the difference between Raphael and me. Whilst his taste is still into Western ladies, mine turned almost desperately into Asian, starting already while living in the Netherlands.

I suspect it was fuelled by a Dutch girl I met online. She was a couple of years younger and lived on two hours driving distance from my hometown. As a result, it did not last long, but her beautiful brown Asian influenced eyes always remained a benchmark for future relationships. She wasn't my first love, but surely the first one I fell into love with. Later I started dating a Chinese girl, and from that moment onwards I was poisoned by what they call the yellow fever.

Now the music stopped, and the lights on the stage went on. A few people whom I could not recognise walked up and two dull sounds filled the nightclub when the organiser tabbed the microphone.

"Ladies and gentlemen…" He started with a Chinese English accent,

"Welcome to the fifteenth Shanghai International Film Festival after-party. What an incredible week it was…"

Guests started to cheer and applauded. It felt increasingly as if we attended somebody else's party. Another movie of *Wedding Crashers* except this was not a wedding.

"This week many awards have been given to outstanding performances delivered by great actors and actresses. It is, therefore, an honour to have here on stage with me Vladas Bagdonas, who won an award for the best actor in "The Conductor", and Ursula

Pruneda, the prize winner as best actress in "The Dream of Lu" and last but not least Paula Ortiz, who won the best music award for the American movie Chrysalis!"

The audience cheered even more. Raphael and I looked at each other. I could see from the expression on his face that he wasn't familiar with these actors and actresses too. As the nominees and the movies on the SIFF are not the Hollywood blockbusters broadcasted in global cinema's, we did not know anybody here except Heather Graham. The winners on stage showed their award to the audience, said a few words of appreciation and the evening continued with club music. I reached for another glass of wine, my third one since we arrived.

"How do you like it here?" I asked Raphael.

The expression on his face seemed satisfactory. I looked around. It was getting more crowded now. All guests had drinks in their hands and talked in small groups. I did not feel like to start a conversation with a stranger that much, apprehensive that the conversation would end up embarrassing because I am nothing related to the movie industry. I already have a hard time recognising Chinese actors and actresses by face. I do not often watch Chinese movies. I started to sense that there must have been many famous Chinese actors and actresses because numerous pretty Chinese ladies and handsome men were welcomed with applause and photographed extensively on the red carpet. Raphael handed me another glass of wine.

"It's free buddy, let's enjoy it!"

Because of the loud music, we could not talk a lot. But who cared because there was so much to see around us.

While enjoying this fourth glass filled with red wine, an astonishing Chinese lady approached me. Her hair was tied up in a traditional style, and her lips were finished with dark red lipstick. She was slim, wearing a long red dress made from a shiny material. As the dress did not have any sleeves, her skinny arms where uncovered from her shoulders to her hands, with one of them holding a small red leather handbag. It was just big enough to put a mobile phone and a home key in. Or an access card to a hotel room. The dress fitted her body well and had a cut on both sides, showing her legs. The red high heel shoes with strings around her feet were the reason that she looked so tall, but that did not matter and diminish any of her beauty. She was astonishing. I could imagine her being an actress or at least an upcoming one. She looked me in the eyes. The world around us just moved on, but I felt like I was in a little bubble. The music around us continued with a flat beat, and I heard conversations around me, but I could not understand what it was about. She walked three steps towards me, just close enough to have a decent conversation. Without introducing herself, she asked me:

"Hi, are you an American movie director?" Within a fraction of a second, my thoughts were going in two directions. Should I be honest and just tell her that I represent one of the nobodies within the movie industry and try to enjoy my evening at M1NT? Or... what if I say yes? What could happen next? She would probably ask me which movies I have on my resume. Or ask me to show my personal Wikipedia page with filmography. Would she believe me if I say *Titanic* or *Forrest Gump*? I don't quite look like James Cameron or Robert Zemeckis but do you think she will notice? Would she introduce me to her hot actress friends and ask me to join their exclusive after-party somewhere in a five-star hotel's suite? Or a private penthouse party on the fiftieth floor of a residential tower right next to the Pudong river with a view on Pudong's financial district? As I did not have much time to decide and did not want to embarrass myself too much, I answered:

"No, I am actually working as a part-time project manager in Shanghai Jiao Tong University."

Straightforward and fair. I could see a disillusioned expression on her face. She did not have time to respond because immediately after that, she was pulled away by somebody to join a conversation in a group of people happening right next to us. Without saying bye or something like it was nice talking to you, she continued her evening.

"Wow!"

I heard behind me. I turned around.

"What was that?! Or... who was that?!" Said Raphael.

He must just have witnessed one of the shortest conversations ever.

"Was she hitting on you?!" I stared at my empty glass. I reached for a new glass of red wine and took a big sip.

"No, I don't think she was."

"She approached you and talked to you!"

"Yes, but she just asked whether I was an American movie director. I mean, do I look like one? As soon as I said no, the conversation was over."

"Well, then she probably wasn't worth it anyway." Raphael grinned.

"You would not go for a Steven Spielberg no. But maybe a Woody Allen?"

"Ah fuck you," I poked Raphael's shoulder.

"Woody Allen never played in or produced a movie that I actually enjoyed."

Raphael lifted his glass in the air, waiting for me to do the same and cling towards a cheer.

"To free booze!" Raphael said.

"Cheers, buddy," I answered.

It seemed the music got louder now, or was it getting more into hardstyle? I thought again... what if I would have said yes? Just something like yes, I am a movie director. Small movies, though, but they are promising and starting to get the attention of a bigger audience. My life could have turned into a totally different direction, this night here in M1NT. Probably not, but still. I looked around. The astonishing lady was still talking with the same people as for whom she left our conversation. What if she was a Chinese actress? I would never know who she is. If I just randomly Google Chinese actress I may recognise her face. On page seventeen. Anyway, never mind. I poked Raphael into his side.

"It is just before eleven o'clock, and I have to go back home. You have weekend tomorrow, but I have to work on a project management lecture."

Raphael nodded.

"Alright, let's go. I may go for a massage on the way home and catch an early sleep." We bottomed up our fifth glass of red wine, and without spending a single RMB, we left M1NT.

"Good choice to come here tonight Victor,"

Raphael said while we passed the shark tank once again on the way to the elevator. Two of them swam along with us.

"Let's do this again next year. And by then prepare yourself a hard copy of a screenplay in case you are approached again by a pretty Chinese movie star."

In the taxi on the way back home, I checked my emails on the phone. There was a Keane fan email with a title that they would play a concert in Beijing. At first, I couldn't believe my eyes, and I opened the email. It was true! Keane is excited to play their first-ever show in China, during the Burberry launch event on invitation by Burberry's chief creative officer Christopher Bailey. My excitement faded away when I further read through the email, which mentioned that this was a closed event and for invitees only. How could I ever get myself access to such an event?

There might be backdoor access similar to the SIFF event tonight. I started to think about the people I know in Beijing. There is one girl I met during my first trip to Beijing, but I did not contact her for a long time. It would be a bit embarrassing to contact her for this reason. Suddenly I thought about Serena. She is from Beijing and might be able to help out. I'd send her a message whether she knew anybody that could get us tickets for this evening. She would be my only chance, though. But never tried is never done, so I sent a message to Serena. Soon I received a reply that she would contact some family members and friends and would keep me posted. I looked outside the taxi window into the sky, as if a short prayer would increase my chances. But if anybody was listening, the low hanging clouds may have blocked my prayer. I could only hope from now onwards.

21

Xinhu Riverside Residence, 09:10

From: Gerald van Tatenhof
To: Victor de Lange
Send 09/12/2008

Hi Victor,

In reaction to our last meeting in office, I have bad news. HR has frozen all budgets to hire new people or create new positions. We'll have to postpone the position discussed till further notice – let's stay in touch.

Regards,

Gerald van Tatenhof

Back at square one.

22

Huaihai Road, Central Shanghai, 18:40

It was raining on this Thursday night. I rushed to be on time for the second dinner with Mr Wang. As he invited me for the first dinner and did me two offers to start a business with him, I thought it would be fair enough to invite him this time. As I couldn't afford the luxury kind of place he took me to last time I thought it would be a good idea to invite him to Brick. It's both a formal and romantic place, so good for both occasions. I took a taxi from home where I was working all afternoon on my project management classes. Looking back, I could have taken the subway, which would be cheaper and probably more convenient. But then I had to walk in the rain from the subway station to the restaurant. Now I was stuck in traffic, in the middle of a rainy Thursday evening rush hour, and still had forty minutes left to arrive at Brick in Sinan Road. By all means, I wanted to arrive there earlier than Mr Wang so I could choose the best available table.

The taxi driver seemed annoyed by the weather and the traffic jam. I looked outside the window of my yellow taxi. I saw a tricycle full of flowers under a retail overhang. The owner was sitting in front of it on the other side of the pathway. There are thousands of these small businesses in Shanghai, either selling flowers, fruit, mobile phone accessories, clothes, food, offering a shoe repairing service, hairdressing or you can even find dentists operating on the sideways of Shanghai. You can actually find everything you need on the street. Next thing I saw was a fruit store, with a ginger cat sitting in front of it. The cat seemed to enjoy the accompany of the people passing by. The fruit looked incredibly fresh, from banana's to lemons to blueberries. A big measurer was hanging near the entrance where the fruit could be weighted to measure the right price. The driver indicated and took a left, into a street that was smaller and not as crowded as the main road we just drove on. I noticed Shanghainese residents enjoying dinner on the sideway of the street. It seemed like a husband and wife, under the shed of their home while hiding from the rain. Their plates looked empty. The husband was looking at his phone, while his wife kept an eye of what happened around them on the street. I could imagine them sitting there throughout the year just out of curiosity what is happening in their street and catching up with passing by neighbours.

Meanwhile, the rain turned into a drizzle. While I glimpsed my watch, I noticed it was now twenty minutes before seven. In this speed we could make it at least on time. After a few turns left and right, the taxi stopped, and I arrived just in time and before Mr Wang did. The waitress welcomed me in. The atmosphere was good. Dimmed lights, piano music on the background and surrounded by brick walls.

"Do you have any table preference, Sir?" the waitress asked.

"I'd prefer one of those tables on the side please, with a bit of privacy if possible."

"No problem Sir, will the table over there be alright?" She pointed to a corner table on the side. I nodded.

"That should be fine." The waitress pulled out the chair so I could slide in. Next, she handed the food and drink menu for my first orientation.

"I am waiting for a friend to arrive."

"No problem. I will come back to you later."

I looked again at my watch. It was just a few minutes after seven. Mr Wang did not arrive yet. He must have been stuck in traffic as well. He is certainly not the kind of person to travel by subway. He would have his driver dropping him off in the front of the restaurant. I glanced at the menu for a bit while keeping an eye on the front door. It opened a few times, gradually filling the restaurant with guests.

Once I started to feel a bit nervous - did he forget we would have dinner together tonight? - the door opened. It was Mr Wang, poring the rain drips from his suit that ended up there on the way from the car to Brick's front door. He looked well dressed as always, in a tailor-made suit from his private company. He looked around for a second before he noticed me.

"Hello, Mr Victor," he said when he stood next to the table.

"Hi Mr Wang," I answered in return, and I stood up to shake his hand.

"The weather is not good today," started Mr Wang while he observed the table I selected for our dinner tonight. It was one-sixth the size of the table during our first dinner. I wasn't sure what went through his head. Mr Wang sat down.

"How are you today?" he asked.

"I am fine, spent the most time working on the project management class. Quite productive. How about you?"

"I'm working on a presentation I have to deliver next week for a board of directors. Your presentations always look very nice and ordered. Can you please have a look at it?"

I nodded.

"No problem. If you wish, I can optimise it where necessary without changing the presentation content. Just send it to me by email."

It was good to see that Mr Wang started to trust me for this kind of tasks. And it is fair to do something back after the expensive dinner he treated me last time.

"Let's order food." I started.

"I chose this restaurant as they serve brilliant Western food. I wanted you to experience this, as well. They have a variety of fish and meat dishes in both their starters and mains. And an extensive wine list. Shall we order a bottle of red?"

Mr Wang was browsing through the menu and reading the dish names out loud as if he was practising his English. Meanwhile, more people walked in. It was perhaps good that I reserved a table for tonight. I looked over my shoulder. The red seats in the middle section of the restaurant were all occupied now. Mr Wang, who was facing the restaurant, said:

"Okay Mr Victor, let's order food." I felt Mr Wang was a bit in a rush or seemed not feeling totally comfortable eating here. Maybe he was afraid of being recognised in a middle-class restaurant as Brick? Treating Mr Wang dinner in a restaurant like we did last time would at least be a month worth of teaching in Shanghai Jiao Tong University. Or a month worth of rent. Meanwhile, Mr Wang waved to the waitress who just passed by. It must be new for him that tonight he'd have to share one waitress with at least nine other tables. Usually, he has at least five waitresses just for himself.

"I'd like to have the smoked salmon salad to start with, and I go for the grilled salmon filet as main." He looked at me.

"Ehm, I'm going for the beef carpaccio and the lamb rack." I reached for the wine menu, which stood in the middle of the table. If I knew Mr Wang well, he would probably like French wine. Last time during our dinner he brought a 1970 Great Wall wine which tasted surprisingly well. Or, at least the label indicated 1970. I should probably not order Chilean wines for him. I browsed through the menu until I saw a Domaine de Toasc from the Provence, in the south of France. Every red wine I had from the Provence was good, so that made me comfortable selecting it.

"Let's go for the French one, can we have one bottle of this one please?" I pointed to the Domaine de Toasc. A quick calculation in my head told me that this dinner would cost me around one thousand RMB. Quite a significant amount for me at this point. But comparing this with a restaurant in the Netherlands it can be considered pretty cheap.

"So, Mr Victor, have you considered the business opportunities we discussed last month?"

Mr Wang went straight to the point.

"Yes, I have given it some thought. Both opportunities seem very good. The business training concept will stand a good chance of success because of the valuable network of business owners you have in Shanghai and China overall. It opens doors where they would remain closed for entrepreneurs starting from scratch. A corporate training company is in line with what I am doing now as I am teaching a business curriculum to graduates, young professionals and middle management executives. I think that a consultant in wedding arrangements will be more challenging from a background point of view. Yes, I have an eye for detail and deliver a high level of service, but a traditional Chinese wedding is what the name says, traditional. I am not sure whether you should let a foreigner deal with traditional Chinese weddings."

During my reflection on Mr Wang's business proposals, the wine was served. We now both had a wide bowl glass with wine in front of us. The burning candle behind the glass intensified the dark red colour of the wine.

"Gan Bei," I said while I lifted my glass. Mr Wang followed me, and the sound of our crystal glasses clinked through the restaurant.

"Let's then focus on the consulting business if you feel more comfortable doing that. Wedding consultancy will indeed be more challenging but is ultimately a better business model as people spend a lot of money on their wedding. It marks one of the most important milestones in the life of a Chinese person. More than it does for you foreigners."

"What is the price paid for a wedding here in Shanghai?"

"More than two hundred thousand RMB."

"That is indeed a lot, considering that Shanghai's GDP by capita is currently just below seventy-five thousand RMB."

After putting things quickly into perspective, Mr Wang was right. Business consulting is a very competitive market, especially now with the economy facing a deep crisis. The Chinese economy is still growing, but many multinational companies have frozen their budgets until the situation gets better. In that case, we would first and only focus on Mr Wang's network. On the other hand, wedding consultancy is a competitive market as well, but couples are prepared to pay a lot. Their families have been saving money for that special day all of their life. As well, the majority of each wedding is paid by the content of red envelopes given by the guests. The money in these envelopes can contain up to a few thousand RMB per envelope. I swirled my glass of wine and took a sip.

"You've given me two truly great opportunities," I continued.

"But at this stage of my life, I am not sure whether I should go for it or not. I feel I need much more practical experience before I am confident to start my own company."

Mr Wang interrupted me.

"Look, I am an entrepreneur all my life. Yes, I had the benefit of having a good family that backed me up financially in the first projects I wanted to take on. But it required hard work and faced a high risk of failure when starting each of the twelve businesses I own today. You have to go for the unknown sometimes."

"True, but you are in your own country. I am ten thousand kilometres away from home."

"If one day, everything you've built up in China will collapse, you always have a home in the Netherlands to go back to. You can disappear and start anew in the Netherlands or elsewhere in Europe while I still need to face the consequences of a business failure here."

"But that should make you more determined not to fail."

While I said that, the waitress arrived with the starter. She served Mr Wang the smoked salmon salad, while I got the beef carpaccio in front of me. This was going to taste great together with the wine.

"Enjoy your dinner, Mr Wang," I said.

Mr Wang was looking for the fork and knife. It was clear that he was not very used to have meals with forks and knives. He started cutting the smoked salmon in a bit of an uneasy way.

"Thank you, Mr Victor."

Meanwhile, the restaurant was full of people. Even at the bar, where a limited number of guests enjoyed a glass of wine with a snack. Because of the increased noise, it became more difficult to have a conversation. I could see this made Mr Wang a bit uneasy. He seemed as if he was in a hurry for the next appointment. Did I take him to the wrong restaurant? I thought it would be nice for him as a change and as well because he specifically interests himself in Western culture for his business. We both finished our starter, and Mr Wang lifted his glass to cheer.

"Thank you, Mr Victor, thank you for dinner here tonight."

I hope he meant this and did not say it just to be polite. Next time I treat him dinner, I should consider bringing him to a Chinese restaurant. Mr Wang started:

"If you feel like you're too inexperienced to start your own business, you can become my personal assistant if you like. In that way you can gain first-hand experience first."

Wow. This was the third option he offered within two dinners. He is really trying to help me here. But becoming his personal assistant means I will probably lose touch with international business and its manners. Chinese business etiquette is a skill itself, and it comes with its own laws. Working for him would most likely involve preparing presentations and join him during business dinners and lunches. It would probably increase his status, having a foreigner on his side as a personal assistant. If these lunches and dinners are very business traditional, Mr Wang's business partners would be in to test my drinking skills. And not in beer and wine, but with Baijiu.

Why do I always see the negatives of his offers? Can I say three times no to a man like this?

"I can pay you maximum eight thousand RMB per month," Mr Wang added.

I quickly calculated. Including teaching that would make me earn about thirteen thousand RMB per month. That's not too bad to start with.

"Thank you. That sounds like a nice offer Mr Wang," I started.

"But I am going to have to think about this one too. I do not want to link myself to a new job with an impulse decision."

"I totally understand that Mr Victor, please do not feel obligated to accept any of the three offers. I just want to help you settle."

I nodded and I felt happy that he did not expect me to choose anything. If I ultimately would decide none of the three offers would be it for me, he would understand.

"If I am honest, I am really hoping that I can resume working in Philips, Mr Wang.

"This is where I did my internship and where I gained interest in lighting. That is my highest priority."

"I understand Mr Victor. Just see what is best for you and where your interest is. That is most important."

Just when he finished his sentence, the main dishes were served. Mr Wang looked at his grilled salmon filet while I got my sizzling lamb rack in front of me. The waitress refilled our glasses with wine.

"This is looking good, Mr Victor,"

Mr Wang said. It made me feel a bit better about the decision to bring him here.

"Now tell me about your family." Mr Wang looked slightly better now with the fork and his knife when he cut his grilled salmon. I took my glass and sipped some of the wine.

"I was born as a first child in what would become a family of four. I have a brother who is two and a half year younger than me. My parents both work in education, with my dad just retiring this year."

Mr Wang nodded while I continued:

"I grew up in a middle-class family in the south west of the Netherlands, two and a half hour driving from Amsterdam. From a population point of view, that place could probably be compared to the compound you live. Just three thousand people."

Mr Wang chuckled.

"But I was raised relatively free. My parents let me explore the world in a controlled way. They gave me the trust to do what I liked and what I was interested in. But if, or before I screwed up, they would be there to point me on what went wrong. Luckily that happened not very often."

"I see, Mr Victor, and that is why you are in Shanghai now. Your curiosity brought you this far."

"Well, without the support from my parents I wouldn't even be sitting here right now."

"I see you have good parents, Mr Victor."

I wanted to ask him something in return.

"Have you travelled to the Netherlands before?"

"Yes I did,"

"I have been to Amsterdam and Doetinchem. Both trips were for business though."

"When was that?"

"Ehm," Mr Wang thought for a while.

"Seven or eight years ago. It was only for a few days."

"How did you like it?"

"Your country is very beautiful, Mr Victor."

This was Mr Wang as I knew him. He would compliment you about something, without mentioning any details. Just how it is.

"Have you travelled to more countries in Europe?"

"Yes, I surely did. For work, I frequently travel to the UK, France, Switzerland and Italy."

"Just for Baromon, for the distributors we have in those countries."

We meanwhile ate our grilled salmon and the lamb rack. The bottle with wine was nearly empty now, even though I did not feel we drank a lot. That's the thing when you eat, drink and talk. Time flies. I looked outside. Seemingly the rain stopped now. People passed by from left to right, some of them glancing inside Brick. The brick walls, dimmed spots in the ceiling and the line with candles on each side of the wall towards the bar must look cosy from the street. The unplayed piano in the back of the restaurant. There are often live jazz music performances on weekend evenings. Today it was just a comfortable playlist with piano and jazz music. This place deserved much more credit than they actually got. The food, the ambience and the service are great. I looked at Mr Wang. He sipped the last bit of wine out of his glass.

"Do you wish to have a desert?" I asked.

Just to make sure that he left the restaurant fully satisfied.

"No Mr Victor, thank you." He looked at his watch.

"I have to leave now."

I checked the time too. It was eight forty-five. Mr Wang was not the kind of person to have late-night drinks with. Before I could pay for the bill, Mr Wang already wiped his mouth with his white napkin and stood up after putting it back on the table.

"Thank you for the dinner, Mr Victor." I smiled.

"You're welcome, I hope you enjoyed it."

The uncertain feeling for dinner that night came back now. It could be that Mr Wang was in a hurry, or maybe still had some work to do. Walking away from the table before its cleared and the bill is paid for seemed a bit strange to me.

"Think about the business opportunities we discussed. And I will send you my presentation by email. Thank you very much for looking at it."

He looked me in the eye, and while he passed by, he put a hand on my shoulder.

"I'll see you soon." He walked away.

And there I sat. Two empty plates still on the table, a sip of wine left in the bottle and an unpaid bill. While I waved to the waitress, I poured the left-over wine from the bottle into my glass. Quite a good bottle of wine, matching perfectly with roasted meat. I finished the wine, paid for the bill, and stood up to leave the restaurant. The waitress thanked me and wished me a good evening while she held the door open. Sinan Road was quiet although it was dry now. I decided to take the subway back home. It would probably take me forty minutes to arrive in Zhenping Road. Arrival time at home would be a perfect time to shower and sleep. Tomorrow would be a busy day again with preparations for the project management class.

23

Hong Kong Plaza Mall, Huaihai Road, Shanghai - 21:00

"So you found the restaurant!" Raphael was waiting for me in a Teppanyaki restaurant on the fifth floor of a shopping mall on Huaihai Road where he had dinner earlier tonight with a group of friends. It was just after ten PM; I had spent a quiet evening with Linda. She felt too tired, so she decided to go home and not join me on another Saturday night out in Shanghai.

"Yes, the shopping mall itself wasn't a problem, but the restaurant was a little bit difficult. But I'm here."

"Good buddy, let's order a beer for you." Raphael waived to the waiter, who walked up to our table and noted the order of two beers.

"Qingdao please," Raphael added. "And cold, cold, cold beer!"

The poor waiter did not seem to understand a single word of English.

"Pin Te Pijiu!" Raphael added.

Now it was clear. The waiter nodded and walked away.

"You can't make this clear enough. Anyway, how have you been? How is teaching?"

"Fine, I taught a couple of classes now. Feedback from the students is good. And yourself?"

"Good, Good Victor. Busy in office. There are issues in the supply chain this week, so I left office a few times at midnight, to be back in front of my laptop again at six am. Maybe I shouldn't go out either. But life is not all about work."

"That's true. It's good to meet you again."

"How is Linda? Are you guys still seeing each other regularly?"

"hmm yes. We are doing well. We're meeting for dinner, coffee, sometimes drinks. She's staying over occasionally, but I feel her boss is constantly telling her that she shouldn't date a foreigner, and that is making her hesitating about us."

"Shouldn't date a foreigner? Why?"

Raphael asked this question with a smile on his face, as if he knew that dating a foreigner could bring more harm than love.

"Because apparently in her eyes, foreigners are not trustworthy. Or maybe she is just jealous."

"Could be yes. How about you? Are you seeing anybody?"

"Naah not really. I am just too busy with work to invest time in a proper relationship." I nodded. I had time enough to invest in two or more relationships if I wanted. But that would ultimately break hearts, possibly including my own.

Meanwhile, the beers were served, cold as Raphael asked for. We cheered, and I took a sip from the bottle. The good thing in China is that the Qingdao bottles are quite big, containing almost half a litre of beer. The taste is quite light, so they are easy to absorb. Raphael continued:

"You know, last weekend I went out, and I met this girl who I eventually brought back home. She was quite nice, but definitely not from Shanghai. Her behaviour, by times, was not really civilised. Nevertheless, I was into some adventure, so why not Victor?" I nodded in agreement.

"So we arrived at my place, and you know my small studio apartment basically consists out of my bed. Besides a kitchen and bathroom, there is nothing else."

I remembered that yes. Every girl who ended up in that apartment had no other choice to sit on his bed and that was just the beginning.

"I think she knew my intention. But she was hungry and started to ask for food. I did not have much at my home, so I made her some noodles. But while I was cooking the noodles, I suddenly heard a big fart. Like not the one that comes out quick, but one that lasted for at least seven seconds and went up and down in sound.

Like this." and Raphael imitated the sound. It made me laugh out loud. I totally saw it happening. While he was laughing too, he continued his story:

"And Victor, at first I thought I might have heard it wrong. Maybe it was a sound that came out while I was boiling the water. Or it came from the corridor. I could not imagine a girl to produce such a big fart. For sure, it diminished all my appetite in sex. Firstly because of the sound, but mostly from the smell it produced afterwards. Unbelievable like rotten eggs."

I laughed out loud.

"I think I was very polite by not instantly tell her to leave, but first let her finish her noodles. I can't send that girl back onto the streets of Shanghai in the middle of the night with an empty stomach?"

"You did a good thing, buddy," I concluded.

"Then, when she finished her noodles, which she did by sitting on the side of my bed, she put the noodle cup on the ground and let herself fall onto the bed. This would be the moment to sit next to her, talk to her, softly kiss her... But I just constantly heard the sound of that fart playing in my head. I couldn't do it anymore."

"So what did you do?"

"I told her I was tired and that I wanted to go to bed. Easy peasy. She understood the message and left. We did not contact each other since."

"She probably didn't not feel comfortable about that situation too."

While we discussed this moment, we finished the first bottle of beer.

"Shall we have one more before leaving this place?" "Sure, no problem. Your story made me feel thirsty," I joked with a smile on my face.

"So how did your meeting go with that rich Chinese guy last Thursday?"

I had told him about that earlier this week.
"It went pretty well, we met in this huge empty luxury hotel on an hour driving distance from Shanghai. I'm sure there must have

been more staff working that night than actual guests staying in the hotel. The restaurant was there just for us.

"Probably because you're paying a small fortune to eat there," Raphael interrupted me,

"Exactly, but the food was marvellous. Absolutely top notch."

"What did you guys talk about?"

"Just about some possibilities to start a business. He offered to start a business in consulting or wedding arrangement."

"And what did you say?"

"That I would give it some thought.

"What?" Raphael asked. "This is a good opportunity! He must have a big network; you can take advantage of that. High profile people like him do not start companies without carefully considering it. He must see a need for it among his professional network."

"Yes, that's true. But if at this moment I could choose between a start-up company or first gaining experience in a multinational company I would not have to think long. He is like you write the business plan, I come in with money."

Raphael thought for a few seconds.

"Yes, I would have to think about that too actually. A decision like that can have quite a radical impact on your life."

"Besides that, I am still trying and hoping to get back into Philips. That's my first priority."

I looked around and realised that we were almost the only two left in the restaurant. While I took a sip of my beer, a rat ran over the table just two meters away from us. Did I see that correct? Was it really a rat? It happened behind Raphael's back so he couldn't have seen it.

"I swear I just saw a rat running over the table behind you."

"What?!" Raphael almost jumped up.

"Yes, it was a much bigger creature than a mouse."

I looked up to the ceiling and saw another rat walking on the plasterboard of the open ceiling. And another one. I waived to the waiter. This time another one showed up, which would hopefully ease the flow of communication.

"I saw rats running around just now over that table and up in the ceiling."

The waiter did not seem impressed.

"Yes, it happens when the neighbouring restaurants close on this floor. All the rats will come here."

I looked at Raphael to see whether he heard the same inconceivable explanation.

"This can't be true, right?" I asked him. Raphael started to laugh.

"Well, apparently it is. Let's go."

While I stood up, Raphael paid for his dinner, and we left the restaurant. The staff smiled at us, while Raphael said:

"They didn't charge us for the last four beers. I only had to pay for what I consumed during dinner."

"Well, maybe that is to make up for that rat incident. I'm glad I did not have dinner there. Imagine the food you had was pre-tasted by a rat… Or maybe you ordered chicken, and figured out that they run out of chicken meat, so…"

"Ah shut up!" Raphael laughed while he poked me in my side.

We followed the escalators downstairs to the exit of the mall. The street was still full of people. Taxi's passed by. Some were looking for a ride, others on their way to a destination. I saw people coming out of restaurants, while others like Raphael and myself were looking to extend their evening into Shanghai's bustling nightlife.

"Where do you feel like to go?" Raphael asked me.

"Hmm… Cotton Club? We're not too far away from there, and I am in for some good live music."

"Cotton Club it is," said Raphael while he waived for an upcoming taxi to stop.

At least we could enjoy our drinks there without the presence of rats.

24

Element Fresh, Ritz-Carlton Hotel - 13:20

I planned to meet with Camilo for a coffee on Sunday afternoon. After waking up on Sunday mornings, I often went for brunch to Element Fresh on Nanjing West Road. Among other delicacies, they offer a big American breakfast with a free flow of coffee for eighty RMB. The restaurant is located in one of the shops of the Ritz Carlton Hotel. I usually purchase *The Wall Street Journal* so I could enjoy some reading time while enjoying my brunch and coffee. I already finished my brunch as it took too long for me to wait for Camilo, and he already ate breakfast anyway. While I was reading the markets section in *The Wall Street Journal* and enjoyed the third refill of my coffee, I heard:

"Hi Victor," in English with an authentic Italian accent.

Different compared to Dutch people, Italians always put more emphasis on the "i" in Victor. Easy to recognise.

"Hi Camilo, good to see you again, how are you?" I said while I stood up to shake Camilo's hand.

"Fine, fine," Camilo answered while he slid the seat in front of me away from the table so he could just fit in. "Busy here," Camilo remarked while he looked around.

"Yes, it tends to get busy here after ten-thirty on weekend days."

It did not seem to bother Camilo much, or at least not enough to consider moving to another restaurant.

"How's life?" Camilo asked.

"Good! Busy with teaching. Or actually, the teaching itself does not require so much time. It is the lecture preparation that's nearly a fulltime job."

"Ah, yes," Camilo answered while he ordered an espresso.

"The research and creation of PowerPoint presentations take a lot of time." I nodded.

"How long does one class take?"

"Three hours."

Camilo looked surprised.

"That's long for you as a lecturer."

"Correct, but the actual presentation takes maximum an hour and a half. There is a break of fifteen minutes to split the lecture in two, and there is a case study. The group completion of the questions and discussion take approximately an hour as well."

"How long do you prepare per class?"

"Roughly twelve hours,"

"Ouch, that is long."

"Yes, but you'll have to look at it from a long-term point of view. Considering the number of hours I spend preparing this first set of classes, I do not make much money indeed. But once I do this class again with minimum changes, that's where I start making money. Best case scenario is when I can teach this class to companies. They easily pay seventy thousand RMB for a three-day training."

"You can use the network you're building up in the University," Camilo added.

"Yes, or take advantage of a situation where price negotiations with the University get stuck and offer my own price to do business with them directly. Instead of the hourly rate paid by the University, the big bag with money is for me."

Camilo smiled.

"You're off to a good start with this,"

"Yes, if it all works out. The situation I face now is that the University is only running courses on demand, which means if they can fill a class with about eight students minimum, they start one."

"So that can be each month or in a worst-case scenario six months."

"Exactly. It's not a stable source of income. I could make it work if I could run one class per month."

When Camilo's espresso arrived, he carefully added a bit of brown sugar to it by ripping off the top of the small sugar bag supplied on the saucer. He pressed his fingers halfway the bag so just enough sugar could drop into the espresso.

"Now this is coffee, Victor." Camilo had a disapproving look on his face while he looked to my big mug filled with Americano. "Whoever came up with the idea of adding water to espresso?"

"The Americans? But this one comes with my brunch," I answered with a smile on my face.

"Never mind. How do you spend your time mostly?" Camilo asked. "I sometimes think it is difficult to spend time with the right people."

I took a sip from my coffee and thought for a few seconds.

"Well, the first eleven days after arriving in China, I explored the city as much as I could. Armed with the Shanghai Lonely Planet, I went out to discover the hidden places, walking tours, restaurants and sightseeing venues, you know? It made me understand the culture and places better."

Camilo nodded in agreement.

"When I arrived here, the real invasion of foreigners in Shanghai didn't start so much yet. An individual white male object walking through Shanghai was an almost guarantee to get in touch with locals. For good and bad without you having to reach out first."

"Yes, that's true. I remember walking on the Bund during one of those first eleven days where a Chinese guy of my age approached me. He was kind and had an interest in my wellbeing in Shanghai. So, I just talked for a while and thought what a polite guy! After a while, he offered to call his cousin. So that was fine for me. I remember her name was Chrissy, she showed up and joined our walking tour."

Camilo started to laugh, and I could see on the impression on his face that he already knew how this was going to end.

"You know the funny thing is, I did not even realise that I was part of a set-up. After our walking tour through freezing Shanghai, we walked to Yuyuan Garden, where we had dinner together."

"And? How did it finish?"

"Well, I remember meeting her once or twice afterwards, but it did not really work out."

"Ouch, why not? Did you mess it up?"

"No. Imagine this girl coming from the middle of nowhere in China. She had different norms and values. Besides that, the evening I was going out with Chrissy I met Cecile. I had a better feeling with Cecile, so I did not contact Chrissy that often anymore. Our contact ultimately faded away."

"You are so lucky, being a free and single man in Shanghai at the age of twenty-five." Camilo commented. I knew he was ten years older than me and had a family back in Europe.

"This is a golden time for you."

"I'm sure you enjoyed your time too, but then in Italy. Italy must have been conservative twenty years ago, but so is China today." Camilo smiled.

"Society will always have extremes. That was the case twenty years ago, and that's still the case today."

"How do you feel about meeting people in bars?"

"I generally doubt seriousness and good intentions in bars and nightclubs. Never did I meet a girl in a bar or nightclub that ended up in a long-lasting relationship. I mean, did you?"

"No. Relationships often started as a result of friend introductions."

"Exactly. Nightlife intentions seem just different. The last time I tried during my internship was with a girl who was literally drunk during most of the three times we met. No matter it was Saturday night or a random Sunday afternoon. The combination of vodka and dating just didn't work for me."

"Don't you think that compared to the Western world, many Chinese choose to date and eventually marry their high school or university lover? I mean at least in the Netherlands I do not see that as such a big thing."

Camilo looked up from his espresso.

"I think so, yes. But in addition to the Western world where dating on the work floor is not recommended, I feel it actually isn't such a big deal in China. I've encountered several colleague couples in my company and friends' companies. As well, company babies are nothing new. Where do you see that in Europe?"

"Perhaps the office or factory environment offers a promising arena for many to practise their dating skills. Girls would normally go for a caring, slightly older and experienced male colleague with if possible, a good family background, where for guys prettiness, character and a stable background are prerequisites to go for."

"So that gives you many opportunities here, Victor," Camilo said.

"Except for the fact that I am a foreigner. That comes with advantages and disadvantages on a whole different level."

"Such as?"

"In many cases, the traditional aspect and expectations of a wedding will become due. They don't ask you for an apartment or car. But her parents might object."

"Well, as long as they see you are a good and serious guy, you'll be fine. It is just that many traditional Chinese parents do not trust foreigners. From their point of view, we come to China just to work and have fun. Chinese girls waste time in such a way as it becomes more difficult to find good husbands once they are in their late twenties. On that age, I have had friends falling in the often-short lasting trap of dating their boss with hopes and good intentions of career perspectives. I do not think they do that with a long-term perspective in mind. Eventually, it is the laoban…"

"Laoban?"

"That's Mandarin for a boss, abusing his power and taking the opportunity to fuck outside the doors of his arranged marriage."

"Ouch," Camilo said again. "That does not sound good."

"I agree, but there are girls who think they can get a benefit out of this. Anyway. If I am ever doomed to end up alone, I will probably visit People Square on a Sunday afternoon.

"Why? What's going on there?"

"Oh, have you not been there? We can go there this afternoon if you wish." I giggled.

"It already sounds like I don't want to go there. I am not going anywhere until you tell me what I can expect."

"Well, it offers an opportunity for parents to advertise their son or daughter to potentially interested families. In return, they offer a single and aged son or daughter, one who is unlucky in love or possibly divorced and based on a few criteria, and they look for a potential match."

Camilo made a face as if I just told him that ghosts exist in real.

"It is actually just a market. But only the parents are there. They approach other parents with attractive profiles - which are self-written papers hanging in trees or bushes and based on the quality of the conversation or what both parties have to offer, they recommend this person to their son or daughter and set up a date. Criteria's could be age, profession, income and hukou, which is the household registration in a city."

"Have you been there?" Camilo asked, but now with a smile on his face.

"You seem to know it quite well."

"Yes, but not on purpose. I once crossed People Square on a Sunday afternoon, and so I unintentionally ended up in that situation."

"Did you approach some parents?" Camilo seemed still in his joking mood.

"No, of course not. But they looked at me in a way that I was there too to find a lover, but I didn't."

"It could have been your lucky day."

"Do you think they would have negotiated directly with me? I mean, my parents were not there? And I am foreign. That's like going to the market with the aim to buy oranges, but you ultimately come home with fish."

Camilo laughed.

"But fish could taste good too."

"Well, let's agree that on the day you'll divorce, and I am desperately looking for a wife we go to People Square Park on Sunday afternoon to find the love of our life."

"That sounds like a credential story," Camilo said now with a smile on his face.

"Anyway. You have any travel coming up?" I asked Camilo.

"I plan to go back to Italy to make use of my home flight. Should be within now and eight weeks."

"You? Have you anything coming up?"

"I am mostly focussed on my project management class right now and hopefully launch myself a job in Philips. Once I saved enough money or got a fulltime job, it is time again to travel."

"Not even to Beijing?" Camilo said with a smile on his face.

"Beijing? Why? I have been there two times now. I would rather go somewhere I haven't been yet first."

"Raphael told me some flashes of the adventure you encountered while in Beijing."

"Oh, did he?"

"Yes, tell me what happened. You travelled there with your brother, did you?"

"Correct. He visited me during my internship and wanted to see the Great Wall with his own eyes. So I took him to Beijing."

"And what happened there?"

"We went out to Sanlitun and…"

"Of course you did!" Camilo interrupted me.

"That's where people go out indeed," I continued my story. "We were in this lousy looking bar, you know one of those bars where you don't hope a fire outbreak occurs because the bar is overfull of people, ceilings are low, and the only exit is the front door. While enjoying a drink, we were approached by two girls to dance with. One of them was too drunk already. So, after a weird conversation, I let her go while my brother continued to dance and talk with her friend. She was still reasonably sober. Meanwhile, I started talking with another girl and ended up dancing with her. Her name was Lyla. We had a good time together, but at some point, we felt like going back to the hotel because it was about two in the morning. My brother said he said he would come back to the hotel later."

"So, you asked your brother to give you the room for like six minutes?"

"Ha ha," I said instead of actually laughing.

"No, I didn't. I can control the time fairly well. So we went back to the hotel, we stayed in a room without windows I remember. Lyla took a shower. The shower had a prominent place in the room, but the shower curtain could provide some privacy. In preparation for her shower, I closed the curtain, and she warned me not to look at her while she took her shower. She felt a bit shy. But I noticed a small gap."

"You motherfucker!" Camilo said a little bit too loud, and some of the people around us pointed their eyes in our direction.

"After she finished her shower, we played and had sex in the darkness. At some point, I looked at the alarm clock on the table beside the bed. It was already four-thirty, and my brother still wasn't back. I could not imagine him being kidnapped by one complete drunk and another tipsy Chinese girl"

"He would be lucky to be kidnapped by two girls, that would provide him with a better night than yours!"

"Maybe yes. I called him, and after the phone rang a few times, he answered. "I am in a hospital now, and I just saw a girl's stomach being emptied by a medical team."

"Apparently the girl I talked to first suffered an alcohol poisoning."

"Did you do that, Victor?" Camilo asked.

"No way. She was asking for drinks but given the disastrous state she found herself already in, I did not give her any alcohol. As we talked, Lyla was still naked, covered by the white sheets of the hotel bed. He told me he drove the girls in a brand-new white BMW through the streets of Beijing towards the hospital because her friend couldn't drive. Apparently, the one who got sick originally still planned to drive back. It was a risky thing for him to do, as he had quite a couple of drinks already, and he did not have a Chinese driver licence."

"Ouch," Camilo said again.

"He could have been in trouble in case the police caught him."

"Exactly, it all ended up quite well. We laughed about it, but it could have ended up a whole lot worse." Camilo nodded in agreement.

"The police are not mild here towards foreigners breaking the rules. Your brother might have had a point because he was rescuing this girl by driving her to the hospital, but they could have taken a taxi or call an ambulance too."

"Exactly. That's what I told him."

"So, what happened to you and the girl?"

"My brother came back around six in the morning after taking a taxi from the hospital back to the hotel. Lyla left around eight in the morning."

"That was a short night for you," Camilo said.

"And did you talk to that girl afterwards? I hope you did not take advantage of her?"

"Well, afterwards I learned that she actually fucked me because she just got dumped by her boyfriend and was looking to get over that break-up."

"Oh, I hope you helped her getting that feeling out of her system."

"I think I succeeded because she liked to join us for dinner the next day."

"And your brother? Did he see the girl he danced with afterwards?"

"Yes, that same night. After we came back from dinner, he met with her. I offered the hotel room to them, and I ended up watching *Californication* in the lobby of the hotel." Camilo laughed.

"That's quite a story. I'm sure you still talk about this when you're both old."

"I hope so," I said.

"Or even better experiences."

"Alright," Camilo said.

"I have to go and do some groceries. It was good catching up with you."

He waved for the waitress to come so he could pay for the espresso.

"Don't worry about that Camilo, it's on my table number. I'll get it once I pay for my food and consumptions too."

"Thank you, we'll speak soon." And he offered his hand.

"Ciao."

When I saw him walking away, I realised he is a good friend to have. Ten years older, which comes with more experience, and he is a good listener if you need him. Today we mostly talked nonsense, but he would be there in case I need him. I remember Raphael staying with him for a couple of weeks in-between apartments. I believe as foreigners living abroad, it is generally easier to establish friendships, especially in Asian countries. It's probably easier to connect far away from home with not too many Caucasians around.

I opened the Wall Street Journal and continued reading until I felt my phone buzzing. I first ignored it as China Mobile recently sent me quite a bit of commercial messages to upgrade my mobile plan. But now it is Sunday. After grabbing my phone out of curiosity, I saw it was Linda texting me instead with a message I did not see coming:

"My parents asked me to move back to my hometown. They need more care, and I can start working in my uncle's company."

I suddenly felt a lump coming up in my throat. I never told Linda that I actually quite liked her. We spent some time together, which mostly revolved around sex. We never discussed it, but I guess we lived both with the assumption that we were exclusively dating and at some point, we would bring it to the next stage. But that stage may now never come. I typed a reply:

"I'm sorry to hear that. When will you leave? Is there still time for us to meet?"

I could perhaps change her mind by meeting face to face while putting my hands around hers and tell her about the feeling I developed? I pressed send. Linda's feelings for me may not have been strong enough to let her stay in Shanghai. Or the pressure of her parents may be too much overwhelming. In the worst-case scenario, if she comes from a traditional family, they may even have organised a husband for her.

My phone buzzed again:

"No, I don't think so. I'm leaving tomorrow morning."

I swore in public. How could she do this to me? She is relocating and only tells me about it the night before? Is this how important I am for her? She could have had a different understanding of what we had. I decided not to blame her for anything. Fighting over text messages would not solve anything. But why did she not inform me earlier? It could have been a part of her plan to protect herself as she was afraid that I was going to try to change her mind. And that would not be in line with the demand of her family. Chengdu is two thousand kilometres away from Shanghai. Would it be worth maintaining a long-distance relationship with millions of potential girlfriends living around me here within a few square kilometres?

With a heavy heart, I answered:

"Alright, take care then. Have a good trip. Stay in touch."

An immediate reply said:

"I'm sorry, I have to follow the wish of my parents. Let me know when you visit Chengdu. I'll show you what real Sichuan food is like."

I smiled, but I knew we would never meet anymore. This was the end of the Linda chapter. I just had to let her go. While I left Element Fresh, I had to think about a sentence of my former boss in a restaurant I used to work as a student. In a situation like this he always reminded me with a smile on his face that there are more girls than church towers, so there was nothing to worry about. And that saying applies to Shanghai even more than to the Netherlands.

25

Xinhu Riverside Apartments - 16:45

The past few days, I constantly worked on the project management classes. Working hard did not make me think about Linda too much, although, on some moments, I couldn't resist looking at some pictures we took together. I wondered how she was, and whether she missed me too. Or perhaps she'd been on an arranged date already with a guy. I overthought and researched the two business proposals given by Mr Wang too. The universe threw enough opportunities in my direction recently, I just had to outweigh them and see what the best possible solution is. Considering Mr Wang's Communist Party background, I felt a business cooperation could only end up in two possible scenarios': I would either become rich or end up dead. With the connections and money they have, businesses could start-off and develop really well. But once you get closer and at some point know too much, especially as a foreigner, could work out in your disadvantage. The killing of Neil Heywood, a British journalist who knew too much about Bo Xilai, a former Communist Party of China Committee Secretary for Chongqing, is an example of that. Heywood knew too much about Bo Xilai's dirty laundry and was either murdered or commissioned by Bu Xilai's wife, Gu Kailai. I prefer not to end up like that. As a result, I still need a bit of time to formulate the opportunities and threats.

In order not to totally isolate me and be among people, I worked both at home and outdoors. Outdoors could be the Coffee Bean and Tea Leaf on Fuzhou Road so I could have an excuse to visit the Foreign Bookstore. Or I would go to Starbucks near Jingan Temple, which is a bit easier to reach by subway. The clock on the wall of my master bedroom showed it was four o'clock, which meant I had been working eight hours straight, including a short lunch break. The good thing about working from home is that I am not distracted as much as I would work in, for example Starbucks. It's the overall noise or irritating habit of people sitting next to you talking loud on their phone or sip their coffee with annoying distracting sound. Still, working from Starbucks gained me a mobile number and a name two days ago. It was one of those moments. Whilst concentrated on my corporate training, I noticed a couple sharing a table. The girl looked above average pretty, but I assumed she enjoyed a coffee with her boyfriend. They arrived earlier than me, but I noticed them leaving about twenty minutes after I got there. She had long, straight black hair and a white skin as if she never spent a day in the sun. Her smoky-eyes make-up gave her a real pretty look. She wore a white Gucci t-shirt, with black short pants. They covered the upper part of her black panties. Even though she sat down, I noticed the attractive shape of her legs. Since arriving in Shanghai, I learned that Asian girls with tall skinny legs liked to emphasise this with wearing stockings. Or in this case, it could have been the chilly weather calling for warm panties.

While she walked out, I glanced at her white sneakers, seemingly completely new. Without paying attention to their surroundings, they both left, and I continued my work. At that time, it was around nine o'clock and the Starbucks was not as crowded with people anymore. Within twenty minutes after she left the girl suddenly stood back at my table, introducing herself as Joceline and asking me whether I had any interest in getting to know her better. I noticed that now she stood only a few centimetres away from my table, she got only prettier. We had a short talk, we exchanged numbers, and as quickly as she showed up, she left again. In addition to her departure twenty minutes earlier, she looked over her shoulder and smiled while she opened the door and disappeared into the dark Shanghai evening. From that moment we sent a few text messages to each other, resulting in a date - if you can call it that, tonight at nine-thirty. I proposed to bring her to JZ, the place I usually go with Camilo and Raphael on Wednesday evenings in Fuxingxi Lu. There is a nice vibe on Friday evenings with live music. In case we did not want to talk, there was the possibility to stay inside at one of the high bar tables and listen to the live band. Or if things turned out to be romantic, we could spend time outside surrounded by candle lights and the characteristic Shanghai city background noise. Since Linda's departure in Shanghai, I was officially single again so I could do and see who I want. It still considered it difficult that she suddenly left, but the date with Joceline may heal the breakup pain a little bit. Until that moment I could just relax, take the time to fresh up and make sure I would arrive on time at JZ's.

Then my phone rang. Considering the timing I thought it was Johan to inform me that he enrolled enough students to start the second semester of my project management course. But it wasn't Johan. Instead, it was one of the students in my existing class, her name is Danielle. She is Shanghainese and I guess roughly seven or eight years older than me, but single which was of the things I learned from her as a result of the text messages we sent to each other in the past few days. It all started as a normal student and lecturer conversation, in a situation where questions were asked and solved with an appropriate answer. I did not think much about it until she started to ask me questions about my personal situation. At first, this was more job-related in the way of: What else are you doing besides teaching at Jia Tong University? to: Is there somebody waiting for you after you arrive home from teaching your three-hour project management class?

Currently nobody except a glass with whiskey.

I just followed the flow of the conversation without reaching the borders of a lecturer and student relation. She still has to do her exam, and I did not want her to think she would pass it by playing cute. I answered the call.

"Hello Danielle, how are you?"

"Hi, Victor," she answered immediately, "I am fine and you?"

"I am good too, thanks. What can I help you with? Are there any questions you are struggling with?"

"Eeh, actually not," she answered. "Everything so far is clear. The book, together with your PowerPoint and case studies are very helpful. I just finished a work gathering which I believe is not too far from where you live. If you haven't planned your Friday evening yet, would you like to have dinner somewhere near?"

"Well, I will meet with a friend tonight for a drink at nine-thirty, and I planned to have dinner at home. I have enough ingredients in case you wish to join me for dinner."

"What are you planning to cook?" Danielle asked.

"Just some simple pasta, but I will promise you'll love it."

"Alright," she said. "I'll be there in twenty minutes. Just send me your exact address in a text message."

"Alright, I will do so in a minute. Let me know if you have any troubles finding it."

"Will do, byeeeee!" she answered with a cheerful tone in her voice.

While I texted my address, I started to think about whether this was actually a good idea. I never met Danielle outside of class hours. It would perhaps be better to first meet her somewhere outside. But calling her back that I changed my mind would be weirder. So, I texted my address and used the ten minutes before Danielle's departure to clean my desk, make the bed and put some of the clothes that hung over a chair in order. Mr Lu wasn't at home so that would save me the introduction of another stranger in his sister's home.

It did not take long, or the security system was ringing. When I took the handset, Danielle's face came upon the black and white screen.

"Hi Danielle," I said,

"You've found the right building! Please come up."

I pressed the green button on the left side of the screen, which automatically opened the front door. Two minutes later she knocked on my door. When I opened it, she handed me a bunch of flowers.

"I thought your apartment could use some colour."

"Thank you so much, Danielle, you didn't have to do that."

I looked over my shoulder into the living room. She was actually right. There was a lot of white and grey.

"You found my apartment so easily, and how did you know I lived here?"

"Well, during class, you mentioned a few times that you live in Putuo. As I had this work gathering today in Putuo, I wondered that it might not be very far from your place."

"That's very considerate of you Danielle," Danielle looked around.

"You live in a nice place, Victor."

"Yes, it's quite a spacious place with a nice view. You can look all the way to Zhongshan Park. My landlord is an interior designer."

"Well, she surely left her footprint here. I like the interior set-up."

She walked further in and sat down on the couch.

"Do you live here by yourself?"

"No, the brother of my landlord lives here too, but he is not often at home."

Danielle nodded.

"What were you planning to cook tonight?"

"Ah, just some salmon pasta, quite easy. It only comes with four ingredients. Spaghetti, smoked salmon, cream and parsley. I choose to eat simple tonight as I planned to meet with a friend later on."

"What time do you need to leave for that?"

"About eight-thirty." I checked the clock on the living room wall. It was five-thirty now. We still had time enough to relax before I started cooking.

"Can I see your balcony?" Danielle asked. I nodded yes and walked into my bedroom. We passed my bed and the desk, with my laptop open and still a considerable number of papers and books. Danielle glanced at it.

"That is what the preparation of a project management training looks like."

Danielle giggled. She came from an educational background so she should know what it takes to prepare a lecture or training. I opened the door to give us access to the balcony.

"Wow," Danielle said. "This is a breath-taking view." She walked towards the edge of the balcony and leaned a little bit forward.

"It's high, considering we are only on the tenth floor. How long do you live here?"

"Just since September after I came back to Shanghai. It's a nice place to live in a new compound, except that the concrete floor is freaking cold in the winter," I laughed.

"Just after I moved in, it was the October holiday. Many people moved in, and before doing so, they all had to scare the ghosts out of their apartments by using firecrackers. Those firecracker rolls are so loud! And if that's not enough, they light up slammer crackers which seriously reach as high as my balcony until they explode. The red gunpowder and carton pieces ended up on my balcony floor."

"You should be careful with your laundry then."

"Yes. But you can't plan it. Some of them move in at six in the morning and wake up the entire building with their firecrackers. Unbelievable that people accept that here."

Danielle giggled again.

"Chinese people may not approve it but won't express their feeling."

Meanwhile, sunset started, and the Renaissance hotel in Zhongshan Park was light up in blue.

"Do you have a view at home?" I asked Danielle.

"Yes, but not as far as you. I look onto a horizon of compounds. A complete glass and concrete view."

"On most days mine comes with a grey sky included," I joked.

"And there are days I can't even look as far as Zhongshan Park. But yes, the view is good tonight." Danielle looked to the other side.

"I can see the Suzhou river too!"

She was right. But only through a small gap between two buildings. We looked downstairs. The fountain in the pond in front of the building was on. The sound of falling water was bouncing from the building walls. More people came home now as it was nearing six o'clock. It was the start of the weekend.

"Do you have any further plan for this weekend Danielle?"

"Not so much. Mostly relaxing, I think. Tomorrow night I will have dinner with my auntie. How about you?"

"Not that much either. Relax a bit and perhaps catch up with two of my friends for pasta and whiskey." We walked back inside the master bedroom.

"Are you hungry yet? If yes, I will start to cook. It'll take me about twenty-five minutes to have the food on the table."

"I am quite hungry,"

"By the way, would you like something to drink? I'm sorry I did not offer you earlier. I have juice or cola in the fridge."

"Coke please," Danielle answered, and I walked to the fridge to hand her a can of Coca Cola.

"You have cans?" Danielle asked.

"Yes. If I have a bottle, the bubbles will be gone soon as I am the only one here drinking it. And not to mention the plastic waste. With cans, I always have fresh coke."

I turned on some music for Danielle in the living room. My first choice was *Continuum* by John Mayer, it would set for a relaxing mood.

"Let me know if you need any help," Danielle added.

"This dish is pretty straightforward," I said while I heated up the water for the spaghetti. I kept all other ingredients cool in the fridge. When I walked back into the bedroom, Danielle sat on the edge of the couch and had a few DVDs in her hand.

"You have so many DVD's," she said while she browsed through the titles.

"They are not all mine, most of them were here already when I moved in. I usually download movies online."

I noticed her long and skinny fingers. Her skin was darker than mine, and it seemed she recently visited a nail specialist. Her nails were blinking in pink, where both nails of her ring finger had a little diamond attached to them. She wasn't wearing any rings. I never asked the reason of her being still single, which is a bit unusual for a Chinese woman on her age. She possibly came out of a long relationship or simply just did not meet the right person yet. It was up to Danielle to share that with me if she wanted to. I would not ask.

I heard the water cooking, so I walked back to the kitchen. I put all spaghetti in the boiling water and took another pan out in which I heated up the cream. Once it was hot, I added the smoked salmon and the parsley, just to let it simmer for a while. When I turned my head around the kitchen entrance, I saw that Danielle watched through the window. The living room had big windows covering from the left neighbour to the right neighbour's wall. Despite that, the number of sun rays accessing this living room is minimal even though we are facing the West. But that is caused by the building right in front of me. Danielle turned around and smiled.

"Can I lay the table while you finish cooking our dinner?"

She walked towards the kitchen, passing the big glass table. Usually, I just had dinner at the desk in my bedroom while watching a movie or reading news on my laptop.

"Here are two linen placemats, a fork and a spoon. The plates I will keep in the kitchen to serve the pasta on."

Somehow, I could feel that Danielle was not used to the situation where a man was cooking for her. On her looks and behaviour, I could see she really appreciated it, as if it was a big thing to do. To me, it was just fun. I appreciated her passing by. The fact that she even remembers where I live is proof she is actually paying attention in class. Once the spaghetti was well cooked, I added it to the other pan with the cream, smoked salmon and parsley and mixed it all together. Once I divided it between both plates, I added some freshly chopped parsley on top for the look and taste. Danielle was already sitting at the table.

"That looks delicious Victor," she said with a smile on her face.

"Let's enjoy our dinner."

We both took our first bite when I noticed that it became a bit dark in the living room. I switched on two lamps in the back of the living room and lidded up the candle in a silver holder on the table. She got a blushful colour on her cheeks.

"That's so nice of you, Victor, you know how to create a nice atmosphere."

I smiled at her.

"I love parsley," Danielle said. I nodded.

"What was the reason for you to sign up for this project management course?"

Danielle just put a spoon with pasta in her mouth and excused herself, covering her mouth with her hand. A few seconds later she answered:

"Even though I am working as a marketing specialist I am involved in projects. I would like to understand better what a project actually is, exactly what you explained during the first class - the difference between a project and a process. As well, by knowing the different phases of a project, I will be better able to take initiative and so hopefully play a factor to finish our projects on time and within budget."

I nodded. I remember I asked this question to a few students during the first lecture, but the class was too big for each student to raise his or her voice.

"You did a good thing to sign up for the course. And if you have any questions even after the course is finished, feel free to contact me." Danielle smiled.

"So please tell me a little bit more about yourself." I asked.

"I know you work for a school here in Shanghai in a marketing function, but I do not know much more than that. What are your hobbies, where are your interests and so on?"

"Well," Danielle started,

"I am quite involved with my work during the semesters. I really like what I do. But in my free time, I play badminton or have dinner outside with friends."

Apart from going out for dinner with friends, I could feel she lived a different life than me. Outgoing but in a different way.

"How about you?"

"During weekdays, I spend most of my time working as well, but I regularly hang out with friends to go out for drinks, or we have dinner at one of our homes. Or I just go to Fuzhou Road and check out the bookstores. I love books."

"It sounds like you have a good life here, Victor,"

"It was a good choice to come back to Shanghai, yes. The entire world is in a recession, but here everything is booming like crazy. Okay, partly because of government stimulus, but still."

"It's a good time to be in Shanghai."

Meanwhile, we finished our dinner.

"Are you still hungry?" I asked.

"There is still a bit of pasta left if you want."

"Oh no," Danielle said. "I've had enough, thank you."

I noticed now that she had a bit of a British accent. We left all dishes in the kitchen.

"Just leave it here, I will clean it tomorrow."

We still had two hours until I had to leave. Maybe just enough to watch a movie? But a movie meant that we couldn't talk too much. Watching a movie together is something you would propose to somebody you do not wish to talk too much with. We walked out of the kitchen, and Danielle followed her way into my bedroom. I walked towards my desk chair and turned it into the right direction so I could face Danielle, who sat on the edge of the bed. I was glad to make up the bed earlier. Danielle glanced at my little bookshelf.

"What's the last book you've read?" she asked.

"Aside from project management books?" I pointed to the shelf. "It's the red book there on the right side of the shelf. *Good to Great*. It's about the transformation of good to great companies - and what is required for that. Conclusion, the companies that became great companies are the ones that adapted technology, like computerised logistics first. It made them ahead of their competition."

"Thank you. Now I do not have to read that book anymore," Danielle said, giggling.

"But I did not tell you which companies the research is about." I smiled.

"It's American research though, you only read about companies as Wells Fargo, Wallgreens, Gilette and Coca Cola," and I pointed to the two cans on my desk.

"By looking at the number of books you own, I can conclude that you prefer physical books over e-books." Danielle browsed over the titles on my shelf.

"Yes. I want to have a physical book in my hand. Carry it in my bag on the subway. Fold it when I want, and leave it on my shelf after reading, so it becomes part of a collection."

"Since when did you start collecting these books?"

"I carried a few from the Netherlands, but most of them I purchased in Shanghai. Why?"

"It will tell me whether you are a fast reader or not," Danielle giggled.

"I can even just tell you if you are so curious about this, but actually I am not. Unless I am really attracted to the story, it usually takes me a month to finish reading a book."

"Based on a 300 pages book, that's about ten pages per day," Danielle concluded.

"Yes, but there are days I do not read."

"Have you visited Shanghai Library?" Danielle continued asking.

"It's not far from my home."

"I have a library pass, but I never went in."

As a book lover, I felt a bit embarrassed to confess this.

"They have quite a big assortment of English books. We can go there together sometime if you like. It's not far from Jiao Tong University either." I nodded.

"Let's do that sometimes. It would be good to have a local guide by my side." Meanwhile, my back started to hurt a little bit. Danielle still sat on the bed. She looked at me. For a Chinese woman, her eyes were actually quite big. Her straight black hair reached till just over her bony shoulders. Her brownish silk blouse could use epaulettes to make her shoulders stand out a bit more.

"What are you thinking about?" Danielle interrupted my thoughts.

"What?"

"You're staring in the distance."

"Ah, my back starts to hurt from this desk seat. I probably spent too much time sitting here. I will have to ask my landlord to replace it."

"Come sit here next to me then, if that is more comfortable for your back."

Danielle said while she tapped the white cotton bed cover on her left side. I hesitated but accepted her invitation. After all, I was in my own rented apartment. I moved to the bed. As a result of the sagging mattress, our hips touched each other. With Danielle so close to my side, I could smell her expensive opium perfume.

I turned my face to the right side. Danielle looked at me with an abashed smile on her face, biting her underlip.

"Oh, oh, teach…"

She said, with her rouged lips coming closer to mine. Before I realised, they touched mine, first softly as if she was waiting for my approval and then firmly as if she had to unload a shipload of emotions. She moved over so she could face me, placing her knees on each side. She pressed her breasts against my chest and continued to kiss me from my cheek into my neck. She took the highest button of my blouse between her pink nails and asked:

"May I…?"

The expression on my face said more than a hundred words, moving Danielle to open the first three buttons of my white blouse while she slowly moved to my lap. While she undid another button, she pressed her breasts again to my chest, which was naked now. While looking at my left nipple, she said:

"I knew you had a nipple piercing!"

"What are you paying attention to in class? You're supposed to look at the presentation screen, not my nipples!"

She now had a naughty smile on her face and took it in her mouth while she sucked on it. I was carried away by Danielle's seductions. I had let her go until I felt uncomfortable or embarrassed or conflicted to move on because next week Tuesday, she would sit in front of me again in class. But that feeling did not appear yet. Would others be able to tell what happened by the way we looked at each other? For sure it would be more difficult to face her next week if I objected now. If I would push her away from me and tell her I couldn't do it would leave us both in embarrassment.

"Why are you holding up?" Panted Danielle in my ear.

While my arms were still in both sleeves, she already uncovered my shoulders. She was now waiting for me to do the same in return.

"Aah, nothing Danielle,"

I answered while I placed my both hands on her shoulder. I held back a little bit, so only my fingertips touched her silken blouse and moved both hands to the side of her breasts, where I pressed both hands against her again. Danielle softly moaned, and I opened the first two buttons of her blouse. With her collarbone now laid bare,

I started kissing her while I went down to the upper part of her breasts.

"Wait," she summoned. She got up from the bed and walked towards the door, and closed it. "Let's avoid the awkward situation where your housemate walks in," Danielle giggled. "And we may as well close the curtains."

She was right. With open curtains, we would potentially expose ourselves to roughly seven floors of the building right in front of us. With the door and curtains closed, it seemed all reservations disappeared. Laying back on the bed, it was only a short matter of time until I felt her naked warm breasts against my chest. Her nipples felt hard, and on purpose, she pressed one of them against my pierced nipple. I put my hand around her breasts, held them together and kissed them. Danielle leaned backwards while making blissful sounds. I opened the top button of her jeans. I turned her around, so she laid with her back on the bed. Her hand firmly gripped my neck while she drew my face towards her and kissed me on my mouth. I kissed her gently back while she pulled her jeans down. As if she matched it, she was wearing a pink G-string, the same colour as her nails which just softly rubbed my back. I pulled my pants down and took off my socks before I lay beside her. Danielle turned on her side towards me, and my hand went from her back down to her buttocks. They felt soft and warm. I further pressed her against me, so her vulva rubbed against my hard cock. From both sides, I pulled her G-string down. She lifted her legs and threw her underwear on the cold concrete floor of my bedroom. Danielle was now completely naked, lying beside me. She giggled.

"Did you ever think you would ending up having sex with one of your students?"

She went with her hand inside my boxer short, gently stroking me.

"Not exactly, Danielle," I answered. "I promised to myself to be a good teacher."

"But you are a good teacher..." Danielle whispered in my ear.

"Just this will make you even better..." She pulled down my boxer short.

"You're so big Victor, I want to feel you so badly deep inside of me…"

She said now with a husky voice in my ear. I grabbed a condom from inside my nightstand and quickly pulled it around my cock.

"I want to feel you now,"

Danielle assured me. She opened her legs, and I moved on top of her. I noticed she had pubic hair, but well maintained. I softly pushed against the entrance of her vagina, and while I did so, Danielle moaned in my ear. With both hands, she pulled me closer, making me slide in faster than I intended to. Soon enough, I answered her wish as I was deep inside and slowly went in and out.

"This feels so good Victor," Danielle said while she firmly pressed both of her arms around me. She kissed me in my neck while I searched for her lips to kiss her back.

"I want to be on top of you," Danielle said. "I want to cum before you do…" She giggled. I pulled out and turned on my back. I pulled the condom back, and Danielle put both of her knees on each side of my body. With sparkles in her eyes, she reached for my cock behind her back to point it in the right direction. Then she slowly lowered her position, while I made a soft noise of the bliss I felt when her tight pussy slowly surrounding me. From the movements, I could feel she was looking to hit her G-spot. This was the orgasm stimulation she was just mentioning. She moved quicker and quicker. Her moaning and the view of her moving breasts turned me on even more. Now I had one hand touching her right breast, and the other hand was holding her left buttock. I noticed she was massaging her clitoris with her right hand. This went on for a little while until I had to tell her to slow down a little bit, as I felt myself getting close towards an orgasm.

"Just move on a bit slower," I said to Danielle while I tried to think about something to distract myself from having an early orgasm.

Thinking about the Netherlands' soccer team 1-3 defeat against Russia during Euro 2008 worked. Suffering two goals in extra time against underdog Russia after both qualifying and winning the group stages with maximum points was a hard one to digest.

When I was back with my thoughts in my own comfortable playfield, Danielle leaned over me, and I felt her hard nipples going over my chest. She moved slowly up and down. I put both hands around her hips to control the speed, which I aimed to increase. Soon enough she was back in the game, riding with the same speed as before.

"Don't stop, don't stop," She summoned me. I felt I could still go on for a while without risking a premature orgasm. As if we moved in the final stage of this lovemaking session, she kissed my lips extensively and firm and moved on. I could feel she was getting close to her orgasm, which turned me on again. Hopefully, I wasn't going to be earlier than her. After a little while, she softly moaned, and her body made shocking moves. Feeling the strength of her orgasm, and the liquids that came with, it made me ejaculate almost immediately after she finished her orgasm. Danielle laid on top of me for a while, while I was still inside her. She was breathing quickly, and I could feel her heartbeat slowly decreasing. After a little while, I pulled out, put the cover over us and we lay next to each other in bed. We did not say a word, we both listened to the music that was still playing in the living room. While we made love, I did not notice it at all, but it was still John Mayer. It switched to *Room for Squares* album, and I recognised the song as *City Love*. Actually, quite suitable for this moment. We both listened to the music and enjoyed the moment. I could feel Danielle's warm skin against mine.

"I do not want to push you out of here soon," I said,

"but I have to get moving in a little while. What else will you do tonight?"

"I'll take a taxi back home and probably watch a movie," Danielle answered.

"Have you seen the movie *Marley and Me*? It was released end of last year."

"That's a Christmas movie about that dog, right? With Jennifer Anniston?"

"Yes. But I still want to see it. I saw the DVD shop near my home sold it. Have you seen it?"

"No, if I remember correct Owen Wilson is starring in that movie. I've seen two or so movies of him, but I can't watch that exaggerated acting style of him." Danielle giggled.

"I did not notice that yet. But I let you know what I think of him on Tuesday."

Tuesday.

The day we'll have to pretend that none of this happened. Pretending that I wasn't inside her just four days ago and that we are nothing but a lecturer and his student. I should have been stronger than this. On the other hand, she is eight years older than me. She's supposed to be wiser and more experienced and mannered than me. This isn't a situation where I abused my power or trust in a sexual act with a younger female student. And whatever happened tonight would not affect my decision to let Danielle pass her exam or not. She will still have to study for it.

I'm probably overthinking.

I gave Danielle a kiss on her forehead and pulled the cover away from me. I searched for my boxer short between all the separate pieces of clothes laying around the bed. The floor beside the bed was ridiculously cold and it's not even winter yet. I quickly moved to the carpeted part of the floor. From the corner of my eye, I saw Danielle sitting straight up in bed and navigating her way around in search of her underwear. I reached to the floor and handed it to her. She quickly slipped into it, got out of bed and tripped to the bathroom.

"I'd like to offer you another drink or so, but I'm sorry to be a bit in a rush right now," I said with an apologetic tone. "Let me make up next time with dinner or drinks if you like."

I meant this just to be polite, not exactly to provide any hints for future dates. I did not want to give her the feeling I just used her. On the other hand, and again, this was her call. And to be honest, with Linda's departure, it came exactly at the right moment.

We got dressed and left the apartment. Without even holding hands, we walked through the compound towards the street where we waited for Danielle's taxi to arrive. A yellow coloured taxi just dropped-off a rider nearby. I indicated to the taxi driver, who stopped in front of us, and Danielle turned to me for a firm hug.

"See you Tuesday Victor." I smiled.

"Enjoy your movie and be prepared for next week's class." Danielle smiled.

The taxi drove off in Wuxing Road direction. Through the back window, I could see Danielle raising her hand in the darkness, and I waved back. I had to hurry up a bit to be on time to meet with a girl I knew nothing more about than a name and a mobile number. And that she might even have a boyfriend - if at least the guy she sat together in Starbucks with was her boyfriend. But that's not my responsibility. If she's looking for a fresh breeze, I'd like to spend a nice evening with her and possibly learn a new thing or two. Or I am home within an hour and end up watching a movie just like Danielle. But for sure a movie without Owen Wilson.

Tonight, the public in the subway consisted of a mixture of people coming straight out of work on their way home. Some wearing oversized office pants, pulled together around the waist with a belt while holding their office bag and staring at a phone, reading an evening newspaper gathered for free at the subway station entrance or just simply staring in the distance. The easiest for me to walk to JZ was getting out of the subway at Changshu Road station. From there, it would only be a short walk covering a few blocks. Meanwhile, I felt my phone buzzing in my pocket. It was Joceline:

"I almost arrived."

"Me too, I am two subway stops away from JZ."

"I am in a taxi with a creepy driver with nose hairs and I hope he wouldn't drive me off to a suburb where the worst will happen."

"Ask him to stop in case you feel like you're going in the wrong direction. I will come to pick you up from there. Take care, and I see you soon."

It remained quiet from Joyce's side. Once I got off the subway, I had to navigate myself first well to make sure I wouldn't take the wrong metro exit. I walked past the shops in the subway corridor. Some of them selling hundreds of fake movies on DVD. Another shop sold cheap-looking female clothes, maybe for that reason the shop was completely empty. The salesgirl was standing behind the cash desk with an uninspired expression on her face. Towards the end of the tunnel was a fast-food restaurant. The fetid smell of it made me feel sick while I passed by. Despite it being almost half-past nine, it was still remarkably crowded here. As well on the street. The shops were still open, but most of them were ignored by passers-by.

The next block I headed into was more a residential neighbourhood. As crowded as the main street was, this street looked like as if a night clock ruled the local residents to stay inside their homes. Yellowish street lanterns unevenly illuminated the street, leaving dark spots in between them. The city noise created a familiar background noise, but it was overruled by conversations taking place behind curtains where windows were opened to let the cool breeze in. All homes I could see had this white light in their living room, making it look like a factory floor to me. In front of the entrance of a residential compound, a line with bikes and electric bikes was lined up in an allocated area between white painted lines on the street. Some of them reminded me of bikes I saw on second world war pictures from the Netherlands in 1945. All together it looked like an organised mess. The homes here seemed old, but the rooms are spacious. When I looked upstairs up to the third floor, I saw a lot of cables running down the wall. These buildings must be part of Shanghai's heritage protection, preventing owners from digging holes in walls to despatch cables. The owners of these homes do not have to worry about property developers buying the lot for cheap and being kicked out of their homes with a compensation far below market values. I had to keep looking in front of me as there were trash and gutter left on the street to be picked up by street cleaners tomorrow morning early. The only shop in this street was just about to close. When looking at the trash on the street, I could only conclude it must come from this single shop. A plastic box in the front was filled with bamboo sticks, ready to be cold pressed into a drink. A cat sitting on a box against a shop wall looked at me and followed me while I passed by.

"Hello," I said with a mousy voice, but I did not get any reaction back.

The white shop facade was in desperate need of a new layer of paint. The bamboo pressing device had left brown coloured splatters and smudges on the wall. The windows of the counter were so hazy that it was hardly possible to see what was displayed behind it. I could only imagine the level of hygiene in this shop. If the word hygiene was worth mentioning at all. Despite it being messy, I particularly enjoy walking the tiny streets of Shanghai. This is where you can experience real Shanghai, unlike the big shopping malls on Huaihai Road, offering every possible luxury brand. I came closer to Fuxingxi Road, where empty taxies were passing by looking for riders. From here it was only a short distance to JZ Club. I glanced at my phone, and I saw that Joceline had sent me another message:

"I'm waiting outside for you."

When I looked up, I could see her already in the distance and increased my walking speed. When I got closer, I saw her face being light up by the reflection of her phone's small display.

"Hi Joceline,"

She was wearing a glittering blue navy evening dress as if she dressed herself up for a long night of partying. It fell perfectly over her waist. Her golden high heels made her look taller than she actually was. I would guess her roughly one meter seventy-five, including high heels. She smiled when she saw me.

"Hi Victor," she said.

"Wow, you look like a movie star!" Joceline smiled politely.

I could notice the effort she made to look good tonight. Good was actually an understatement. She looked stunning. Her make-up was enough to maintain her natural look. She wore a different eye shadow compared to when we shortly met in Starbucks just days ago. Her long hair was hanging loosely over her shoulders. She wore a silver neckless with a white pearl surrounded by a silver circle. It perfectly matched with the dress. I felt a bit underdressed in my Armani Jeans with a blue and white striped Scotch and Soda shirt. And in the worst-case scenario, I still had Danielle's expensive opium perfume on me.

"Shall we go inside?" she suggested. I paid fifty RMB entrance for each of us and let her enter JZ in front. I noticed the dress actually left her back nude down to just above her buttocks. She reached for my hand while walking down the stairs towards the seating area. Walking such stairs with high heels came indeed with a risk. People inside watched us walking down the stairs. I could see them thinking something like "a foreigner with a Chinese girl, way out of his league." and "why for God-sake does she choose a guy like this to go out with?" I didn't care. She chooses to go out with me tonight, even though this appears way much more than it actually is. Nobody had a clue that I just met this girl three days ago, and that I did not know anything of her, except her name and her telephone number. And that it looks like she might have a boyfriend, unless the guy she was with the night was a study friend. Or her brother. But that did not seem reasonable knowing China's one-child policy. Unless she had rich parents. I should find out.

Joceline guided me to the front of the bar, where there was still a bar table available for two persons. The way how Joceline ventured on the high seat made me realise that she did not have a lot of space to move in this fancy dress.

"What would you like to drink?" I asked after we both sat down. It was a round table, but to be able to have a conversation, we sat at like a twelve and two pm distance from each other. I could feel her leg against mine.

"I'm going for… Hmmm, let me see."

Joceline browsed carefully. Immediately one of the waiters came up with a mini lantern so she could see things clearly.

"I'd like to have a Piña colada please," she said. The waiter directed the beam of the lantern to the menu laying in front of me.

"For me a whiskey sour please." The waiter nodded and walked away. It would be a little bit longer until the band would start to play.

"Which part of China are you from?" I asked to kick-off the conversation.

"I'm from Zhejiang Province," Joceline asked.

"Oh, that's actually not far from here, right? Two hours by car?"

"Depending on where you live yes," Joceline confirmed.

"My hometown is a bit further. Roughly three and a half hours from here. But that's not during public holidays. I've driven seven to eleven hours to drive home for Chinese New Year or the October holiday."

I thought for a second. The other option is to go by train, but there is always a run on train tickets. Only people with the best of luck would be able to purchase one.

"How about yourself?" Joceline asked curiously.

"I'm from the Netherlands. Arrived in Shanghai just over a year ago for an internship in Philips. I finished my internship, graduated in the Netherlands and came back to Shanghai. Since a few months, I am part-time teaching project management at Jiao Tong University." Joceline nodded.

"And I am hoping to get back into Philips," I added.

"What did you do in Philips?" Joceline asked.

"Market research for their first LED lamp launch in the hospitality market."

"Ah, you were in lighting?"

"Yes."

Joceline looked around us. Couples, friends and colleagues around us continued their conversations and sipping their drinks.

"Lighting is all around us," she noticed. "It must be an interesting job."

"Yes, it is. Especially when you consider what lighting can do with the atmosphere in any given space." Joceline nodded.

"How about you?"

"I'm an executive assistant for a general manager in a multinational company."

"That sounds interesting too! What kind of company?"

"It's a branding and design company."

"You must be a busy girl then…" I said.

"Sometimes yes - but my boss is travelling quite frequently so the days he is not in Shanghai it is not too busy."

"Where's your boss from?"

"From Germany, living here with his family in Hongqiao."

Hongqiao is where all the expats live. There are entire villages of multi-million dollar homes - if not small castles occupied by Shanghai's rich and expats. The roads are wide, and every compound is heavily secured. Some of the Philips expats live there as well.

The waiter arrived with a Piña colada and whiskey sour and a small bowl with peanuts at our table. He placed all on the table, and I grabbed the whiskey sour and lifted it for a cheer.

"Cheers," I said when our glasses clinked.

"Nice to meet you earlier this week, and even nicer to meet again and talk."

Joceline giggled.

"Were you surprised that I walked up to your table?"

"Eeh, a bit to be honest with you." Now she giggled even more.

"Me too actually... I never did something like that before, and I could not imagine I would ever do something like that." I laughed.

"But I am glad you did."

I thought about the guy she was in Starbucks with. She probably thinks that I did not noticed them, so I don't want to ask who that guy was. That's none of my business at this point. We're just here for a drink. Two strangers surrounded by twenty-four million people in a metropole city. She would perhaps have more reasons to question me. It was in fact only two hours ago that I had sex with another girl. And to make matters worse, I did not even have time to shower before I left home. I felt like a half-eaten sandwich.

"What are you dreaming about?"

Joceline said while she abrupted my thoughts.

"Nothing, about... It was about a training I have to deliver."

I was glad I could make something up on the spot.

"I understand you're a busy man,"

Joceline said while she put her hand over mine. I looked at her, and I felt my cheeks blushing. After the leg touch earlier, she was looking for physical contact again. I took a sip of my whiskey sour. They taste best directly after being served because the longer you wait, the more the ice is melting and adding water to the whiskey.

"Can I ask you a question?" Joceline said.

"Sure, go ahead." "If you could have the answer to any question, what question would it be?" I thought for a second.

"I would be curious to know at what age I will die. And how, so I can be prepared. Or is that a second question?" Joceline giggled.

"Yes. It is either when or how."

"If I know how I will die, for example in a plane crash, I would always feel anxious before taking flights. It's better to know when."

Joceline giggled, while she put her hand off mine to reach for her glass, gently putting the straw between her lips and take a sip of her drink.

"How old are you now?" she asked.

"I'm twenty-six."

"So, what if the answer would be twenty-six?"

"That would mean I would still have a maximum of six months left because that's how long it takes till my next birthday."

"I bet it you reach at least ninety-something years," Joceline said.

"Let me ask you another question in return," I said.

"If you lived to a hundred years old, would you rather keep the body or the mind of your twenty-four-year-old self?" Joceline laughed.

"That's a difficult question. For the long term, I think the mind is more important than the body. It's good always to be independent and to make your own decisions. I mean, what's the point of having a 24-year-old body but a brain full of Swiss cheese holes?"

"Yes, you have a point. I think I would rather go with a young mind and an old body too."

Right on that moment, the band walked up the stage. I recognized the singer as the lady who often sings on Wednesday evenings. Those are the evenings I usually spend here with Camilo and Raphael as the breaking point of the week. The singer introduced herself and the band before they started to play the first song. After visiting multiple live music venues in Shanghai, I noticed that there is a big group of musicians who play live music at night. They are part of different bands and step in when friends are not available. You can meet the same artist or band in different venues. The songs they play are mostly jazz, eighties or nineties music, so if you play the drums, it doesn't really matter who you're playing with as long as you know how to play the song. And they often teach in music schools or one-on-one classes during afternoons. I noticed Joceline enjoyed the first tones of this jazz song.

"What music are you usually listening to?" I asked. Joceline turned to me again.

"Usually, Chinese music from artists like Tanya Chua. Do you know her?"

"No, unless my colleagues or friends sang her songs in KTV." Joceline giggled.

"Good chance they did. She is quite famous now."

"You like KTV?" Joceline asked in return.

"Yes, as long as we are with a group of people and with enough booze."

"Booze?"

"Liquor. Order a bottle of whiskey and the more we drink, the better we sing."

Joceline giggled.

"I like KTV too, but I do not go there very often."

"Me neither actually. My Western friends are not very much into KTV. Chinese colleagues used to be." Joceline turned her attention to the stage.

"The drummer of this band is outstanding; you can see the excitement of playing the drums on his face."

"Yes, I think so too. His name is Johnny, he comes all the way from Mauritius."

"Mauritius?" Joceline asked.

"It's an island East of Madagascar in the Indian ocean."

"Ah! Máolǐqiúsī!"

She repeated in Mandarin. It sounds like something as Mauritius to me.

"Do you know him?"

"Not personally but I know his name and whereabouts. He sometimes comes to have a talk with my friends and me on Wednesday evening."

"You go out a lot," Joceline concluded.

"Just twice a week but Wednesdays are not extremely late because we have to work the next day."

I noticed how Joceline finished her drink. The band played their third song out of the usual ten songs they play in a session. I lifted my glass and sipped all whisky sour mingled with the icy water. The ice cubes froze my lips for a second. I could feel the combination of alcohol and icy whisky sour stream all the way down to my abdomen. I was ready for a second round, but I did not want to appear to Joceline as an alcoholic. Neither did I want to give her the impression that I wanted her drunk as soon as possible. But Joceline finished her Piña colada as well. All that was left was dispersed transparent ice without taste.

"What is the funniest thing that somebody asked you here in Shanghai?" Joceline asked. I thought for a second.

"I was once approached whether I was interested in becoming a duck."

"A duck?"

"Yes, that's another name for a male prostitute. A gigolo." Joceline howled with laughter. "What?! How did they ask?"

"By Skype, probably based on my location and Skype picture."

"And what did you say?" "I rejected their offer. But they said I could earn like ninety thousand RMB per month. That made me think afterwards."

"What's that amount in Euro's?"

"Like thirteen thousand Euro's a month."

"Probably work every night and visit lonely women in need of a perfect boyfriend experience. Women have a different perception when they hire a gigolo. They like to talk extensively before going physical."

"So why didn't you do it?"

"I think I was a bit shocked when they asked me. But thinking about it again, I could have done it for one or two years and buy an apartment in Shanghai. It could have secured my retirement in forty or so years from now."

Joceline nodded understandably. And I continued:

"I don't think that a gigolo lives a healthy life. And what will you put on your corporate resume for those years?"

"Well, you never know who you will meet and which opportunities you get," Joceline said.

"True. I once told my mum about this, and she said I should have done it for a while." I laughed.

"Really?"

"Yes. Anyway. That opportunity has passed. Would you like another drink?"

"Sure, why not," Joceline giggled.

Unlike many other girls, the first Piña colada did not have an effect on her behaviour. She seemed sober. I had to be careful of her mixing drinks to avoid a Cecile evening scenario. I waived to the waiter to let him know we were in for a second round. I turned back to Joceline.

"I'm good at drinking," She confirmed as if she could read my thoughts.

"People in my family drink a lot."

This kind of information I would personally not share the first time you meet somebody, but Joceline seemed comfortable enough to share this fact.

"Why if I may ask?" "My dad has his own company. Drinking is part of maintaining business relationships - or guanxi and an important negotiation strategy. In this way, he is able to negotiate the best deals for his company."

"That doesn't sound healthy to me at all." Joceline lifted her shoulders.

"It's the way things are."

"If I were your dad, I would just have an arrangement with the restaurant I bring my business partners to serve me grape juice instead of red wine and water instead of Baijiu. Just for my own sake of health." Joceline laughed.

"That's a good idea until people find out."

"Why?"

"Well, the better he can drink, the stronger he appears. So, he will lose face or prestige if that ever comes out."

We sat for a while and listened to the music. The band was performing well tonight.

"What do you like most about Shanghai?" I asked while the waiter arrived at our table with a tray and two drinks. I handed him a one hundred RMB bill, and he left again.

"I think first of all the options we have when it comes to food. There is actually no better place in the world to eat a bowl of Xiao Long Bao than here in Shanghai."

"What's that?"

"Pork filled soup dumplings! How could you not know? How long do you live in Shanghai?" Joceline giggled.

"I know the dumplings, just not the Chinese name for it sweetheart."

Joceline looked me straight in the eye. A shy smile appeared on her face. She continued her talk: "But you can actually find food from any other region of China. From spicy Sichuan food to oilier vegetables from the northeast of China."

"Which food is Zhejiang province actually famous for?" Joceline thought for a second.

"Zhejiang cuisine is actually one of the eight culinary traditions of Chinese cuisine. It's related to traditional Zhejiang Province cooking, which is located south of Shanghai and centred around Hangzhou. Have you been there?"

"Yes, once. But just very short. But then how do you define the taste of Zhejiang food?"

"Generally speaking, Zhejiang cuisine is not spicy, but prepared with many fresh ingredients resulting in a soft flavour with a mellow fragrance."

"Similar to Shanghai's food, indeed." I concluded.

"But immigrants from basically every corner of China introduced their own food culture to Shanghai." Joceline nodded in agreement.

"Yes. Think about hotpot! Or Sichuan food!"

"There is a good Hunan restaurant near where I live. Even though both serve spicy food, there is a difference in spices they use." I giggled.

"Yes. And for us foreigners, there is so much choice too if you do not feel like eating Chinese food." Joceline looked surprised.

"Are there evenings you do not like to eat Chinese food?" I laughed.

"Plenty of evenings."

"How come?" Joceline asked immediately.

"There are so many different sorts of Chinese food. There is more to choose from than you can eat for every day of the week!"

"Yes. But you have to consider the food fundamentals our parents raised us with."

I said with a serious expression on my face.

"I grew up with Western food, every single day of my life. Our food contains more dairy, and I grew up with bread for breakfast and lunch. We usually had one warm meal a day while you have three!" Joceline nodded.

"As well, many of the spices used in Chinese food are different compared to Western food. And I think the food here is cooked with too much oil. That makes me long for Western food sometimes. The good thing about living here is that there is nothing you can't find in Shanghai."

"I feel like we can continue talking about food all night! Now I want to know what you like about Shanghai?"

I could feel Joceline having a genuine interest in me, or at least in discovering cultural differences we have.

"I love Shanghai's architecture," I said determinedly.

"On Sundays, I can walk for hours through the city. From Xujiahui to the Bund, and it makes me feel that Shanghai is like eight cities in one. Don't you feel that?" Joceline nodded but waited for me to explain further.

"When walking on West Nanjing Road and see all the shops, I feel like I could be in any city. There are big brand shops, malls and brands you see everywhere. Then there is the Shanghai Exhibition Centre combining Russian and Empire style neoclassical architecture mixed with Stalinist neoclassical innovations. But when walking into a side street, it can suddenly feel like you enter a new world. The real China. The life where street vendors and tricycles determine the street view. You can visit the dentist on the corner of the street if you wish." Joceline laughed.

"If you continue to walk in this traditional part of Shanghai, you eventually end up in the French concession, making you feel like you are in France. Then I did not even mention the British and German influences in design and architecture."

"What I consider amazing in contrast between cultures and design is the fact that Jingan Temple is surrounded by brand new skyscrapers. The golden roof and wooden structure are in such contrast with its surroundings."

"Yes. When you are inside Jingan Temple, you don't get much of the city surroundings and sound."

I noticed I hadn't touched my whiskey sour for a while as a result of all the talking. The cold drink caused condense on the outside of the glass. The glass left a wet circle on the table when I lifted the drink to sip. Joceline played with her hair while she looked at me. She looked marvellous. The candlelight illuminated her face, making me imagine how she would look like in front of an open fire in a small cottage in the Swiss Alps. Just the two of us, sipping wine, talking and listening to the crackling and snapping sounds of the open fire. How nice and romantic would that be? I did not know where this sudden imagination came from. Possibly from a movie I once saw. Or a song I listened to. Or was it just lust? Meanwhile, the band finished their final song of the first set. The people around us applauded, and the DJ immediately started a dance song.

"Did they finish already?" Joceline was obviously not familiar with the bands playing here.

"No, this was just the first set. They have a short break now and be back on stage in like thirty minutes."

I noticed Joyce's drink was pretty much finished too. It was just ten o'clock. The night was still young.

"What you're up to?" I asked.

"I don't know, it's a bit noisy here to talk. I like to talk with you more."

"We can go for a walk instead?"

I suggested, but I was immediately reminded by the fact that she was wearing high heels. I could' t let this poor girl wonder the streets of Shanghai on a pair of high heels.

"Do you have any drinks at home?" Joceline asked.

Esteemed by her question, I answered that I just had a couple of bottles of beer and wine, but nothing to make her another Piña colada. Joceline giggled.

"That's no problem. I like beer and wine. Let's go."

Joceline slid from her bar seat and stood right next to me. Right now, she was exactly my height. Our lips were at the same wavelength and not far from each other. Her hair felt naturally over her shoulders, and with a seducingly looking smile on her face, she said:

"Come, let's go."

She grabbed my hand and took the lead towards the exit of the JZ. Whilst walking up the stairs, I noticed her gorgeous looking buttock. The open dress let me glance again into her lower back. I couldn't help watching as Joceline walked up the stairs to the exit while still holding my left hand, resulting in me following very closely. She left a scent of sweet perfume behind her. It made me feel excited. We were still holding hands when we were waiting for a taxi. Joyce's hand felt cold to me. It did not take long for a taxi to arrive and I opened the door so Joceline could enter first. "Wuning Lu, Dongxin Lu," I told the taxi driver and after he gave me a nod of understanding the vehicle started moving. I felt relieved that this driver instantly knew where we had to go. Sometimes it took me minutes to explain this destination - either caused by my considerable level of Chinese or the stupidity of the taxi driver.

"Where do you live?" I asked Joceline.

"Geographically actually not far from where you live, but just on the other side of the Suzhou River."

When looking onto the street, I noticed street barbecues started to emerge, and the smell of barbecue reached as far as in the car. It made me feel hungry again. Joceline looked around, she seemed happy.

"I love this city, because it never sleeps."

"True. Sometimes when I go home after a party, I see elderly people already doing their morning exercise." Joceline giggled.

"I never make it so late. But sometimes I do see people coming back from a party when I have to get up early for work to prepare a trip for my boss. So yes, you're right."

"I think Shanghai is at its best on an early summer day morning. I should actually enjoy it more but nine out of ten times I am still sleeping."

"It's worth to wake up for," agreed Joceline.

"You can even get breakfast around that time."

After telling each other a few more pros and cons of Shanghai, the taxi stopped in front of my compound. I handed the taxi driver a fifty RMB bill which he studied well before accepting it and giving me my change. It happened to me that I was handed a fake fifty RMB. As I was naive at that moment, I accepted it, thinking the best of human beings and some of them are pretty damn hard to recognise as fake. On purpose, they target foreigners for this as we at first pay less attention to this. Especially when we are drunk. Sober tourists have no clue at all. I've had fake twenties and fake tens that I kept, but once I started to receive a fake fifty or one hundred, I just tried to pay with them again in taxies or street shops. Sometimes I succeeded, sometimes they gave the paper money back to me again. As I usually carried more paper money, I could always take a real note and play naive that I did not know about being cheated in my change. Everybody knows foreigners are a target, so nobody would get angry if a foreigner tries to pay with fake money. In the Netherlands, one could get three months to up to a year in jail for this. But this is Shanghai.

I opened the door and got out of the taxi. I offered Joceline my hand to get her safely out of the taxi too. While she stood next to me, she pulled her dress a little down before we started to walk. The building security greeted me and opened the walk-in gate for us. Joceline looked up to the tall buildings we were suddenly surrounded by.

"Wow, you live really nice," she said.

To my surprise, all building tops were illuminated tonight. This only happened on special occasions. Not sure what today's occasion is but it provided the compound with an extra touch of class. We walked over the small bridge leading towards the entrance of the building where I lived.

"Be careful with your high-heels on this bridge," I said to Joceline.

"It is easy to get stuck."

Joceline took this as an opportunity to reach for my hand again. That was exactly how we entered the elevator to the tenth floor. We looked at each other in the mirror. Joyce's slim and bony shoulders, her arms aside her body while her right hand was still holding mine. Compared to her I looked like shit in my jeans and polo shirt. The long working hours on project management classes resulted in dark circles below my eyes. I feel like I'm losing my baby face. The doors behind us opened, and we turned around to walk towards the front door of my apartment. I opened the heavy wooden door of the apartment and saw that Mr Lu was not at home. I handed Joceline some new hotel slippers so she could get more comfortable.

"Wow," she said when she looked around. "You live in a very nice apartment."

She dropped her handbag on the floor and walked straight to the window. The living room was merely dark towards the windows, so the outside lights created a more spectacular view.

"There you can see Zhongshan Park," I said when I pointed to the right. I felt like a tour guide recently on my own balcony.

"And when you look to the left, you can see the Suzhou river."

"I can see the Suzhou river too from my balcony," Joceline said. "But I do not live so high as you do."

"It's only the tenth floor… it goes up to twenty-eight. The people living there oversee the Shanghai skyline."

"Do you have a balcony?" Joceline asked.

"Yes. Follow me," and I walked into the bedroom.

The bedsheets looked messed up, reminding me of what happened here just three hours ago. I opened the balcony door, and Joceline walked out. She walked to the railing, put both hands on it and looked over the edge.

"I'm afraid of height," she confessed.

"Be careful then, although the railing is high enough. Let me hold your hand."

She slowly reached out to me with a shy smile on her face. Her eyes moved quickly from direct eye contact towards the floor. The confidence she showed in JZ seemed all faded away.

Holding her right hand, I turned Joceline around, so she faced the view, and I put both arms around her waist. Her hair tickled my cheek and nose, while her sweet perfume really turned me on. I put her hair aside and softly kissed her in her neck. Joceline closed her eyes out of excitement and lifted her head a bit back. I continued to kiss her, as she did not object. She placed her hand in my neck, pushing it with soft press against her. Then without releasing her hand, she turned around and looked me straight in the eyes. Compared to just now, her eyes were full of confidence. She French kissed me back with her eyes closed. I pressed her waist against me while she comfortably leaned against the railing. In the far distance, an ambulance siren filled the sky. It could even be close, but right on this moment, everything close could be kilometres away.

"I want to go back inside,"

Joceline said while she slowly pushed me towards the glass door. I walked back in reverse until I felt the door. I opened the door behind my back and continued to amble in reverse until I felt my calves touching the bed. I stood still for a moment and lowered myself on the bed. Joceline was standing with her stunning body in front of me. She let me enjoy that moment for a few seconds and pushed me back. She climbed on the bed, pressing her legs on both sides of me and leaned forward. She pressed her breasts against my chest and continued to kiss me. My hands went from her waist over her ass towards me, touching her full breasts. This was picture perfect for this moment, so hot. I had to put a little break to this.

"Wait, sweetheart," I said.

"Let me grab a condom from the bathroom. I'll be quick..."

"Hao, Quai Dian,"

Joceline whispered in Chinese, which made her sound even more attractive. She moved from the top of me, and I got up, closed the curtains and made my way to the bathroom. I closed the door and quickly washed myself. I found a condom in one of the bathroom cabinets and opened the diffused glass door back to the bedroom.

While I was in there, Joceline had quickly made up the bed and was laying there on her belly on my virgin white bedcover. Her black hair fell over her right shoulder, making her back uncovered and she lifted her ass a little bit up. I looked at her all the way down her long legs. Her calves were crossed. She looked stunning. She looked me in the eye, saying

"Come, Victor... I want to feel you close to me..." and she winked her finger.

Showing no objection to this wonderful invitation, I walked towards the bed, just to let me indulge with Joceline's irresistible invitation.

26

Philips Office, 888 Tianlin Road, Shanghai - 10:45

Are you able to pass by the office sometime later this week? Perhaps on Thursday? The email did not contain many more words, but it was all I could wish for. Gerald's intensive travel schedule had refrained him from sending any emails lately, but he kept his promise to contact me in case he saw a suitable role for me in his organisation. And that's how I ended up taking the subway to the Philips office this morning. It would give me a chance to see Serena too, as she got the internship as a result of the interview she had when we first met. She mentioned having a surprise for me, which based on the question I asked recently, could only mean one thing. I tried not to hope too much, but I could not think of any other options. Unless she bought me perfume or so.

As I was a bit too early, Isabella offered me a cup of coffee and a seat at an empty desk, so I could wait for Gerald. Isabella had checked on me whether I was fine and if there would be anything else I needed. I took a sip from the coffee out of the white carton cup with the blue Philips logo. It still had the same nice and strong taste as during my internship. Towards the end of my internship, I could drink five cups a day of this brew. Three in the morning, two in the afternoon. If I had the opportunity to work here again, perhaps I would have to limit myself to three cups per day.

I looked around the office. About half of the team was sitting at their desk, focussing on their screen. About a third of them were talking to others, and a couple of desks seemed normally occupied but empty for this moment. People talked with a low voice, which was regularly drowned out by the noise of the coffee machine and the copier. Then a door from one of the side office opened, and I heard a laughing voice, which I recognised as Gerald's voice saying

"That's going to be fine. Good luck."

When Gerald turned around, he immediately noticed me.

"Hi Victor, good to see you. Take a seat in my office. I will be there in a couple of minutes. I need a quick bathroom break and a caffeine fix."

I got up while shaking Gerald's hand and walked towards his office. There was a table with four chairs in front of his desk. On the left side was a glass wall which was used as a whiteboard. I could see a list of tasks written in neat English letters. It did not have anything to deal with project management. His laptop was left alone in the dock station on his desk. Since I sat there for a few minutes, I heard the email notification sound three times. I remember hearing Gerald talking about the two hundred emails he received each day. Even as an intern, I did not have to remind him to reply to my emails. He mentioned once that he only gets in trouble during holidays. His wife books holiday locations where there is no internet available, so he doesn't have any chance to secretly check his emails. On my question how he solved that, Gerald had answered, laughing: the first week back in the office I just sleep two hours a night, so I have more time to read emails. I never met somebody with a work ethic like Gerald. On that moment Gerald walked in.

"Are you still okay with your coffee? Or would you like any water?" I nodded yes, and Gerald pored me a glass of water out of the vase on the table.

"The reason I wanted to talk to you today..." Gerald started,

"Is that I had a look on your LinkedIn profile, and I noticed you've been teaching project management for a while now. How's that going?"

"Good, I'm going towards the end of the first semester. The response from the students so far is good. And the university is already doing a marketing campaign for a second semester."

"Good, reason of asking is that I am in need of a project manager."

Again, I felt my heartbeat going up. Gerald looked at me with a smile on his face.

"I have a project I would like to start pretty soon and if possible, already next month. But this is a specific project that requires a full-time manager, and I do not have any headcount I can allocate to this role."

"What is this project about?" I asked curiously.

"Packaging. Right now, every region is doing its own packaging design and implementation. Our bulbs have the same size all over the world. We could save a lot of money if we had one global packaging design. Labels still require local characteristics, but I would like to see a general design. Is that something you would be interested in?"

I did not have to think about that.

"Yes, that sounds like a really interesting responsibility," I answered immediately. This was the moment I was waiting for so long. It finally happened! Gerald was clearly happy to see the surprised and relieved expression on my face.

"Did you think about this possibility beforehand? On purpose, I did not tell you about the reason to meet."

"Of course, I was hoping, but no, I did not expect this offer." Gerald laughed.

"That was my intention. I have informed Human Resources about this position, but this is an internal vacancy. We won't advertise this position on the website. So, in fact, you are the only candidate." I smiled. Gerald was good at making you feel good and important.

"For the sake of formality, you will have to conduct two interviews; the first one is with Human Resources and the second one with the project management director. Do you have anything planned? Shall we otherwise do that now?"

I initially planned to go to Starbucks and prepare my class, but that can wait a few hours.

"No problem to do that now," while I looked to the style I dressed today. Luckily, I choose for a suit, as I wanted to leave a good impression.

"No need to wear a tie," Gerald said. "It will be an informal talk, though they might ask you questions about yourself and experience as a project manager."

"That's fine," I answered while we left Gerald's office to another meeting room.

"I will go to HR to let them know you're here," Gerald said. It did not take long for an HR executive to arrive. She introduced herself as Diana and closed the door of the meeting room.

"Hi Victor," she started while she browsed through a copy of my resume, which I send to Gerald earlier.

"Gerald has told me a little bit about you." I nodded.

"Can you tell me something about yourself? I straightened my back to show more confidence.

"I am Victor de Lange, originally from the Netherlands. I first came to China in the beginning of this year to do an internship here. After I finished my internship and submitted my thesis, I graduated back in the Netherlands in my International Business and Management major. While my internship very much educated and inspired me about lighting, it made me think what to do next. Find a job in the Netherlands? Or go back to America, where I used to study in an exchange program? I decided to come back to Shanghai, as my network was most fresh here and I love the city of Shanghai. Besides that, since I worked for Philips, I did not walk into a room without a glance to the ceiling first to check out which lighting solution." Diana smiled and nodded.

"I reviewed a copy of your thesis, yes. It looked good and very informative. While doing your internship here or during your time as a project management lecturer, have you come across any personal strengths or weaknesses?"

I thought for a few seconds.

"I think I am good at working with people. Either in a team or independent but connected to a team. As well as in working towards deadlines, I will do everything to meet them and usually succeed in doing so."

"I like to hear that," Diana reacted. I continued:

"But I think I can improve myself in setting clear priorities on what to do each day. I encountered days where less important but easier tasks slipped into my to-do list instead of the ones that actually take more time and are difficult to finish."

"That's alright," Diana concluded.

"Those are soft skills that you can still work on. It requires time and experience to have these skills polished and improved. Now when it comes to your future, do you have any goals or targets to work to?"

I knew this question would come. When I wasn't working on project management classes or teaching them, I've had plenty of time to think about this question.

"I am determined to learn and develop myself towards a director in project management or strategic marketing."

"Do you have any timeframe in mind for this target?" Diana asked.

"Within ten years." I confirmed with a serious expression on my face.

"I know this is a challenging target, but I like to give myself a high target. But with the right attitude, hard work and a bit of luck, this is not an unrealistic target."

"That is true," Diana said. "And not entirely unrealistic. We have high achievers who are promoted every two or so years from a manager to a director level."

"It is good to hear as well that a company as Philips recognises talent and would like to invest in the development of those employees." Diana nodded.

"Yes, in some cases, we even offer an MBA to steer a high potential employee in a certain direction. Now we've been talking about your target which already indicated a timeline. But I would like to hear from you where you see yourself in five years from now, and then I mean on a personal level."

"In five years from now, I am thirty-one. By that time, I still hope to live in Shanghai with my girlfriend."

"That's good to hear," Diana said.

"There are foreigners who just plan to stay in Shanghai for a year or two and then move on. But the fact that you are planning to live for a longer term in China indicates that you are serious about your future. In respect to this, how is your Mandarin?" I smiled.

"Obviously not fluent. I am only in China for almost a year. I'd like to call my Mandarin fluent on a survival level." Diana laughed.

"That's pretty good considering the time you are in China."

"I can have basic conversations with friends, or when I am in restaurants or in a taxi."

"That's important enough for now," Diana answered. "None of the foreigners in Philips speak Mandarin, so from that point of view, you are ahead of them. Even though fluency in Mandarin would be an advantage, we have a prerequisite for Chinese colleagues to be proficient in English. This because of the high number of international projects they are involved in."

"I study Mandarin in my spare time, so I am sure my Chinese language skills will continue to develop." Diana nodded while she grabbed the three pages of my resume and ordered them in front of herself.

"To finalise, could you tell me something about your hobbies?"

"Currently, a lot of my time goes to the preparation of my project management class, but that will be over in a couple of weeks. In my free time, I like to enjoy nice food, either cooked by myself at home or outside in the city. By doing so, I like to have friends accompanying me so we can catch up about what's life offering at us. Besides that, I try to read every day. I have a range of business books and novels. And I like to watch movies." Diana nodded with an understanding expression on her face.

"Thank you, Victor, I will check with Helena, our project management director, whether she can come in to ask you some more project management related questions as well. But before I leave, are there any questions from your side?"

I thought again for a few seconds.

"How would you describe the company's culture here at Philips?"

"You can best describe it as a market culture." I nodded, but I had no idea what that meant. A market focussed culture? As if Diana could read the question marked expression on my face, she started to explain.

"At Philips, we are a result-based organisation where the emphasis lays on finishing work and getting things done."

While Diana walked to the whiteboard, she said:

"We have this with a focus on three value drivers: protecting and gaining market share, achieving goals set, and like every publicly listed company: profitability." Diana continued: "I would say our colleagues are most competitive and focused on reaching their goals. On a higher level, our leaders are hard drivers and producers. At times they are tough to deal with and have high expectations."

"That sound like a competitive environment where people are making themselves and each other better,"

"Exactly,"

Diana said with an agreeing expression on her face.

"The emphasis on reaching targets and winning keeps the organisation together. Reputation and success are the most important. Long-term focus is on rival activities and reaching goals. As you might have learned during your internship, market penetration is a fundamental conception here at Philips. Competitive prices so we can compete with lower-cost producers and market leadership are important."

"Yes, that is indeed something I saw while conducting my research in the Asian hotels. They have a big number of lower-cost products to choose from."

"Exactly," Diana said.

"Any other questions?"

"No, that was a clear answer to my question. I understand the company culture here better, and it makes me want to work even more for Philips." Diana smiled.

"I'll check whether Helena is ready to speak to you."

Diana grabbed my resume and walked out of the room. I looked at the whiteboard where Diana just wrote the three values in neat handwriting. While I reread them, the sun came through the window blinds, leaving sunny and shadow dashes on the white glass whiteboard. I heard the coffee machine on the background, making me hanker to one of the strong double shots I had during my internship. Then another lady walked in, of which I presumed it was Helena. I stood up to introduce myself.

"Hi, my name is Victor." She smiled, took a seat and said:

"Hi, my name is Helena. I am a project management director at Philips Lighting. I heard you are interested in the position of a project manager in my team?"

"Very much yes," and while I said that I wondered whether I did not sound too desperate.

"You know that this is not like the typical project manager role, right?"

"Yes, Gerald told me about a global packaging project." Helena nodded.

"Exactly. I have a team of five project managers, but they are focussed on projects with an objective of product creation. They follow processes, and they are excellent in what they are doing, but the global packaging project is a project with a scope never executed in Philips Lighting before. We are, therefore looking for somebody who is able to design and execute his or her own processes with the objective of a successful project delivery. You'll have to manage and steer international teams in Asia, Europe and America. This requires a different set of skills and background." I nodded yes.

"So Gerald told me you are teaching project management at Jiao Tong University?"

"Yes, I do so since the end of last year."

"How is it going so far? Do you like it?"

"Yes, I like to go out and inspire young professionals in project management."

"Can you describe the achievement that you're getting out of this?"

"The fact that students walk into the classroom the first lecture, and sometimes do not know much about project management. Eight weeks later they walk out being able to manage a project as a result of the theory, real case examples, case studies and group discussions we had in class after passing an exam with excellence."

"That's a good sign indeed," Helena added.

"Now would you tell me something about the project management lifecycle?"

"Sure, can I make use of the whiteboard for that?"

"No problem, you can use whatever you need to give me a clear indication of your project management lifecycle."

I stood up and walked towards the whiteboard. Helena turned her seat in my direction, so she had a clear view of what I was going to write. I took the black marker and drew five vertical lines on the whiteboard.

"These represent the four stages of the project management lifecycle," I started.

"The first phase is the initiation phase."

I wrote the two words down as good as I could.

"In this phase, you identify the business need, a possible problem, or in Philips' case the need for a product or new global packaging concept and organise a brainstorm session that the project team can deliver this need, solve this problem, or seize this opportunity. This is as well the phase where you agree on an objective for the project and organise a feasibility study to determine whether the project is feasible or not. Once the team agreed that this project is worth starting, you draw the deliverables for the project."

"So far you are almost exactly telling what I am thinking," Helena said. As if she knew it would give me more self-confidence to continue this explanation. I continued:

"Once the management approved the project based on your business case or project initiation document, you move into the planning phase. In this phase, it is your task to understand what needs to be done while breaking break down the larger project into smaller tasks. Based on what exactly needs to be done, you build your team, with the skills in mind, you need the team to deliver the project well. This is as well the moment where the project manager creates smaller goals within the larger project, making sure each is achievable within the time frame."

"But you do not always have the resources available when you need them," Helena said. "Teams are working on a specific number of projects, and their span of control is only allowing them to work on a maximum number of projects to make sure they are not overworked."

"True, but that is even a matter of planning," I said.

"Here in Philips, we have about seventy projects going on at the same time."

"You know when projects will finish, so you have eventually headcount available for a new project to start." Helena nodded in agreement, and I continued.

"The execution or delivery phase will need the team to start working on this project. This is the phase that turns everything you've planned in the initiation and planning phase into action."

"So, what is your role here?" Helena asked.

"It is the project manager's role to monitor and control the planning, team, and smaller goals to make sure the project is on track to meet the milestones of the original plan."

"Yes, that's correct," Helena added.

"Once your team has completed work on a project, you enter the closure phase. In the closure phase, you provide final deliverables, release project resources, and determine the success of the project. Just because the major project work is over, that doesn't mean the project manager's job is done. There are still important things to do, including evaluating what did and did not work with the project."

I kept silence for a few seconds and overviewed the words I wrote on the whiteboard. For every project management phase, I listed a few keywords, providing a clear overview. Everybody without understanding about project management would have at least an idea what this was about.

"That was very good Victor," Helena said.

"I can see you're a competent lecturer."

"Not only a competent project management lecturer," I added.

"Due to my deep understanding of the project management lifecycle, I know what is expected from the role of a project manager." Helena nodded.

"What is from your point of view the most important skill of a project manager?"

"Communication," I said without any hesitation.

"If a project manager isn't able to communicate well on scope and deliverables during a project, the project is doomed to fail."

"That's correct," Helena said.

"So, how would you describe your communication style?"

"As direct, but fair. I know in China, communication does not always happen in a direct manner. I will have to keep this in mind when talking to a project team."

"There is no reason to tell somebody he or she did not perform well, or that you expect a better or different performance or way of working to achieve a milestone. But if you have to do it, do so in a closed-door room with just you and that person. Avoid criticising colleagues in groups."

"Correct," I answered.

"This is a topic I have discussed in class. The majority of the students come from abroad, so it is important to understand this."

"That's good, indeed. Now how do you keep your project members motivated? Projects can be long, and one team member is dealing with around thirty projects at a time."

I thought for a second.

"By communicating well and keeping the project members involved in the process of the project. I like to make them feel valued and create the environment that they are valuable resources in this project." Helena nodded yes.

"So, while keeping your team members motivated, how do you monitor and control your project to make sure all deliverables are met?"

"Monitoring and controlling are about comparing planned results with actual results. Those results are summarised in different project stages but subdivided into milestones and tasks."

"Correct," Helena said. "Do you use any software for that?"

"The work breakdown structure of the project which gives an indication of the tasks, milestones and project phases. But this does not happen at the deadline of each task or milestone. Because of meetings and conversations with project team members, you continually monitor and control the project. If you figure out that a team member is having difficulties with meeting a task, deadline or milestone, it is my responsibility to provide solutions for the issue he or she is facing."

"And if you as a project manager cannot bring this solution?"

"Well, projects naturally change over time. These changes are often initiated by the project manager and the project team. They are the ones applying corrective actions or process improvements throughout the project."

"But which software do you use?" Helena asked again.

I had to be careful not to talk too much just for the sake of talking. It was better to carefully listen to her questions and just straight go to the point.

"I just use Excel." I answered instead and supplying Helena with all the information she initially wanted to know.

"Not Salesforce or Clarity?"

"No, just Excel so far."

"Alright," Helena continued.

"The reason I asked is that we are seeking to integrate project management software into our project management office. It would be of great benefit if you had already experience in working with these."

Hearing what Helena just said, my body felt overtaken by nervousness. I thought I was on the right track to impress Helena in explaining how to be a valuable addition to her team, but the last two questions made me realise how easy it is to possibly mess up an interview. The question whether I had any beneficial experience in a project management software tool had an impact on my overall feeling of this interview.

"Well," Helena added when browsing one more time through my resume,

"I think I know enough for now. I will further discuss the position with Gerald, and either he or HR will contact you with the outcome."

This sentence made me feel she was now the gatekeeper between a Philips career and myself. If she went back to Gerald with a green light, the next thing what would happen is that HR would contact me with an offer. If on the other hand, it was a red light the chance was big that Gerald would not support my return in Philips neither. I did not feel so uncomfortable in a long time. My heartbeat was up, and I could feel sweat dripping down from under my armpits.

"Do you have any questions for me?" Helena asked. I thought for a second.

"Yes. What is the biggest challenge your project management office is currently dealing with?" Now Helena needed a few seconds to think.

"I wish it was just one challenge I had to deal with," she answered.

"There are quite a few things that sometimes literally keep me up at night."

Helena opened herself a bit now. "I can imagine that with a team developing products with a global focus," I said.

"The biggest challenge I have is to keep up with technology improvements in the market. An average project takes six months to complete, but within those six months new, cheaper or better components can be available. If we miss out on that, the product may end up not price or specification competitive and ends up not selling well. On the other hand, if we change the specs or components after project stage two, we will face delays in delivery. It's a dilemma we have to deal with quite frequently because the pressure of the competition is high." I nodded yes.

"I can imagine that it is tough, yes, finding that balance between cost and spec while keeping ahead of competitors."

"Do you have any other questions?" Helena asked.

"No, not for now, thank you for your time, Helena."

"Sure, no problem. Thank you for coming in as well. I will further discuss our conversation with Gerald."

I stood up and offered Helena my hand.

"Thank you again, Victor," said Helena while she smiled at me.

It made me feel a bit nervous knowing that she probably already knows whether she considers me a valuable add in her team or not. It probably still had to wait a few days until I had the answer. I saw Isabella waiting for me at the door of the meeting room. Once again, I glanced at the white glass board on the wall. My project management phase description looked quite sophisticated. Hoping that it had helped me in launching a job, I walked towards the entrance door. Helena followed me, leaving the glass wall for what it was.

"Hi Victor," Isabella started with a smile on her face.

"Gerald is in a meeting now but have instructed me to let you know that human resources will be in touch with you fairly soon."

"Thank you, Isabella, I will be on standby."

Isabella giggled while I turned around to wave to Helena and walked towards the elevator. It was getting towards lunchtime now. From my internship, I still remembered that some colleagues go for lunch as early as half-past eleven. That resulted in an almost empty office floor. I did not feel famished yet, all the talking had made me rather thirsty. The elevator door opened, and I pressed the button back to the ground floor. As there were only five floors in this office, it did not take long until I walked out and found my way back to the reception. I took my phone and rang to Serena.

"How did it go!' She said immediately after answering the call.

"Not too bad, I think? I feel like I did quite well, based on the conversations I had. I hope they thought the same."

"That's good! So where are you now?"

"I'm at the reception."

"Okay, wait for me there. I'll be there in about five minutes. But I have to attend a meeting in ten minutes so it will be quick."

I sat down on the couch and watched people walking in and out. Soon Serena was among them. She held her right hand behind her back as if she wanted to hide something and smiled when she walked towards me.

"Hello Victor," she said while she gave me a quick hug.

"How's your day going?"

"Aah, good but busy. We'll have to finish a marketing draft proposal by the end of today, and we're not even half-way yet. I am glad to hear your interview went well! We may become colleagues soon," giggled Serena.

"That would be funny. Hey, I have something for you," and she took her hand from behind her back and handed me a small wrapped box.

Would it still be the perfume, as a recognition of our friendship? With a smile on my face, but a bit of a disappointed feeling started unwrapping the box. Serena waited patiently but excited as if she could not wait for me to see what was inside. It was indeed a box from 'L Oreal, a men skincare product. But somehow it felt like an empty box.

"Don't you want to open it?" Serena said.

When I opened the box, I saw an envelope inside. I quickly took it out and opened it - and it had a self-written note inside.

Valid for two entrance tickets to the Keane concert in Beijing.

"Oh, wow! Really?! Thank you so much! How did you manage to get them?"

"Via my cousin. She works in media relations."

"I can't thank you enough for this, Serena!"

"You're welcome, Victor," Serena said when looking at her watch.

"I better be going now. Otherwise, I am too late for my meeting." And she hugged me again.

"No worries, we'll catch up soon!" And there she left again, leaving me behind with a handwritten note in my hand. When I walked outside the sun was still shining, making it excellent Spring weather for people to go outside and have a walk through the business park. I found my way to the subway station and headed back home to further work on the second final project management class. I thought about the interview, but there is nothing I can change anymore now. It is what it is, and all I can do is wait. I've had some doubts about whether Helena left the interview with a positive feeling. When I came closer to the subway station, I heard the announcement that the subway in Xujiahui direction would arrive in five minutes. That would give me a bit of time to get a bottle of water from the vending machine and wait for the train to arrive. Time to focus on things that I could influence right now - the quality of my project management class.

27

Hohhot Baita International Airport, Inner Mongolia - 08:46

It's been nearly a calendar week now since the interview with Philips. So many things happened in the last couple of weeks. Linda disappeared from my life, teaching and preparing lectures for the university and a glance in my passport taught me that my visa will expire reasonably soon. I am on a business visa which is recently harder to extend, so that would mean I would have to leave the country and get back on a tourist visa. I would like to avoid that if possible, as it comes with a high expense and a risk of visa rejection.

And then there is the taste and experience of pointless sex I recently have in my mouth after the dinner with Danielle and date with Joceline. I thought it might help me to move on quicker from Linda, but it did not make me feel much better. In the end, I am looking for immersion rather than variety. A stable relationship comes with immersion, where casual sex with a couple of girls feels perfect on that exact moment, but still leaves you with an empty feeling afterwards. It's causing emotional peaks on moments when you meet, but you feel surrounded by dark, quiet valleys when you are alone. I just wish to have a soulmate around.

I felt tired and have to change the scenery for a few days. Experience new things. I wanted to be alone, but that is not easy in Eastern China.

Thinking about the challenges ahead, my flight touched down in Hohhot, which is the capital of Inner Mongolia in northern China.

It's hard to imagine but a two hours flight time from Shanghai to Hohhot is enough to let you end up in a whole different world. It must be one of the only regions in the world where you can witness running horses between grazing sheep on an endless looking green grassland and riding camels on the same day. Inner Mongolia is an autonomous region counting for roughly twelve per cent of China mainland. In many other countries in the world, such size would be a fairly small piece of land. But not in China. The autonomous region represents one point two million square kilometres of land, the same size as Peru or South Africa, and is subdivided into endless grasslands and deserts. Inner Mongolia offers a home to roughly twenty-four million people. Roughly eighty per cent of the population is Han Chinese, and seventeen per cent native Mongol. A few other minorities complete the total balance of the ethnic composition. Compare this to Shanghai, wherein the municipality area as many people live as in Inner Mongolia. But to put it more into contrast; Shanghai covers just a half per cent of the Inner Mongolian land, but both have the same population.

While the aeroplane slowly taxied to the gate, one of the flight attendants welcomed us to Hohhot while mentioning an outside temperature of only seven degrees. That's cool compared to Shanghai, where I left with a comfortable twenty-three degree Celsius. Hohhot Temperatures in October are mostly above zero degrees, up to fifteen degrees on average. In the months up to February, it can go as low as minus twenty-degree Celsius. I was the only foreigner aboard, which is always good for extra pleasant smiles from the cabin crew. During the flight it came to my imagination that if this plane would have crashed, I would at least be mentioned in the news: "Aeroplane crash in China leaving one hundred seventy-seven people including cabin crew dead. All passengers were Chinese except one passenger with a Dutch nationality." That is at least how I would be remembered.

Once the seatbelt sign was off, everybody stood up as soon as possible, making the aisle filled with passengers in a matter of seconds. I had a window seat, so with my physical height standing up would be impossible. I looked through the window, where the airport crew already surrounded the aeroplane to check the engines and offload the luggage. I could feel the air pressure being released immediately after the door cabin opened. There was a bus parked right next to the aeroplane so we could be transported to an entrance leading to the luggage collection hall. Once I set foot out of the aeroplane, a cool and dry air welcomed me. While on the bus to the luggage belt, I noticed the semi-cloudy sky above the airport. The screens confirmed that only five flights had landed this morning and all of them had a message "all luggage on the belt" - changing from English to Chinese characters.

It did not take long for the first luggage to arrive. Soon after that, I could not see the luggage belt anymore despite a clear yellow line where people are supposed to stay behind. Apparently, nobody cared. Everybody expected his or her luggage to arrive first. It's an interesting process to witness. I saw my suitcase coming closer, and I pushed myself in the middle to grab my suitcase. Realising that they were blocking the process, a Chinese man laughed at me and set a step aside. I turned around to search for the exit, and the first illegal taxi driver approached me already. They must have noticed me already from long distance.

The airport is located about fourteen kilometres from downtown Hohhot, so I decided taking a bus to save money. I feared that regular taxi drivers would not turn on the meter and ask me for at least a hundred RMB to drive me to the city. A primitive bus trip would only cost me twenty RMB. I searched for a bus into Huimin district direction where the Holiday Inn is located, and where I would stay for the following two nights. The airport itself is not very far from Hohhot.

"One ticket to Huimin please,"

I asked the ticket seller in Mandarin who was looking at me with a bored expression on his wrinkled face. His brown skin colour revealed a man who actually enjoyed a lot of sunshine. While I searched for cash, I could smell his cigarette was at the point where he was actually smoking the filter. Without saying a word, he shoved a ticket into my direction, and he pointed into my left direction covering a one hundred thirty degrees angle with six busses lined up. At least it was clear I would have to take one out of those six. Every bus had a board with some Chinese characters at the entrance, but no English translation was provided. I checked the ticket in my hand and the characters matched with the destination description of the fourth bus. While I walked in the direction of the busses, some Chinese tourists ran in the same direction as if the busses could leave any time. None of the busses was equipped with drivers, so I assumed we still had enough time to walk.

 I slide my suitcase in the luggage compartment and walked up the stairs. I took a seat right above the luggage compartment so I could see exactly which suitcases would go in and out when the bus had to make stops before arriving at its final destination in Huimin district. The good thing with these airport busses in China is that they leave every twenty minutes, so you never have to wait long. The driver said something in Mandarin and set the bus in movement. We shortly drove up north before taking a left turn onto the highway towards Hohhot. Other passengers took this opportunity to take a nap. I felt exhausted because of waking up early but still wanted to explore the Inner Mongolian surroundings. I expected to see endless beautiful green grasslands under an unreal blue sky. The reality was different. The G6 highway leading to the city was surrounded by dry farmlands and smoke-producing factories. Nothing here looked like the Teletubbies grasslands I always imagined. There appeared mountains on my right side, which must be the enormous gateway to the neighbouring country Mongolia. It looks like it rains regularly on top of the mountains. But the local inhabitants in the valley are praying for rain every day with hopes that their farmlands won't change into deserts, which will devastate the local economy. An economy that is largely depending on livestock, forestry and tourism industries. And because of a large number of sheep and goats on animal husbandry acts as an export base for meat, milk, cheese, wool and cashmere. But all of this is only possible with rain. Without rain, the region can only rely on its mineral-rich ground deposits in rare earth and coal. That trend is reflected in the view I have from the bus now. Besides the ongoing industry, I saw countless apartment compounds under construction. Cranes created a major impact on the Inner Mongolian horizon, where just the sun appeared through the clouds. A grey and depressive looking landscape seemed now slightly more liveable.

I heard the bus driver turned on his direction light to leave the highway. We were almost the only vehicle on the road. Once we drove into Hohhot, civilisation and the density of people increased. Most of the cars on the road were taxi's while the majority of people used a bike or tricycle to go from A to B. I had no idea where the bus would stop and how far this would be from the Holiday Inn hotel. It could be two or fifteen blocks. I tried to spot a Holiday Inn logo, but all I saw was yellow and white painted commercial buildings with green and golden coloured domes on their roof. Big sized Chinese characters filled the building facade as huge banners. Some of them I could read but not enough to distinguish any names.

The bus abruptly came to a stop. The other passengers on the bus woke up, and while judging their reaction, I could sense that we reached the final destination. The driver pressed a button to open the front door, and I saw the luggage compartment moving open on my right side. All passengers lined up in the small aisle. I joined the line and slowly found my way towards the exit. The noise of the traffic and horning cars increased. I passed the bus driver and asked:

"Holiday Inn?"

I only got a nod back, not providing me with any information on whether we were close or not.

Locals would only know the hotel name in Chinese.

After getting my suitcase out of the luggage compartment, I checked my watch and noticed that it was just before noon. The hotel would not accept my check-in yet, and the aeroplane breakfast had made me quite hungry. After walking one block, I saw a street with restaurants. The restaurants were based in traditional Chinese buildings, something that once must have been homes. It looked a bit like Shanghai's Xintiandi although the luxury shops, restaurants and nightclubs were missing. A place like this has the potential to grow into something as exclusive as Xintiandi. The street was separated in two lanes because of the stall shops in the middle selling local products and the usual cell phone accessories you're not looking for. The characteristic streetlights were all built in a T shape with traditional looking lanterns on each side of the horizontal bar but were ruined by commercial banners. This could be so pretty. Locals occupied each of the benches under characteristic street lanterns, involved in serious conversations, playing Mahjong or just stared in the far distance. They take life as it comes. There is no such rush as I always see in Shanghai. Nobody seems to have the urgency to be somewhere soon.

I passed a couple of restaurants with terraces so I could understand what Hohhot has to offer from a food perspective. Most of it was local fast food, which I was looking forward to trying. I ended up on one of the terraces with white plastic camping chairs and tables. It was one of the better-looking terraces in this street. Five waitresses were lined up and welcomed me to the restaurant. After I sat down, one of them walked into my direction with a menu in her hand.

"Welcome to our restaurant," she started.

I smiled and nodded as if I left my voice in the aeroplane earlier this morning. While she pointed me through the menu with pictures of each dish, I made up my mind:

"I'd like to have a local beef noodle soup and a coke, please."

"Sure," the waitress answered.

While she walked away, I thought about the afternoon to come. After I finished my lunch, I would have to go to the hotel and see if I could travel to the grass fields. While the waitress came back with my Coke, I asked her about any tours she might know, but she confirmed that the hotel might be one of the best places to inquire, as they have the best relations and can protect me in not being overcharged for a tour. She had a point.

"Thank you, I'll keep that in mind."

She nodded and walked away. Minutes later the beef soup arrived, a dish you generally do not have to wait long for. Once all ingredients are put in a bowl, including the thin slices of beef, soup is added, and it is ready to be served. It looked delicious.

"Enjoy,"

The waitress said when I reached out to the left side of the table to grab a pair of chopsticks. I smiled at her. After this local lunch, I walked to the hotel.

***

The Shanghai Expat

"Your luggage will be carried into your room after two pm today."

Said the receptionist when he made a copy of my passport and visa. Curious as I was, I asked about the possibilities of a tour or driver to the grasslands. He looked at his watch.

"We have one leaving at 1pm this afternoon, that's in twenty-five minutes from now." Could that be even more perfect?

"There is a small bus that will pick up guests from other hotels too, before it will drive you to the grasslands on approximate an hour drive from here."

"And how much does it cost?"

"It's six hundred RMB per person, Sir. Dinner is included. You'll be back at the hotel tonight around 8pm."

The receptionist acted very politely. He sounded like an undergraduate reading hospitality language sentences from a textbook.

"I'd like to join this tour if possible," I said.

I paid the six hundred RMB in cash and took a seat on one of the comfortable couches in the hotel lobby. This looks like a brand-new hotel. Much of golden accents in the ceiling while the floor and stairs had a marble finish. And in contrast to the hotel I had dinner with Mr Wang, this hotel actually had guests walking around. I noticed a coffee machine in the lobby corner, so to kill the time I made myself a black coffee. A bit of caffeine would be good. I asked for a glass of water too, as the beef soup I had for lunch had made me feel thirsty. After enjoying my coffee and a well-needed cup of water, a representative from the tour agency walked in. The receptionist pointed into my direction. The tour representative walked into my direction and reached out his hand to introduce himself.

"My name is John," he said. "Please follow me. This hotel is the last one on the list, so from here we drive directly to the grasslands."

When I entered the small bus, roughly ten pair of eyes stared at me. All of them were Chinese tourists. As if John could read my mind, he said:

"I will do the talking both in Chinese and English, unless you understand Chinese."

"Not really, so English would be good for me."

John nodded understandingly and told the driver in Chinese that we were complete and ready to start the tour. I took a seat in front of the van, giving me a nice front view through the big front window. The other tourists immediately fell asleep as if for them the tour would only begin once we arrived in the grasslands. Not for me. The Inner Mongolian infrastructure is so much different compared to Shanghai, it would be a waste to close my eyes right now. John seemed in a good mood. Despite most of his group preferring to sleep instead of listening to him, he took the microphone and started to talk in Chinese. I could understand the part that it would take about an hour to drive to the grasslands. For everything else, I was waiting for the English version.

"We are now on our way to the highway," John started in English.

"From here it will take about an hour to arrive in the grasslands." John smiled and continued:

"Once we arrive there, you will have time to visit one of the nomad villages. But keep an eye on the time, because dinner is included. You'll be served roasted lamb meat, one of the local specialities in a Yurt that is turned into a restaurant."

From the research I did before starting this trip, I knew that a Yurt is an often portable, round tent covered with skins or felt lived by nomads. Yurts are relatively easy to relocate when the nomads move to another piece of land with fresh and untouched grass. Meanwhile, John continued:

"Let me know in case you have any questions while we are driving. I am more than happy to answer you."

I nodded again and looked over my shoulder to the left side of the street. We passed a neighbourhood of which it was hard to tell whether it was abandoned or still in construction. It appeared to me like a war zone, as if affected by a bomb explosion. It seemed John could read the impressed expression from my face:

"The homes you see here were once in construction, but either the contractor or the owner ran out of money. As a result, nothing is happening right now. They might continue development once new money is on the table."

From the so-called warzone, we entered a regional road, and from now onwards, the scenery started to look greener. The bicycles and tricycles in downtown were now replaced with small trucks and cars.

A blue truck full of workers sitting in the alloy tray passed by. All of them wore wrinkled blue shirts covering their tanned skinny bodies and wearing a yellow helmet. The majority of them had a cigarette in their mouth. None of them was buckled up in seatbelts. If this truck would end up in an accident, probably none of the passengers would survive. Workers like this are usually not insured for accidents during working time. If one of them would die in a work-related accident, the local government pay the family a ransom as compensation. The height of the compensation usually depends on what the government or their employer is prepared to give them. If the accident got a lot of media attention, the settlement is usually higher. In this case and for these workers I'd expect the worse. The family of fallen miners in remote areas usually got paid not much more than a hundred fifty thousand RBM or barely twenty thousand Euro per person. This compensation covers about four years of salary while many of the workers have many more years to go until retirement.

While our trip continued, the landscape continued to change as well. The view of occasional small villages changed into endless hills with grass fields. Not perfectly green but a bit yellow caused by a lack of rain. As if John could read my mind, he stood up and instantly started talking in English:

"This area is geographically far located from the sea and has parts with higher altitudes. Thereby Inner Mongolia has a temperate monsoon climate. This means there is only a little and irregular rainfall, and summers and winters have a big switch in temperature."

The explanation of John reflected the environment I witnessed when looking out of the window. John continued his tour talk:

"You're lucky to visit Inner Mongolia now as it can get freezing in January with temperatures between minus ten and minus thirty-two degrees Celsius. Summers are warm but very short here, usually only one or two months per year. Some parts of Inner Mongolia don't even have summer!"

Good that I carried an extra coat and a warm pullover. Trees outside the car blocked the view to the endless grass fields I just had. They had a healthy green colour, and of them had white paint at the bottom so wild animals wouldn't eat the bark.

It did not take long before we arrived at a collection of Yurts surrounded by grasslands and located in front of a dusty parking area. The Yurt village was surrounded by low brick walls to indicate their territory. The entrance was between two tall pillars with both a harpoon shaped sign with three golden tender hooks pointing into the clear blue sky. After John opened the door, three local girls in traditional clothing offered us a shot of what looked like baijiu. John was just in time to explain to me what I was about to drink.

"This is a local baijiu Victor, but not produced from grains. Have a try, it is safe to drink."

Without explaining more, he waited for me to try. I tried a sip, it tasted much like a grain distilled baijiu. A heavy pungent taste entered my mouth, and right after I swallowed it, I could feel it running down all the way to my abdomen. This must contain at least forty-five per cent of alcohol.

"How do you like it?"

"It's nice," I said just to keep John on my side. I would not drink this for fun.

Usually, baijiu only tastes acceptable in combination with food, and this version did not taste much different.

"This is made from horse milk," John added.

"Horse milk and it is still as transparent as water?"

"Yes."

I finished my shot and continued to walk towards the gate. I wondered whether people really live here or whether this is just a commercial collection of Yurts for tourists to visit. I saw a big Yurt in the middle of the community, which could be the restaurant location where we would have dinner. On the roof, it had the same tenterhooks sign as I saw at the entrance gate pillars. John, now equipped with a little red flag showing the logo of his company in his hands ran a few meters in front of the small group, just to inform us that from now onwards we could walk around by ourselves as long as we would be Back in time for dinner, to be served at five o'clock in the main Yurt. That would allow me to walk around and make myself familiar with this interesting culture. The Yurts here weren't the ones that could be relocated every once in a while. They were built from stone, with a roof made of concrete. The walls and the roof these Yurts were painted in white, with a blue tribal shape coloured in blue on the roof. Entrances were identified with a small shed.

I continued my walk. I passed by a series of Yurts that were available for rent, aligned in a row of twelve next two each other. Some of them had the door wide open. Inside was a small two-person bed, a table and a bathroom. A fireplace could keep the guests warm during the cold winter nights. Imagine renting this Yurt with minus forty degree Celsius outside! A dusty path led to the edge of the community were a few more Yurts where build. One had a few people lining up, and when I came closer, I could read "WC" in blue letters on its white walls. Interesting to see how nomads accommodate toilets. As I couldn't see any drainage tubes in the distant surroundings, I wonder where all the turd would end up. Or would there really be underground pipes?

As far as I could see, there were no other communities until the horizon, which could be at least fifty kilometres. The only thing what I saw was a herd of sheep on a few kilometres distance. The shepherd tried to keep his herd together by waving his arms in the air. As the grass wasn't green, they must have a hard time finding decent food these days.

When I walked back towards the Yurt community, I discovered a KTV Yurt. Actually, there were several KTV Yurts for people to rent. There was a small red and white billboard outside, supported by two poles. At night it must be light up because it had an electricity cable running from the ground to the top. From the outside, the Yurt itself did not look different compared to the other Yurts. It was decorated with plastic canvas with a Chinese girl pop group. As well it had a picture of a mahjong table and a Chinese lady in traditional clothes standing next to it, creating an inviting appearance.

When I walked closer and looked through the window, I saw a beamer hanging in the middle of the Yurt, pointed to a projector screen on the wall. A red couch stood on the side against the wall, creating a little bit of space in the middle for visitors to dance if they wish. This KTV had its own charm. I could imagine spending a few hours here with a bunch of friends, in the middle of nowhere. As long as there is good music and drinks the environment does not really matter.

When I walked around the Yurt, I saw hundreds of empty beer bottles accurately stalled to the brick wall that bordered this Yurt community with the endless hills and fields of grass. This is proof that there have been some good parties in this KTV. John walked up to me to notify me about a show that started not far away from us. We walked a dusty road towards a herd of horses. They were waiting there, with five horses on a leash to a wooden pole. By counting the poles, there must have been fifty horses. First, we were guided to a sand circle. Several tourist groups came together, I estimated that a hundred people were watching what would happen next. We would witness a wrestling event. The men from this Yurt community, wearing leather boots, jeans and a light blue skirt, looking like traditional clothing. Over this light blue skirt, they wore a leather vest. Four couples stood in front of each other on a similar distance, holding each other's shoulders while both were looking at the ground. They were waiting for a sign to start wrestling. This came from a ninth guy shooting in the air with a gun. As guns are prohibited in China, I suppose that this wasn't a real gun, but just to enhance the wild East feeling a bit. The four couples started wrestling, and it did not take too long until the first guy lay on the ground. People started to cheer. With every new round, the losers were out. The four remaining wrestlers took their position as before while waiting for the gunshot. It was quiet now. All I could hear was the sound of the horses standing beside us. Once the shotgun sounded, both couples were off to wrest each other. The audience around the sand circle started to yell louder with every round leading to the final. The two remaining wrestlers made a show of it, not creating a risk to make a wrong move and lose the game. The final took slightly longer compared to the other rounds, but ultimately one guy ended up on the ground, and the audience applauded for the winner. I'm not sure what the winner earned in prestige, but it seemed that he was happy with his victory. While we were watching the final coming to an end, the guys who lost earlier already prepared a few of the horses for the next event.

We all moved to the side of the sand circle, creating an almost one-hundred meter line for the horses to run. All nomads took position on their horses on a far distance from us, and an older man closer to us laid stones in the grass. The horses started to run after hearing the gunshot. They ran towards us with five horses and their rider on top. Once the riders came closer to the location of the stones, they hung on one side on the side of the horse so they could catch the stone laying on the ground. So, this was the purpose of the game. The one who would catch most of the stones will win this round. As the stones were lying right in front of me, it was quite a spectacular view once the horses passed by with their men hanging on the side. The one closest to me ultimately won. While the audience cheered with enthusiasm, I felt a hand on my shoulder. It was John.

"Come, this is almost the end of this competition. We'll have our early dinner soon so let's go to the restaurant before all the other spectators go and have a good seat. I know where to sit best."

John knew his way around here. Curious as I was to see how this competition would end, I followed him. Interesting enough he forgot about all the other tourists that joined us before in the bus, it was just him and me walking away from the crowds onto a dusty path on our way to the biggest Yurt in town. We entered the Yurt, and the first thing we saw were long tables. At full capacity, they should be able to accommodate over one hundred people here.

"Come, follow me," John said. We walked across the long tables where staff, all dressed in traditional clothing, placed chopsticks and sauces on the table.

"They all live in this village, it's their job to offer the best service to tourists."

I saw it all happening. John walked me to a table right in front of a small open space.

"This is where they soon serve the lamb," he said.

"You'll be first in line once they start cutting the meat."

Impressed as I was by John's actions, I looked around. At the other end was a bar. On the white wall, three boards were installed, all filled with a variety of baijiu. A thick pole made from an old tree in the middle of the Yurt kept the roof up. Vertical wooden sticks, covered in red paper material, held the surface up towards the ridge of the roof. On the wall hung some local calendars, with famous quotes and beautiful pictures of Yurts and grasslands.

Now the other tourist started to walk in. The game was finished. I was the only one missing out on who won the horse race competition. The number of tourists in the Yurt proliferated. I looked at my watch. It was only four-thirty. It would mean we had a very early dinner. The noodles I had for lunch today were anyway a light meal for me, so a bit of roasted lamb meat would fit right in. We got offered another glass of baijiu. John looked at me.

"The first one is for free," he said. I nodded yes to the waitress, and with a smile, she filled my shot glass. I took a sip of the baijiu and again felt it through my oesophagus running down into my stomach. I can't imagine that people can get used to drinking this liquor. Then four Chinese men dressed in local clothes in green and red entered the Yurt. They made traditional music.

"This is the start of the ceremony,"

John said. I looked around whether I could see some of the other tourists who joined us on the bus earlier today. They sat at a table on the side of the Yurt, quite far away from us. I wondered why John had only invited me to come here earlier while abandoning the other tourists for this moment. The four Mongolian musicians walked through the Yurt, while people made pictures of their performance. When I looked at my right, four girls in traditional clothes, beautifully dressed in orange, pink and red dresses presented two roasted lambs prepared on one driving platform. Both lambs stood up, leaning on the upper parts of their legs with the nose pointed in the air. The music continued, and the girls pored a bit baijiu over both lambs. They invited us around the platforms. The majority of people in the Yurt joined the nomads in a circle around the platform. A few of them were making pictures or videos. I looked around. I was the only foreigner here in the Yurt among Chinese people, probably from all corners of the country.

When the ceremony stopped, we took our place at the table again, and the nomad girls started to cut the lamb into pieces.

"Historical records are found with evidence that a roasted whole lamb as we eat it today was Genghis Khan's favourite dish. Do you know who Genghis Khan is?"

I nodded, yes.

"He served it to the noblemen and his soldiers after they won a battle. Back in the days, only those who had distinguished identities could be served a roasted whole lamb. Nowadays it is used as a special delicacy to serve guests from faraway places as we experience now as tourists."

"This is a very nice experience, John, I am glad I signed up for this trip. It's a perfect balance of a tourist trip but still giving an experience to taste the culture of the nomads here in Inner Mongolia."

One of the four girls served me a slice of lamb meat.

"You can get traditionally prepared potato's and sauces on the side of the Yurt. Just a slice of lamb meat may not be enough to cover for your dinner."

Following John's advice, I walked up there and made sure I had enough food for dinner. John was right to put me on this side of the Yurt. When looking at the lamb served, the size of the slice I got and the number of people waiting for food, I think there would not be enough to provide all people. I walked back to the table where John got himself a slice of lamb as well.

"How many times do you get to eat this?" I asked him. "You're not getting sick yet of roasted lamb meat?"

"No, in fact, this is my favourite food. I am lucky to be here at least once a week and enjoy the food provided by the locals."

"Yes you are," I said after I tasted a part of the lamb. It did taste very well.

"How long does it need to roast a lamb-like this?"

"A few hours," John said. "But according to tradition, you can't just roast every lamb you see outside in the field. There are strict rules. They need to be one to two years old, well-fed and strong. These are prerequisites leading to a good, fresh taste and rich nutrition."

"Yes, I can imagine. The taste of this roasted lamb is extraordinary. I did not have it as tasty as this before. Which ingredients do they use? Anything special?"

"Not really. From what I know, they add salt, chilli pepper and cumin to the meat. You can furthermore add sweet sauce, shallots, onion, cucumber or lettuce but that depends on your personal taste. As you can see the lamb itself is pretty natural."

"Look, I have the crispy skin as well." I said while I pointed to my plate.

"That's actually the better part of the lamb, but some people do not like it."

Without saying much more, we enjoyed our slice of roasted lamb.

"I'll go check on the bus and whether the driver is waiting for us in the parking area," John said.

"I will tell the other people from our group as well. Let's meet over there in fifteen minutes from now."

I nodded. I checked my watch. If we would leave in about twenty minutes from now, we would indeed be back at the hotel around eight o'clock. The lamb meat with the side dishes had filled me quite well. I looked around and absorbed this unique environment again. Never ever did I spend a day among grandchildren of real nomads. The Ethnic Mongols are one of the fifty-five ethnic minorities officially recognised by the People's Republic of China. There are nearly six million Ethnic Mongols living in China. Roughly four million of them live in Inner Mongolia, mostly in the cities but even in Yurt communities surrounded by endless grasslands. The life they live is incomparable to the life I live in Shanghai. Are the people here happier than we city slickers generally are? Do they live surrounded by less stress, materialism and depression?

This afternoon I developed a little nostalgia for the Mongolian nomad's life. But, instead of buying groceries in Carrefour and simply fill my shopping basket with whatever I need, I would have to forage in droughts, and as a substitute to my comfortable tenth-floor master bedroom, I'd have to sleep in yurts instead. Cooking would happen on fires fuelled by dried dung instead of switching on my gas pits.

Could I consider this as an option in case Philips would not come with an offer? Move to Inner Mongolia and live a quiet life?

The need for project management training would be significantly less here. Perhaps I could teach English instead. Due to the lower cost of living a ten thousand RMB salary would provide me with more spending power here compared to Shanghai. But that nostalgia melted when thinking about my original future objectives. Moving here would certainly slow-down the path to a director position in a multinational company. And who needs horses now when there are cars?

Meanwhile, the four girls took care of what was left of both lambs. I could distinguish the bones of the ribs, legs and the head. Both were entirely consumed. The first tourists started to pack their bags and coats. I did so too. I'd love to come back here someday. Alone or with a new love. Stay for a night or two in a Yurt when the temperature during daytime is acceptable but gets cold during the night. Experience the extreme quietness and the beautiful sky full of stars.

I walked the dusty path towards the parking area. Six small busses were waiting, and when I got closer, our driver greeted me. I took place in the same seat as at the beginning of the afternoon and closed my eyes. I felt the bus moving, and the next thing I noticed was a hand upon my shoulder from John.

"Victor, wake up, we'll soon arrive at your hotel."

I must have slept in a wrong position. I felt my neck hurting when I looked out of the window. I did not recognise the street we entered.

"Tomorrow we're back at eight in the morning to pick you up for the day trip to the desert." I nodded with a sleepy expression on my face. It was nearly eight pm now. After arriving in the hotel, I just wanted to watch TV and fall asleep, to be energised for the desert trip tomorrow.

28

The Holiday Inn Hohhot Hotel - 08:03

After a good night of sleep and a breakfast consisting of black coffee that tasted as raw motor oil, paired with deep-fried dough sticks, the same bus passed by the hotel to pick me up for the desert tour. To make things a bit easier for John, I waited outside the hotel. There was a different group of tourists compared to yesterday. Where I was the only foreigner yesterday, I noticed a few Western faces in the back of the bus. They appeared like Russians or Eastern Europeans to me. As the Holiday Inn was again the final pick-up spot, I had not much choice for a seat. I walked halfway through the bus and choose to sit next to a Chinese gentleman in an aisle seat. From the way he was dressed and styled his hair, I could tell he was a civilised person. A carefully ironed white linen blouse and pants and white sports shoes. Dressed to visit the desert but in style. He smiled at me, and I shortly introduced myself as Victor.

"I'm Wilson, pleased to meet you."

Right at that moment, John took the microphone in his hand and introduced himself in Chinese to the tour participants. The same story followed as well in English. We were now on our way to the Gobi Desert, which would take a three-hour drive from Hohhot. John proposed to let us take a rest first, and once we got closer to the destination, he would come back with some Gobi Desert related information. I decided to close my eyes when Wilson poked my arm.

"Where are you from? America?" That's an assumption many Chinese have. You're foreign, so you must be American.

"No, I'm from the Netherlands, and you?"

It's one hundred per cent clear that Wilson is local, but when you ask a Chinese in China where they come from, they won't say China but the region or city they are from.

"I'm living in Shenzhen."

I knew Shenzhen. Once a fisher's village but since the Chinese government made it a Special Economic Zone in 1980, over fourteen million people moved in. That made Shenzhen today China's the highest ratio of migrant population to the total population (almost sixty-eight per cent), outstripping Shanghai, Beijing and Guangzhou by about thirty per cent.

"I flew into Shenzhen airport once but only saw the city skyline from the highway on the way to Huizhou. I've never been to downtown." Wilson nodded.

"My parents moved to Shenzhen after it became a special economic region because of its increasing economic prospects. They are originally from Inner Mongolia. I'm here to see how my parents and grandparents lived."

"Is this your first time to visit Inner Mongolia?"

"Yes."

"How old are you if I may ask?"

"Twenty-one."

It's not strange that a Chinese never visited his or her hometown, or a national landmark like the Great Wall. The distances between cities are long, after all. Shenzhen to Hohhot is nearly twenty-five hundred kilometres. That's not a distance you can easily bridge as a Chinese teenager.

"I live in Shanghai. I'm on holiday here to experience Inner Mongolia. Or at least a part of it. Where did your parents grow up?"

"In Baotou, it's a city on about a hundred and eighty kilometres from Hohhot and the largest city of Inner Mongolia by urban population."

"What do you know about your family background? Or are you here to search for that?"

"I know my families historical footprints. I am curious to link the stories I've been told with the places I visit on this trip. When looking at what happened back in the days, I think I should be lucky still to be here."

"But shouldn't we all? I mean, the impact of the industrial revolution, First and Second World War... I remember my grandfather used to play for a soccer team during the second world war and had to take a ferry back home. Together with some teammates, he preferred to stay the night and leave the next morning. The majority of the team took the ferry back, which was bombed by German soldiers, and they all died. If my grandfather had been on that ferry, we wouldn't have this conversation here."

Wilson had an impressed expression on his face.

"You had two world wars, but Inner Mongolia's history is a complicated one too. In 1931, Manchuria came under the control of the Japanese puppet state Manchukuo, taking some Mongol areas in the Manchurian provinces. Then Japan openly and fully invaded the Republic of China in 1937. The years that followed were hard for my grandparents. They faced different kinds of resistance movements. That changed in 1941 with the Soviet–Japanese Neutrality Pact after which Inner Mongolia was geographically used as a buffer zone between Japanese forces and the Soviet Union. Ten per cent of the Inner Mongolian population was trained to use weapons and fight a war in case things ran out of control. Inner Mongolia supported the Soviet Military against the Germans with the finance of several war units and half a million military horses. It had three hundred persons volunteering army fighting in the Eastern front. My grandparents were both kept under arms. They lived under occupation by Manchuria during the Second World War, but once this came to an end, the Chinese Communists gained control of Manchuria and the Inner Mongolian Communists with Soviet support. They established the Inner Mongolia Autonomous Region as we know it today in 1947."

"Wow, that is an impressive story too. I never heard stories of my grandparents using weapons in the second world war, though. But you know your family history well." Wilson nodded.

"We often talk about this during dinner. It is good to realise what your grandparents and their ancestors have done to give us a better life. They have ultimately built the fundament of your well-being today. I think we should have respect for them." I nodded yes.

"But when you are young you do not realise that enough. That only comes when you grow up and it for me it was too late to tell them."

"True," Wilson said.

"So, we have to keep their spirits alive by sharing their stories."

"I think you should become a historian. Or a travel guide like John."

I pointed into John's direction, who was taking an opportunity to have a nap on our three-hour journey.

"You know so much about Inner Mongolia's history." Wilson smiled.

"That's only a result of the many family dinners I had."

"True, but the topic has to interest you as well." Wilson nodded.

"I am interested to learn about history."

"What's your major in university?"

"Foreign Languages."

"I suggest you add a history minor to that."

I looked outside the window and noticed a change in the landscape again. The further we drove yesterday, the greener it became. Today shows the complete opposite. The longer we drive, the dryer the scenery looks. We're really heading towards the Gobi Desert.

"I'll close my eyes as well if you don't mind," I said to Wilson.

He nodded at me and did the same. The movement of the bus made me fall asleep again, and I woke up twenty minutes before we arrived because John had taken the microphone for a preliminary arrival talk.

"We almost arrived at our destination," John started.

"Allow me to give you a brief introduction." Wilson looked attentive.

"Did you know that the Gobi Desert is one of the largest deserts in the world? To be precise, Gobi is actually the largest in Asia and fifth largest desert in the world. It's stretching over China and

Mongolia. Actually, thirty per cent of the Mongolian territory is absorbed by the Gobi Desert, quite a bit."

One of the other foreign tourists raised her hand.

"I've heard that the Gobi Desert was once a sea, is that correct?" John nodded.

"Some geologists say so yes, after discovering fossilised coral heads and shells. For them, this was a clear indication that in ancient times, the Gobi Desert was once the bottom of a sea. As a result of this, many Chinese refer to Gobi as Han-Hal, which means dry sea in Mandarin."

"How can a sea transform to a desert?" the same tourist asked.

"Well, you're talking about a time-span of thousands of years," John explained.

"Throughout the years, Gobi suffered from having most of its rain blocked by the Himalayas. But this doesn't mean the desert receives zero precipitation. It still rains approximately a hundred seventy-seven millimetre on an annual basis. In comparison; Beijing receives an average of six hundred and ten millimetres per year."

Now Wilson raised his hand.

"Only five per cent of Gobi is actually sand dunes, right? Will we go there today?"

John smiled.

"Yes. We'll make sure you experience exactly that five per cent of the desert."

Some people on the bus looked relieved. I knew that most of the Gobi Desert is covered by steppes, yellow sand, mountains and because of the rain it received it is a home as well for camel breeders. In addition to other deserts, Gobi offers wildlife and vegetation a place to live. John continued:

"The Gobi Desert is home to some Silk Road communities. The Venetian explorer Marco Polo visited a couple of them during his thirteenth-century travels. This triggered the economy of then luxury trade goods such as silk, medicines, perfumes, jewels, glassware, spices and slaves. Those communities still use those visits in their marketing to lure tourists to their villages."

"Will we visit any of them as well today?" one of the other tourists asked, probably a Marco Polo fan.

To my satisfaction, John mentioned that this wasn't the case. I could totally envision how a community like this would look like; a small marketplace where we would be dropped for an hour just to walk around and shop tourist gadgets you actually don't need. I mean, it's not that Marco Polo visited that community just yesterday and that his footprints are still out there left in the sand, right? It's been seven hundred years ago. I would rather see endless sand dunes, have a camel ride and experience a desert in real life. In Western Europe, we do not have such a place we can visit. Yes, we can visit the Dunes of Loon and Drunen National Park in the Netherlands, which is called the *Brabant Sahara* but that's of course a joke compared to the Gobi Desert. I felt like we got a bit off-track now as the environment around us became noticeable dryer and less colourful. This was a piece of land in-between civilisation and what looks like the end of the world.

Soon the bus came to a stop on a gravelled parking place which was literally the border of us between the Gobi Desert. I got out of the bus and witnessed endless white golden sand dunes with every now and then little islands made of green grass and trees. We were pointed to a cable-car not far from the bus, which would transport us from the parking place to a camel community a few hundred meters away. I could see the cable cars slowly moving.

The last time I took a cable car must have been nearly twenty years ago in France. We used to have our family holiday in a ski resort in Tignes, located in the French Alps near the Italian border. I remember going there twice. I never understood why we as a family that never skied before visited a ski resort in the summer. The only objective of my parents was to get as close as possible to the sun during the summer holiday. The cable cars we took in France were closed to protect you from an eventual snowstorm. This cable car we would take in just a couple of minutes was completely open. Our feet would be hanging loosely in the air. The possibility of a sandstorm on the way to the camel station would leave us completely sand screened.

John made sure we all lined up in front of the cable car, counted all the tourists, and we accessed the incoming cars one by one. We first followed a steep hill up, which gave me a beautiful view over the Gobi Desert for as far as I could look. Ten meters below me, I could see the untouched sand altering from one dune into another. The low hanging morning sun created dark shadows in the little valleys. Not long after that, I noticed the camel community appearing on the horizon. There must have been a hundred camels gathered together on a flat part in the Gobi Desert, waiting for tourists to climb on their back. When we had our feet back on the sandy Gobi Desert ground, John took a moment to explain what was going to happen now.

"We are surrounded here by Bactrian Camels, they have an estimated population of more than one million, and approximately seven hundred thousand of them live in China and Mongolia combined."

I looked around. Some of them were standing, while others kneeled down in the sand. They looked healthy and calm.

"Unlike bears or koala's, camels are actually social animals who roam the deserts in search of food and water in groups with up to thirty other camels."

"Can camels be aggressive?" I asked. John laughed.

"There is no need to sign a waiver in case anything goes wrong. Camels are peaceful animals, where only the males might get aggressive when competing for females." I smiled.

"So, if I end up on a female camel and one of the male camels get jealous, I'm in trouble?"

"No, within this community, the hierarchy has been settled already. As well, you don't have to be afraid that in the middle of the trip your camel feels exhausted and makes a half-hearted attempt to do its job. They are pack animals and able to carry up to two hundred fifty kilos at a rate of forty-seven kilometre per day. But we won't get that far."

The camels looked into our direction now, as if they clearly knew what would be happening next. But before that, John added:

"Camels sleep roughly six hours per night. They can even sleep while standing, as this makes it easier for them to escape from any possible threats."

"What is the highest speed they can walk or run?"

"In case of severe danger, they may be able to run up to sixty-five kilometre an hour, but they rarely ever go this fast."

Some people had a relieved expression on their face. The first group of camels lined up, ready for the tourists to climb on their back. They waited in a line of seven camels, all with a ring through their nose and a chain to the saddle of the camel in front of them. After the shepherd said something in Mandarin all camels kneeled, and we all climbed up. It reminded me of the only time in my life I sat on the back of a horse and fell down, even before the horse started walking. When I comfortably sat on this back between two humps, I felt not only safer compared to sitting on a horseback but noticed the camel's long eyelashes and sealable nostrils, which help it cope with intense sandstorms. That's a comforting thought as well, even though the weather seemed as comfortable as it possibly could be.

The camels lifted themselves up in synchronisation from first to the last one and on another sign of the shepherd we slowly started moving. Many people think that camel humps are used for water storage, but that is not true. There is actually fat inside. The camel uses it as nourishment when food is scarce. Given this fact, all camels that accompanied us on this tour did not appear limp, which meant that they all enjoyed proper food and rest. When looking in the far distance, all I could see were endless sand dunes under a blue sky.

"Isn't this beautiful?" Wilson said.

I looked behind and noticed that he was right behind me.

"I do not hear anything except camels breathing and their foots moving in the sand." John sat on the first camel. On this moment, I did not know what to expect. Would we be walking here in a circle for an hour without any particular destination in mind? We slowly moved forward for about forty minutes until we came across a high dune, from where an oasis was visible next to a peaceful temple. An ancient Chinese tower was visible surrounded by lower rooms and a courtyard surrounded by a wall. John started explaining:

"The oasis we see here in front of us is according to Chinese legends the first one under the sun. There are many stories of what is actually in the oasis. We Chinese believe that this is a medicine oasis because there is grass growing, called seven-star grass. As well there is a special fish swimming there, called the iron back fish. The story is that if you've eaten both, you can live forever."

The tourists behind me mumbled to each other in not understandable Chinese. Maybe they thought both would be served for lunch?

"Business people travelling the silk road have stopped here for centuries to sleep and relax. Throughout those years it became a temple as well for pilgrim Buddhism. As of today, thousands of pilgrims are still coming here every year."

While we neared the temple, it seemed that we would be the only visitors. At the beginning of a paved road leading to the temple, the camels stopped and kneeled back in the sand so we could get off. We'd have to walk the last one hundred or so meter, which I welcomed. While we got closer to the temple, John continued talking:

"One of the most interesting stories of how this oasis came to be is that many years ago, all of the dunes around us were mountains."

To articulate this, John pointed in the far distance around us.

"They believed that demons were living in those mountains. One day, there was a traveller named Jiang Guo Lao who travelled with his donkey through this area. On both sides of his donkey, he had one large bag of sand to protect themselves from the dragons. At some point, they've met a naughty young boy who unsolicited opened the bags of sand hanging on the side of the donkey. The donkey got scared and started running all around, while the sand poured all out of the bags. This is the sand laying around us, and the donkey's hard stump on the floor created this oasis. People believe that on windy days you can still hear the demons cry covered in their mountains by a thick layer of sand."

Wilson, who was walking next to me now poked me and said:

"That's probably just the sound of moving sand." I giggled and raised my hand.

"That iron back fish, was it on the menu back in the days?"

"No, if that was the case everybody who visited this temple would live forever after simply ordering this fish from the menu. You had to actually fish in the oasis, and only the luckiest ones would catch one."

"And then one would run around to find the seven-star grass." Wilson added.

I could feel he believed in this story was as much - or actually as less as me. Just like the Bible, people will always find comfort or strength in this kind of stories.

We walked around in the temple while witnessing in the main hall a big statue of a goddess made out of camphor wood. It must have been five or so meters tall. The next hall, filled with gold characters on a green painted wall, hung a Ming Dynasty copper bell of three tons, I learned after Johns explanation. The temple had a greyish colour on the outside, similar to the sand environment it was surrounded by. A tree in the middle of the courtyard looked grey caused by the dust. The only shining asset here was the golden Buddha in front of the entrance to one of the main halls. John was making an effort to get the group back together. It started to look cloudy. We walked back to the camels, who were still there patiently waiting for us. While I climbed on the camel, I felt my phone buzzing. An unknown number from Shanghai. Who could that be?

"Hello, this is Victor speaking," I said while the camel chain started moving again.

"Good morning Victor, this is Diana from Philips. I'm calling with hopefully good news. We reviewed your interview and came to the conclusion that you are suitable for the position of project manager."

I jumped up, but as I was sitting on a camel, I could not run around and celebrate.

"Thank you! I'm so happy to hear that!" "Let me confirm your email address, that's just your full name @ Hotmail dot com, right?"

"That's correct."

"Keep an eye on that, I will send you a letter of intention and a job offer later this afternoon. That will have all the details on your package and benefits. Let me know if you have any questions regarding that."

This is the call where I was waiting so long for. Tomorrow I would arrive back into Shanghai with a job offer in the pocket. Who could have thought about that?

"I will check and let you know. Thank you so much again, this made my day!"

"Thank you as well Victor, we'll talk soon."

I put the phone safely in my pocket, I did not want to lose it here in the desert. Right on that moment, the sun came out, lighting up my world even more. Should I call Gerald to say thanks? Maybe not yet. As the initiator of helping me back into Philips, he would anyway know about the offer. He must have even approved it. I would send him an email back later tonight in the hotel.

"You seem excited," I heard from behind. It was Wilson.

"Was that your girlfriend calling?" I laughed.

"No, it was the human resource director of a company I had an interview with last week with a job offer.

"Congratulations Victor!" Wilson said while our camels slowly moved forward.

"I've been waiting over a week for this!" "Which company did you have the interview with?"

"Philips Lighting, have you heard about them? Most people know Philips from consumer electronics, not from lighting." "I've seen Philips lights in the supermarket near my home,"

Wilson confirmed. Just like after I got the job offer from Jiao Tong University, I wanted to call my parents and friends to tell them about this exciting news, but it was just seven in the morning in the Netherlands. That would have to wait a little bit. Who could have imagined this? For almost a year I've been hoping to get the opportunity to re-join Philips, and right on the moment I'm sitting between two humps on the back of a Bactrian camel in the Gobi Desert I receive the redeeming call. The camel had exactly the same expression on his face since the moment we first met, and did not seem to be bothered with my jump at all. We continued walking, and the camel station appeared back on the horizon. There were water bowls installed as refreshment for the camels who spend most of the past one and a half hour walking. John had thought about us too with bottled water. Wilson grabbed two bottles of water, walked up to me and handed me one. Despite the fact that we sat down most of the time, I felt thirsty.

"What is next for you?" Wilson asked me.

"Hmm, not much if you're talking about Inner Mongolia. I will go back to the hotel, have a good night of sleep and take an early morning flight back to Shanghai. In three days I will be back in the north, as I will go to Beijing for a concert."

Wilson smiled.

"And I assume you can't wait to start working now?" I laughed.

"Partially yes. I came here to clear my mind from the recent workload I had from my teaching job and a girl who suddenly disappeared in my life. I had to clear a few things out for myself."

"A girl who suddenly disappeared? How did that happen?"

"Well, we were seeing each other for a couple of months, just not so long yet. We enjoyed dinners together, watched movies, had long conversations... She was funny and cute. I enjoyed every minute we spent together. She suddenly sent me a text message all out of nothing that she had to leave to her hometown to take care of her parents. We did not even have the time to say goodbye. Oddly enough, I never told her how much I liked her and fully appreciated her love and thoughtfulness."

Wilson thought for a moment.

"That's not abnormal for a Chinese girl. If she is an only child and her parents are facing health issues - especially in smaller villages there are no facilities or other people to look after them. She had to do this in expectation of her family."

"But why so sudden? She must have known this earlier than the ten-hour in advance of her flight she told me?"

"Yes, but seeing you on the night before her departure would only make things more difficult. Believe me, it is hard enough for her to leave a stable life in Shanghai with a job and a relationship. She probably did not want to but had no choice. But she would never tell you." I sighed and looked in the far distance.

"I thought she might not have loved or liked me enough."

"No, don't you think that. To me, it seems she was too heartbroken to face you before departure to her hometown. Have you talked to her since?"

"No, we did not have any contact. It's possibly better for now."

We both stared in the distance, not saying anything at all. Possibly because I did not have anything to add and I actually wanted to avoid thinking about Linda, that was one of the reasons to be here. But he could be right. His explanation did put things a bit more into perspective. Wilson probably felt he had entered a sensitive part of me.

"What is next for you?" I asked. Wilson turned back to me.

"I'll be taking the train tomorrow morning early. It will take me roughly three hours to arrive in Baotou. I have family living there, and they have invited me to stay with them for a couple of days. It would be interesting to get to know them better and further learn about our family history." I nodded. Wilson continued:

"Did you know that Inner Mongolia has seen considerable development since Deng Xiaoping instituted Chinese economic reform in 1978?"

"No, actually not."

"Everybody is only talking about the creation of Shenzhen as experimental ground for practising market capitalism bordered by the community but guided by the Supremes of socialism with Chinese characteristics, not so much about Inner Mongolia."

"Actually since 2000, which is nine years now, Inner Mongolia's GDP growth has been the highest in the country, together with Guangdong, which was mainly driven by Shenzhen and Guangzhou. The success here is largely owed to the success of natural resource industries in the region."

I was fascinated by Wilson's intellectual capability. But I realised as well that just like Cindy and hundreds of other million students - he must have had school for six and a half day per week until graduation. And besides that, the start of the Chinese economic reform is still a significant milestone in Chinese history. Something comparable to the European Industrial Revolution in the seventeenth and eighteenth century.

"GDP growth here in Inner Mongolia has continually been over ten per cent, even fifteen per cent and connections with the Wolf Economy to the north has helped development. But this growth came at a cost with a lot of pollution and demolition of the grasslands."

"Exactly like what happened during our Industrial Revolution. But Wolf Economy? What's that?" I asked. I've never heard of that term.

"This was initiated by Ganhuyag Chuluun Hutagt and after that used by Renaissance Capital in their blue sky report about Inner Mongolia. They predicted that Mongolia would become the Mongolian wolf as they described it and would bring "unstoppable" economic growth." I nodded.

"But to get those natural resources out of the ground, you have to build mines and need workers."

"Correct, so the local government attracted ethnic Chinese to migrate from other regions to stimulate the economy, and urbanised the rural nomads and peasants. But this led to huge amounts of corruption and waste in public spending in for example Ordos City. And not to mention uneven wealth distribution among ethnic groups."

"So that resulted in the fact that now roughly eighty per cent of the population in Inner Mongolia is Han Chinese, while the Mongols only contribute seventeen per cent of the population."

"True. And then there are still some minorities called Manchu, Hui, Dofand Evenks. They contribute roughly eight hundred thousand people to the region."

"So are your parents from Mongolian origin?"

"Yes. They were born and raised in Baotou. But when the opportunity was there to move to Shenzhen, they left."

"But I can imagine that everybody wanted to move to Shenzhen after hearing about the opening of the special economic zone. How did they manage that?"

"Only people with a specific profession, education or experience in a particular field could apply for the hukou. You may have heard about this household registration system?"

"Yes."

"My parents are lawyers. With all those new people moving into the city, they could use quite a few lawyers too."

On that moment John walked up to us.

"The bus is ready to leave, will you come too?"

We walked towards the bus, and we were the only two persons still missing. Wilson wrote his number on a small piece of paper in case I would visit Shenzhen in the near future.

"You can stay at my home if you want."

"Thank you for that offer, it would be nice to visit Shenzhen someday, and walk through downtown instead of seeing the city skyline from a highway."

Wilson handed the paper to me, and we entered the bus. As we were the last two to join, we could not sit together anymore.

"Enjoy the continuation of your trip here in Inner Mongolia. I am sure you'll discover more interesting facts about your family." Wilson nodded and shook my hand.

"We'll stay in touch."

Now I had an aisle seat in the back of the small bus. Tired as I was from the past two days, I decided to have a nap on the return to Hohhot.

The talk with Wilson about the possible incentive from Linda to leave Shanghai actually made sense. His explanation made me feel better, or at least more acceptable. I am sure she must be still thinking about me and the times we spent together. I could understand that she would choose her family over me, firstly because we did not know each other long and well, and who says I will live in Shanghai for the rest of my life? Or China? Probably not. I may relocate back to Europe or another country in Asia, which would put pressure on a long-term relationship if she doesn't have the intention to move overseas. I just wish she will be happy and find a guy she loves, rather than living an unhappy life in an arranged marriage. With this in mind, I closed my eyes and dozed off quick, smoothened by the moving bus.

29

Shanghai Hongqiao Airport - 07:40

We were late this morning. Late because we slept too late last night. Friday nights are to enjoy. Serena came to visit me for dinner after she finished work. I cooked pasta, my favourite chicken with cherry tomato, cream, mushroom and Mediterranean herbs, and we opened a bottle of wine. Serena originally planned to go home so she could pack her luggage and we would then meet the next morning at the airport for our flight to Beijing. But she decided to stay over, we finished the bottle of wine and slept too late. This morning the third alarm woke us up. Luckily, I had everything already packed, and traffic was reasonably smooth on a Saturday morning otherwise we may have missed our flight. There we sat at the gate. Both a coffee in our hands. I with a little trolley as hand luggage and Serena in the same clothes as she arrived in my apartment yesterday.

"I have asked my family to prepare some clothes for me." She ensured me when we boarded the aeroplane.

Flying with Air China this morning was one of the cheaper options. Now I understood why. They had a Boeing 747 to fill. When we all sat down, and the aeroplane started taxiing, I looked around and concluded that they did not succeed to do so. While the cabin crew was going through the emergency instructions, I looked outside the small aeroplane window. Shanghai was unusually sunny today. Serena already closed her eyes, ready to catch up with some of the missed hours of sleep from last night. I thought about how quickly things can go and how incredibly lucky I was. Only a month or so ago I met Serena in the subway. We get to know each other, hang out for a few times and two weeks ago I read about this first Keane concert in China. I got very excited because it's not easy to keep up with Western artists and their concerts since I live in China. The problem I encountered was that the concert was organised as a closed party to celebrate the official launch of the Burberry brand in China. It was invitees only, so no tickets were sold to the public.

Now Serena's cousin works in media relations and could get us two tickets via her network. I haven't seen Keane live since their War Child concert in London, which I saw together with two of my Dutch friends. That's two years ago now. A long time ago given the frequency of concerts I visited while living in the Netherlands. I used to see them two or three times per year. The good thing about flying so early is that the risk of delay is small. Afternoon or early evening flights are often standard delayed with at least an hour. We had more than enough time to arrive in Beijing, check-in the hotel, quickly meet for dinner with Serena's cousin and head to the CCTV building where the concert takes place.

Meanwhile, Serena placed her head against my shoulder. She wore her blue caterpillar over a greyish t-shirt with a drawing of yellow flowers, holding her hands closed over her belly. Despite the relatively short time, we knew each other she must have felt comfortable being around me. So did I. It felt natural. As if we knew each other already for a long time. I looked at a passenger on the other side of the aisle, who was reading a book and carefully underlined sentences with a yellow pencil. Should I tell him that research concluded that you actually forget eighty per cent of all the text you underline or mark? Never mind.

Out of boredom, I reached out for the Air China magazine. But it was published completely in Chinese, so I could just look colourful pictures of exotic travel destinations, city trips and commercials of luxury brands. As a result, I went through it quickly and decided to close my eyes for the remainder of the flight. We'd have a busy day ahead of us. The next thing I knew was a hard bump which indicates turbulence or touch-down. I looked outside through the window and saw the brand-new Beijing's International Airport. The wing flaps came up, causing forward pressure and buffeting while the Boeing 747 was slowing down. From what I could hear from the first officer's message is that it was a comfortable eighteen degrees and sunny weather in Beijing. Serena was awake too and smiled at me.

"Did you have a good flight?" She asked.

"Yes, I had. Probably the quickest in my life. I slept all at the time."

I rubbed my eyes.

"It would be nice to have a coffee after we get out of the plane." Serena nodded.

As our seats were close to the exit, it was relatively easy to leave the aircraft. This airport looked brand new. People walked across slimming corridors and gates where numbered in blackboards with yellow numbers. We walked straight towards the taxis. A few people were lined up, but the supply of taxi's was enough to accommodate us to the city in a quick manner.

"Let's go to the hotel first to drop the luggage, then do a bit of sightseeing and meet with your cousin for dinner and head off on-time to the CCTV building for the concert. According to the website, Keane will start playing only at eight pm in the evening, so we do not have to hurry."

Serena nodded again. Meanwhile, the taxi organiser assigned us to taxi stand number seventeen. The taxi drove up and stopped next to us. The car itself was an old yellow Volkswagen with a green line on the side. The windows were open, which indicated that the driver had been smoking in the car just now or the air conditioning did not work. Or perhaps both. The driver stepped out and helped me to put my luggage in the trunk. I opened the door for Serena, and we both stepped in. The seats were covered with a white cotton layer. The dirty look of it exposed how many people had been sitting in this taxi before. We started driving. The strong smell of burned kerosene hung in the car. Serena told the taxi driver in Mandarin where we had to go. It was easier to let her explain this to the driver directly. We started driving, and soon after we got out of the airport, the air quality became better.

I never felt really safe in Chinese taxis. The only benefit you can give Chinese drivers is that they know how to handle situations where a foreigner would end up in a crash. They have skills and reflexes we foreigners do not have. But despite that, the drivers often do not look healthy. They work long shifts. I remembered a taxi driver that dozed away on the highway. I had to keep on talking to him to make sure he did not close his eyes for more than two seconds. This driver seemed awake, but we were driving with all windows open on the highway. The only person wearing a seatbelt was the driver as the seatbelts on the backseat were covered with the white linen sheets. You'd rather not end up in a crash. As if Serena could read my worried face, she put her hand on my leg. The highway between the airport and the city still had special Olympic Games lanes, indicated by the Olympic Games logos painted on the highway surface.

"Have you had a chance to visit any of the Olympic Games Serena?"

"Yes, I went to see a couple of volleyball and basketball games in the Olympic Park and an athletic game in the Bird Nest. Have you seen any?"

"No, unfortunately not. I was in the Netherlands at that time. It was after my internship in Philips and did not decide yet on whether I wanted to go back to China. I remember seeing the opening ceremony in August on TV, it was imposing." Serena agreed.

"The Olympic Games were so important for many of the Chinese people. It was one of the first major worldwide events held in China. It made the people real proud, and many saw it as a milestone in Chinese history. It brought the country a lot of prosperity." I nodded.

"I never really followed the Olympic Games, though. I follow European and World championships in soccer."

Meanwhile, the taxi took a left turn onto another highway.

"Are we still going the right way?" I informed.

"Yes, our hotel is located in Chaoyang district."

The surrounding looked as if we were heading to the city. It gradually changed from the countryside to a developed world.

"We're almost there, Victor." I smiled at her and put my hand on hers.

She was right, it only took us a couple of more minutes to arrive in front of the hotel. The front of the hotel had an authentic Chinese look, as I could remember from one of the pictures on the website where I booked the hotel. It had a red arch with Chinese lanterns hanging on its facade. It did not look like anything in comparison with the hotel where Mr Wang took me out for dinner. I paid eighty-three RMB for the taxi, and we crossed the sidewalk towards the entrance of the hotel.

"I think it's still too early to check-in," noticed Serena.

"Check-in usually starts around two or three o'clock."

She was right. We could only drop my luggage behind the reception as check-in started in three hours from now.

"Let's come back here sometime halfway the afternoon before we get ready to meet with your cousin for dinner."

"Where shall we go now?" Serena asked.

"We are on walking distance from 798 Art District. Let's go there, and we can check out some art galleries, enjoy a coffee and have lunch."

"That sounds like a good plan."

We left the hotel and walked on a paved sideway into the north direction. On our left side cars, motors and bikes passed by. On the right side, several small shops were located. I looked into each of them while we passed by. Some offered lighting products, others pipe equipment, wooden plates for construction, and a beef soup restaurant. The owner had twinkling eyes when he saw us and welcomed us in his restaurant. It did not look as if he maintained a high level of hygiene. We continued our walk.

"See, there in front of us at the square is one of the main entrances of the 798 Art District."

A building with glass facade came closer with every step we set. When we were close enough, we discovered it was built in front of the original Factory #798. Old factory equipment was visible through the dusty windows. A rusted gantry crane made the scene of an old factory complete.

"This place is breathing history, Serena." I said.

"Ground breaking for the factory started back in 1954, as part of a military-industrial cooperation between the Soviet Union and the People's Republic of China. It first saw production in 1957 after a big opening ceremony attended by high officials of the Chinese Communist party and East German government representatives. The East Germans ended up as a part of this project because the Soviet Union did not feel like to accept a project to produce modern electronic components. On the Soviet Union's suggestion, the Chinese turned to East Germany."

"How do you know all that?" Serena asked.

"I did a bit of research to this art district before. And I have to be honest to you that I choose this hotel because it was close to the art district."

"Even you as a foreigner know more about this than I do as a local Beijing girl."

I laughed.

"As a foreigner, I may have more interest in this. After I visited 50 Mogashan Road in Shanghai, I became a fan of these art districts."

Serena seemed triggered by my story.

"By when did the factory turn into an art district? Only recently?"

"Well, during Deng Xiaoping's reforms in the 1980s the factory became a thorn in the eye of the Chinese government. Where many state-owned enterprises received governmental subsidy and support, factories like this could not sustain competition. As a result, by the late 1980s and early 1990s, most sub-factories had ceased production, and sixty per cent of the workers had been laid off. What was left at that point was a management team with one real estate-oriented mission: overseeing the industrial park and find tenants and renters for the abandoned buildings. They succeeded doing so in 1995 when the Beijing's Central Academy of Fine Arts was looking for a cheap location for their workshop away from downtown Beijing. Downtown rental prices significantly increased. That started as a temporary move but became permanent in the year 2000. Rent at that time was only zero point eight RMB per square meter per day. This was for artists a key as they did not charge visitors to enter their galleries. Their income depends a lot on the sales of their paints and art. From the moment when in 2001 an American art bookstore, publishing office and gallery owner moved in, more artists were triggered by low rent and the art community. Ever since then the popularity of the art district was complete with coffee shops, galleries, restaurants, publishing firms, designers and high-end tailor shops. Luxury brands as Sony, Omega, Christian Dior, Toyota, Shell have even organised promotion and launch events."

Serena looked interested at me.

"I'm impressed by your knowledge Victor,"

She said while walked inside the 798 Space gallery. It had a high wall on one side with windows just under the bending ceiling and stretching the entire length. The building was German engineered with windows facing the north, so optimal use could be made from the sun and shadows inside were kept to a minimum. As the weather was cloudy now, neither sunshine nor shadows were visible inside this grey rectangular-shaped building.

"What is written in those big red Chinese characters on the ceiling arches over there?" I pointed to the right. Serena took a few seconds to read what was written.

"Oh, those are old Maoist slogans."

Same as the windows, they stretched over the entire ceiling. Unimpressed as Serena was, she wondered further. She is the perfect example of the Chinese millennial generation who does not give a fuck about politics. Knowing that they can't escape the system they live within the social boundaries set by the government, paying as less as possible attention to propaganda on television and in the media. On the other hand, many of the art exposed in the 798 Art District or 50 Mogashan Road is inspired by propaganda from the Chinese Communist Party in the nineteen fifties and sixties. I can artistically learn about Chinese history. For Serena and a billion others, it is something they must have faced in school daily. They had to know these texts by hard as part of their education.

We left the building through the backdoor and walked onto another square. This was the joint factory 718, with two steal chimney's protruding the building's roof. Horizontal pipelines crossed the road on about four-meter height supported by poles so cars could drive underneath if required.

"Let's check out that gallery," Serena suggested.

We walked inside. The first thing I saw was a big paint of the world map. Countries were coloured in green, yellow, grey and orange. The sea was in blue. I tried to understand why particular countries had particular colours. Could they be linked economically? Or perhaps politically? I could not distinguish any relations. It could only be the imagination of the artist. This is what I like about modern art. It makes you think and wondering what message the artist would like to send.

The next artwork was a meters long keyboard. It stretched in a twenty-degree angle on a white wall. A few meters further three roots used for cooking were laying on a weight measurer. The measurer was on, indicating that the roots had a combined weight of a bit more than twelve hundred grams. An exposition with red light followed, where an entire hall was completely darkened. From different angles, red lasers were illuminating the room, resulting in thousands of red dots all over the surface. Some bigger dots, some were smaller. While I was walking through the hall, Serena laughed.

"You look like you're having a massive disease with all those red dots over your body!" I looked at Serena.

"And so do you," I giggled.

A little bit further, a white table was illuminated as well by a flow of red dots. By walking through this room, you would almost forget that there is still daylight once you walk out of this space.

"Let's go and have some lunch. There must be some good places around here."

We ultimately found a cafe where we ordered two pasta's and a cappuccino. I looked at my watch.

"What time is your cousin able to meet us with your clothes and the invitation to tonight's concert?"

"I don't know. She'll get off work at five o'clock. Let me text her."

I took a sip of my cappuccino. Serena's phone received an answer.

"She can meet with us at five-thirty in a Spanish restaurant near Sanlitun."

"Alright, that's still a little while. We can check-in the hotel now, relax for a little while and head-off towards Sanlitun to meet your cousin."

"Sure thing!" said Serena while she reached out over the table to my hand, with her head supporting on her other arm. She smiled.

"It's nice to be here in Beijing with you."

After we finished our coffee, we walked back to our hotel. Serena did the check-in, and we followed the elevator up to the third floor of the building. In total, this hotel had eight floors. The room looked as traditional as the front of the hotel. It had a green avocado coloured carpet in a small corridor leading first to a small corner where a table was located. All furniture, and as well a part of the wall was made out of dark heavy wood. Another small corridor led to the bedroom. The bed was made from the same dark wood as the other furniture. I was only missing a few red lanterns instead of the small chandelier hanging on the ceiling in the middle of the room.

"I like the traditional style of the room," Serena said.

Where I usually stayed in Western-branded hotels, I actually liked this style for a change as well.

"Yes, it is indeed an interesting design."

I laid and stretched myself out on the bed. Serena first put one knee on the bed, then crawled on her knees towards me. She put her head on my chest.

"You know, it's difficult for us to be exposed to good foreign music in China," Serena added.

"Most of the foreign artists here are commercial mainstream artists like Celine Dion, Beyonce, Elton John and Kylie Minogue. The real good alternative music from smaller bands is hard to listen to."

"Yes, but that is why you have me. I can introduce you to some good music from Europe. You did not listen to Thirteen Senses or A Balladeer yet. They are one of the most underestimated bands of this moment."

I put my right arm around Serena and pressed her firmly against me. I did not know where this was going to end. In fact, we only knew each other for a month or so. This was still all very new for us. We lay there for a while without saying a word to each other. All I could hear was the traffic passing by on the street in front of the hotel.

"Let's get ready and get ourselves in a taxi towards the restaurant where we will meet your cousin," I said:

"I do not want to risk missing out on those tickets." Serena laughed.

"She's not the person to give them away to somebody else Victor, those tickets are safe in her hands." I giggled.

"I don't doubt that. By the way, how will you introduce me to her? She may be gossiping in your family about us being in Beijing."

"No, she won't. My family actually do not know that I am in Beijing now."

"What?! You did not even tell them?"

"We are only here for two days. Actually, not even two full days. It is too short. And I do not want them to think that I am going to marry you."

"Well, you can just explain that to them, right?"

"Explain what?"

"That I am just a friend and that we are in Beijing to enjoy a concert?"

"But then they would expect me to stay at their home, and you stay by yourself in a hotel."

"Hmmm, okay. That makes sense. They must be very protective of you."

"Yes, as long as they do not know in detail what I am doing, they are fine with me living in Shanghai."

"Like accepting a telephone number from a total stranger, you've just met twenty minutes earlier in the subway?" Serena giggled.

"Such as that yes."

We left the hotel room and took the elevator down together with two older couples from a higher floor. I could see they were from other provinces, probably spending their holiday in Beijing. They looked with a decrying expression on their face to us. A tall foreigner with a young Chinese girl in a hotel. The older man stared at me.

"Ni hao!" I said with a smile on my face.

As if he did not expect me to speak Chinese, he nodded something back. Serena giggled with her hand in front of her mouth. Luckily for all of us, there was the ping from the elevator that we arrived at the ground floor. Once the door opened, we went out first.

"Come quickly, let's take the first taxi which is waiting there," I said when I pointed to the entrance.

"What you did there was quite funny,"

Serena said while we stepped into the taxi.

"Well, I am used to people staring at me as if I am an alien who just arrived from another planet. Some of them react shocked or shy when I start talking to them. It seems nobody expects me to say something."

"But you have to understand. They may have travelled from a remote area in China, and you might have been the first foreigner they have seen in their life!"

"Yes. And then imagine you end up with one during the first day of your holiday in a two square meter elevator. No chance to escape. I can hardly think of a more shocking experience."

"Exactly!"

I looked out of the window and saw traffic getting worse towards rush hour.

"This is what I don't like about Beijing." I said.

"No matter where you go, it always takes at least one hour to go from A to B. You're always stuck in traffic, no matter what time of the day."

"That is because many taxi drivers choose to drive on one of the four city rings, so you often get a bit of a city tour."

"But is Shanghai so much better?"

"I think so. Within Puxi, I can arrive pretty much anywhere within twenty-five minutes. If from Pudong to Puxi, probably maximum forty minutes."

"Do taxi drivers try to cheat on you as a foreigner?"

"Not really, I can usually intervene verbally in Chinese quite early when it happens. The fact that I speak already Chinese when I get into the taxi might give them an impression that I am a local foreigner."

"Yes, true. What is the most you ever paid because of a city tour?" I thought.

"Actually nothing. I once ran out of a taxi from a driver who was giving me an obvious city tour. He was driving fine, but at some point, he took a left turn instead of a right turn. He drove basically away from where we had to go to. I started complaining in Chinese, but he said this was the right direction. At some point, the taxi meter was already indicating ninety RMB, where I should have paid no more than forty. So I got angry, and he stopped the taxi because he thought I would pay and step out. But once he stopped the taxi, I opened the door and ran away."

"So, what did the driver do?"

"He shouted at me, but I do not think he ran after me. Then he would have to leave his taxi full of cash behind to chase a foreigner with legs twice as long as his. And besides that, those drivers are smoking and sitting all day, sprinting one hundred meters would probably mean an end to his life."

"I can understand you did that." Serena said.

"Yes, otherwise he felt good about ripping off a foreigner that night. Now I felt good because I wouldn't let this driver cheat on me. I took another taxi a few blocks further and drove back home for like thirty RMB. I just did not want to give him this victory. I did not thought it over and ran. But I hope I do not have to do that again."

Serena looked out of the window.
"So far, this driver is keeping track. I think we can arrive within a minute or ten. Let me call my cousin."

She opened her bag and searched for her phone. Not long after that she said

"Wei...?" and started talking in Mandarin. While she still had the phone on her ear, she put her hand over the phone and whispered:

"She is already in the restaurant." Then she turned back to the phone and said again in Mandarin:

"Okay, we will be there in about ten minutes. See you soon!"

Beijing was actually surprisingly clear now. The sun was positioned between immense skyscrapers in the second inner-city ring.

Within the heart of the city, skyscrapers are not allowed. No buildings are allowed to be higher than government buildings. With all respect, it looks like a big village out there. Once you get out of the inner-city ring, a new cityscape arises. We now drove from the highway onto a smaller road. The sideway was occupied by pedestrians. I keep being amazed by the high number of people on the street during daytime in big Chinese cities. As if they do not have a job? Or is everybody working different shifts?

"Ah, I have been here before," I said to Serena when I recognised a shopping mall and some small shops.

"Yes, we're getting closer to Sanlitun now. What a coincidence that you recognise just this part of the city."

"Well, I even know some of the neighbourhoods around the Forbidden City, the Summer Palace and towards the Great Wall. But Sanlitun happened to be one of the places I have been before yes. At least the fact that I still recognise the neighbourhood of Sanlitun proofs that I wasn't completely drunk when I was here. I'm sure many foreigners can't remember much of Sanlitun anymore." Serena giggled.

"I've never seen you drunk. That would be quite an interesting experience."

A few minutes later, Serena directed the driver to stop, it seemed we arrived at our dinner destination. I paid a little bit over fifty RMB to the taxi driver and told him to keep the change of three RMB.

"There is the restaurant," and Serena pointed to a white building in front of us. It was an authentic Spanish restaurant, or at least that was written on the facade. The name of the restaurant was Carmen Spanish Restaurant. The green blinds were open and offered a nice and cosy view inside. We walked in, and despite the early time for dinner, quite some tables were occupied already. The left side of the restaurant had bar tables, where on the right side, normal tables were settled. All seats were in the same green tint as the blinds. While we walked between tables full of Spanish tapas, fish, paella and ham, suddenly a lady lifted her arm in the air.

"Ah, there she is!" Serena said excitedly. We walked towards the table, and I moved a chair so Serena could slip in. Before doing so, she hugged her cousin.

"It's been a while!"

"It is so nice to see you again. We hardly see you anymore since you moved to Shanghai." Then her cousin turned to me.

"Hi, my name is Janice, so nice to meet you!"

"My name is Victor, nice to meet you too!"

We all sat down, and Janice immediately started to talk to Serena. I browsed the menu and acted as if I was not paying attention, I could hear her asking whether I was the new boyfriend. Serena denied and stated that I was just a good friend. Then her cousin handed over her clothes, and they started talking about life in Shanghai.

"Sorry to interrupt your nice little catch-up, shall I meanwhile order some food for us?"

"Oh yes, sure Victor, no problem."

I browsed the menu, got the attention of a waiter and decided to order a two sort of ham salad and a bowl with paella. I added a beer for myself and for Serena a smoothie. Janice already ordered a tea for herself.

"So how do you like Beijing Victor? Is it your first time to come here?"

"No, it is actually the third time. When I was doing my internship earlier this year, I came here with some friends. And the second time was with my brother. Both trips were just three days, quite short trips. It's nice to be back but honestly, I like Shanghai better." I laughed.

"Why?" Janice asked.

"Well, I think Shanghai is more developed, and the city centre is smaller, so you don't have to travel that far to go from A to B."

I did not mention the pollution, that would probably not be good at this point. Shanghai's air isn't clear blue recently, but at least better compared to Beijing. Here they suffer more from coal mines and the fact that Beijing is not a sea city.

"But never mind, it is nice to travel here. And when I have family or friends over from the Netherlands, I will surely show them around in Beijing."

The smoothie and beer were served.

"Cheers, ladies," I said. "Thank you so much for arranging the tickets for tonight's Keane concert." Janice smiled.

"No problem," she said.

"We had a few left-over tickets in our company, so it was no issue to pass them on to you."

"It really means a lot to me," I said.

"This is the first-ever Keane show in China."

"I actually do not know them," Janice said.

"Well, he listens to them continually." Serena explained.

"Actually, they are not very famous in China. They have done shows in Japan, Taiwan, Hong Kong, and South East Asia but somehow not in Mainland China yet."

Janice grabbed her Gucci bag and placed a white envelope on the table. "Here are your tickets. Don't forget them."

The waiter walked by our table to serve us the drinks with an amuse. I took a sip of my beer.

"What is it you actually do for a living Janice?"

"I'm working as a manager for a local media company here in Beijing. We help companies to advise companies on how and where to advertise, and on how to present a positive picture of themselves to the public."

"Ah, right. Along the way or on a project basis?"

"Both, it depends on how much they have to spend. And as well on the complexity of the project."

"How about yourself?" Janice asked.

"I am teaching project management in Shanghai Jiao Tong University, but on a part-time basis. Although I am teaching for three to six hours per week, class preparation is nearly a full-time job."

"That sounds interesting. Jiao Tong University is a famous and well recognised university in China. We have Tsinghua University and Peking University here which are in the top hundred best universities in the world.

"Yes, I know. In Shanghai, we have Fudan University and Jiao Tong University, which are in the top two hundred."

"Not bad at all, Victor!"

"Well, it's just a part-time job, It doesn't really mean a lot."

"Don't say that Victor," Serena interrupted who followed the entire conversation.

"If you could not inform, educate and entertain a group of twenty students, they would not offer you this job."

I took another sip of my beer. It is good she did not know how I actually got this job. I do not feel there was not such a high threshold to get this job. But getting a job is one thing, keeping it is another.

The ham salad was served, containing slices of Jamón Ibérico ham.

"This looks delicious," Serena said.

"It does. These are two fine pieces of Spanish ham." I added.

There were two beds with lettuce around with drips of green dressing. I let Serena and Janice try first.

"They're quite salty, but taste good." Serena said.

I tried a piece too. We ate the ham in silence, each enjoying the authentic taste of Spain.

"Have you been to Spain?" Janice asked both Serena and me. I waited for Serena to answer first.

"Yes I did, during my study abroad in Italy, I travelled around in Europe quite extensively. Spain was one of the countries. I have been in Holland too," Serena said while she looked at me and chewed on the Jamón Ibérico ham. Ignoring her trip to the Netherlands, I answered Janice first.

"Me too, I have been to Barcelona and the Costa Brava with two friends. It was actually the time I decided to book a ticket back to China."

"How did you like it? Do you recommend me to visit Spain someday?"

"It was nice yes, we stayed on campings though. Next time I would prefer to stay in a hotel."

Soon after that, the paella was served. It was a bowl big enough for the three of us to eat from. The dish looked good. Hips of tiger prawns, mussels and clams with onion, tomato, beans, green peas, smoked paprika and fresh chopped rosemary on top. The attractive smell of it made you want to start eating instantly, but I let Janice and Serena try first. Once they filled their plate, I did so too. We finished the dish mostly in silence, an indication of how good the dish quality was. While Serena and Janice were talking in Chinese, I asked for the bill and paid the dinner.

"Let's get going soon," I said to Serena while the waiter came back with the change.

"I do not want to end up in a traffic jam and miss like half of the concert."

Serena and Janice understood my hurry as they started packing their belongings quite soon. While we walked through the restaurant towards the exit, I noticed that it was full now, we were lucky to be here relatively early. Outside the restaurant, Serena hugged Janice and said in Mandarin that they should stay in touch. Meanwhile, I got us a taxi and explained to the taxi driver where to head to.

"It was so nice to meet Janice for dinner," Serena said.

"We do not see each other enough, unfortunately. I wish there was more time."

While our taxi joined the tale of what seemed a long traffic jam, I comforted Serena by saying that as long as they both wanted it, there would be enough opportunities to meet in the future. Serena nodded.

While we were standing still on a road in the middle of Beijing, I saw two people on a tricycle full of construction trash moving between cars. Assuming they were married, the husband on the bike controlling the pedals and his wife pushing on the back. Both wheels only had a few centimetres to merge between the cars on the road. When they passed us, the taxi driver shouted something to them, something I assumed was not a friendly greeting. The tricycle owners looked at him but ignored his words. Sad to see these people literally surviving in a city where billions of RMB are spend on new infrastructure, roads, apartments, shopping centres and railway stations. Where millions of people buy expensive luxury bags from Chanel, Louis Vuitton and Hermes. Rich Chinese who can afford to spend forty thousand RMB on a bag. Or eighty thousand RMB for a single square meter of an apartment. Those tricycle owners probably have an income of around a hundred RMB per week. Critics are talking about the increasing gap between rich and poor in the

Western world, but in China, this seems a much bigger gap. There is a huge middle class separating the ultimate rich from the very poor. And the taxi driver might still have had some frustrations about something happening earlier today and releasing himself on those poor people. Serena stared in front of her, not paying attention to anything that happened just now. She was lucky to be born in an upper-middle-class family, owning two apartments in Beijing. And they recently purchased another apartment in Sanya, so her parents could retire in comfort once the time comes. Besides all this, her parents could afford to send her to a good university in Shanghai. She is clever, although she doesn't always seem to utilise her capabilities well.

"What did you think of my cousin?" Serena asked.

"She's a nice girl," I answered.

"You should take more efforts to maintain contact with her. She could be a valuable source for possibilities on the day your desire to return to Beijing has become a reality." Serena stared outside the window in the distance without saying a word. Life on the streets of Beijing continued, but I did not think she noticed anything of it. It all just happened. She could be so dreamy by times, living in her own thoughts. Serena nodded.

"Yes, as I mentioned before, we do not talk enough. But she could be good for future connections." We continued our drive. "

Are we getting close yet?" I asked Serena.

"The Keane website said the show would start around eight o'clock. I am getting a bit worried that we will be late."

"It should just be a few blocks, by looking at the buildings around us here."

"Good. I am getting a bit worried."

"Don't be, we have plenty of time," Serena assured me.

"I know the traffic here in Beijing, we will be fine."

We drove a few blocks further, and I recognised the CCTV building. Serena ordered the taxi to drive to the side of the road, right in front of the building gate. Cars were not allowed to get in. The gate was locked with a rollable chain door leaving just enough space for people to walk in and out but not without passing a gate control office. I grabbed the white envelope with the invitation. Serena paid the taxi, and we crossed the street towards the main gate of the CCTV building. While holding Serena's hand, we reached the main entrance, and I made an attempt to take the invitation, made from nice white carton material with golden letters stating the Burberry logo with the time and date of the event out of the white envelope. Before I could actually take the invitation out of the envelope, the security guy already provided us with access to the CCTV building front. White direction boards with a golden Burberry logo in the same style as the invitation led us to a black open door. I could already hear the music of *Somewhere Only We Know*.

"Fuck, we are late!" I said to Serena.

"Or is this still the soundcheck? I really hope so."

Serena looked at me with a face that could not provide me with an answer. We walked through a short corridor and all of a sudden, we entered a big hall with at the lower end of it a stage. It was Keane playing *Somewhere Only We Know*, but not for the soundcheck. The concert was in full play. It seemed it started earlier as previously mentioned on the Keane website. Still holding Serena's hand, I manoeuvred towards the stage. As close as we could get. Between the people was enough space to walk closer to the stage. *Somewhere Only We Know* just finished, and Tom Chaplin announced *Crystal Ball*. A big glitter ball appeared at the back of the stage, creating thousands of light spots all around the stage and the hall. The Keane gents were only a few meters away from us, closer as ever. This Burberry event was a rare opportunity to see Keane live. Tom, Tim, Richard and Jesse were here in Beijing for the very first time, and we were one of the few to witness it. Few as in a couple of hundred people. Usually, Keane is giving gigs in front of thousands of people, if not full arenas or sold-out stadiums. This was a rare opportunity. By looking at the people standing next to me, Keane actually has fans in China. Some groupies at the very front of the stage got very excited when Tom got closer. Soon after *Crystal Ball*, *Bedshaped* followed which was according to my Keane experience the last song of the show.

"On no, did we almost miss the entire show?!" I said to Serena. She did not say anything but looked to the stage.

"How come the show started so early?" I asked again.

"I do not know Victor, this is beyond our control. If they change the schedule last-minute, it is not our fault. Let's just enjoy whatever is left of this concert."

She was right. In my frustration about arriving late, I did not fully enjoy what was happening in front of us. *Bedshaped* ran to its end.

"Thank you very much for having us here, people of Beijing," Tom said, and the band left their instruments to come together while embracing each other. Looking tired and all wet from sweat they made a bow, waved goodbye and disappeared from the stage.

Was this really it? Did we fly to from Shanghai to Beijing just to see three songs of this concert? On the one hand, I felt so excited, it was the first time in two years I saw Keane live. On the other hand, I was disappointed not to be able to enjoy the full concert. But Serena was right, this was beyond our control. The lights on the stage dimmed, people mingled to other parts of the hall. On the left side, there was a huge Burberry logo on the wall, created out of a light beam somewhere from the ceiling.

"Let's go to the bar and get a drink," I said to Serena.

I took her hand, walked up front navigated our way to the back of the hall, where one of the several bars was located. While we walked, Serena looked several times over her shoulder while we passed people.

"There are so many Chinese movie stars and singers here, Victor!"

I looked around. Indeed, there was quite a few good-looking men and women that could go for a singer or movie star. They must have been invited by Burberry directly to build brand equity. I have no clue about who they are. I know Hollywood stars, but if a Chinese movie star passed by in the supermarket, I would not recognise him or her. When we approached the bar, it seemed it was sponsored by Moët & Chandon. Huge bottles were standing in the back of the bar, providing a free flow of champagne for everybody who attended the party. A waiter filled a tray of glasses in one go, to let the foam disappear and fill the glass with champagne to just under the top of the glass. I took two glasses, one for myself and one for Serena.

The Shanghai Expat

"No, thank you," She said immediately.

"I will check on whether they have some juice as well."

Not understanding why she wasted this opportunity to a free flow of champagne, and thirsty as I was from the paella, I bottomed up one of the two glasses. It's better to be seen with one glass in your hand instead of two. Some guests were approaching to leave the party already.

"Shall we leave too? It seems there is not much going on anymore." Serena asked.

"Hmm, let's stay for a while and have at least a few glasses of champagne. We flew all the way from Shanghai to here. I would like it to last longer than just an hour."

We stood for a while without saying anything, while we just looked at guests walking by. Every now and then, a seemingly important star or designer walked by. It was easy to recognise them as they were accompanied by a group of other people. From the corner of my eye, I saw Tom Chaplin appearing. He was with Jesse McQuin, the bass player of Keane. They were posing for a picture with a good-looking Chinese girl. Both Tom and Jesse had a drink in their hand, which could be a gin tonic judging from the look of it.

"Look, there are Tom and Jesse!" I excitedly said to Serena while poking her in her side.

"I want to have a picture with them. Can you please do so?"

And I reached for the digital camera in my small backpack. During all the concerts I hoped to ever meet one of the Keane lads, which is difficult or nearly impossible. Once they finished the picture session with the Chinese girl, I walked up to them.

"Can I have a picture with you?" Tom looked up to me and said:

"Yes sure," and he poked Jesse to join in. Serena got the camera ready, while I had Tom standing on my left and Jesse on my right side. Tom embraced me; I could feel his left hand on my shoulder.

"Are you ready? Are you ready?" Tom joked.

"Where do I have to look?" Both Jesse and Tom laughed, and so did I.

Serena was standing right in front of us. Tom was looking to his left. I did not want to waste this opportunity for a nice picture.

"Tom, look in front of us!" I said while I pointed to Serena. Meanwhile, Serena had made already a few pictures. These must look funny. Me trying to organise Tom and Jesse into a picture. The flashes of the camera were still on my eye frame.

"Thanks a lot, guys," I said to Tom and Jesse while I shook their hands. They moved on while I walked up to Serena to see how the pictures looked like. She took four in total. One of them looked good, I could see myself with a big smile with a blushed Tom and a laughing Jesse on my side. The other picture was a funny one, it was the one where Tom was jokingly looking for the camera. I finished my other glass of champagne and walked up to the bar to get one more. Freshly served, with bubbles appearing from the bottle of the glass right up to the top. I walked up to the other side of the hall, while Serena followed me. Between all the people I saw Tim Rice Oxley standing. Totally left alone. He was standing there just by himself with a drink in his hand.

"Should I approach him?" I asked Serena. I felt a bit nervous about doing so.

"What would you do if you suddenly saw one of the major idols in your life? One you've been listening to for endless hours in your life? The creative brain behind Keane music? The guy who wrote a long list of songs you felt comfort in during bitter and happy times?"

"I would be nervous too," Serena said. "But at the same time, I would not waste this opportunity. It could be the last one in life, and he does not seem busy now. Go for it."

I approached Tim. He looked at me while I came closer.

"Hi Tim," I said while we shook hands. For my own feeling way too formal for this occasion, but it was a door-opener.

"How did you like the show?" Tim almost asked immediately.

"It was nice!" I said excitedly.

"The first show in China." Tim nodded.

"I have seen Keane shows in the Netherlands, United Kingdom and Hong Kong so far," I said.

"Eight in total." Tim smiled.

"Where are you from?" he asked with a clear British accent.

"Originally from the Netherlands, but now I live and work in Shanghai. I flew specially from Shanghai to here for the show."

Right at that moment, Serena started to make a few pictures of us as if she was a paparazzi, and I saw Tim looking up a bit surprised.

"That's my friend," I assured him. Don't worry. Now she is doing so anyway, can I have a picture with you?"

He took all time to make a few nice shots.

"What are you doing for work in Shanghai?" Tim asked. I felt a bit shy, why would Tim be interested in what kind of work I am doing?

"I am currently working for Jiao Tong University as a project management lecturer."

"That's cool," Tim said. "I have never been to Shanghai before. It seems like a great city." Serena poked my arm.

"I will go and wait for you outside," I nodded yes to her and turned back to Tim.

"What do you think about China so far?" I asked.

"It's been very nice here, we appreciate the invitation from Burberry to come and play on their launch party. We'll go to see the Great Wall tomorrow."

"That's an absolute place you should go yes, it's beautiful out there. By the way, I have been listening to a lot to *The Night Train* album lately." Tim smiled again.

"What do you think of it?" I thought for a second.

"It is different compared to the other albums released previously, but I like it. Especially *Stop For A Minute* and *My Shadow*. Overall it's been received well, I think?"

"Yes it did, but we did not think it would be so successful," Tim said and now with a bit of a shy smile on his face.

"My daughter likes it too," he continued. "She likes to listen to it every morning I drive her to school." I smiled.

"That must be so nice." Tim nodded.

"Do you have children?" he asked in return.

"No, not yet," I said. "I did not find the right partner yet."

Meanwhile, a lady passed by with a tray with glasses filled with Moët & Chandon. I don't think she recognised Tim. We both reached out for a glass, took a sip and continued our talk.

"What is important if you as a band or musician would like to break through in China? Tim asked. "Are there any things you have to keep in mind, different compared to Europe?" I thought for a second.

"Most important is that your lyrics are not politically oriented, especially against the Chinese Government. They will prohibit artists from releasing music and playing gigs in China if they have a pro-Tibet or anti-communism history. Bands with concerts planned saw them cancelled because of this." Tim nodded.

"Yes, I have heard about Björk's concert in Shanghai, where she suddenly started to talk about Tibet."

"Another thing is attendance on Chinese social media like Weibo. This can give you quick recognition among Chinese audiences."

I took another sip of my champagne. This was so far one of the best nights of my life. Seeing a Keane concert by invitation, followed by pictures and a nice talk with the band members, with a free flow of Moët and Chandon champagne. What do you want more?

Suddenly Tom walked towards us, with seemingly the same joyful mood as he had when we took a picture earlier this evening.

"Are you alright?" Tim asked, just to make sure.

"Yes!" Tom answered with red cheeks from excitement.

"Where are you from?" Tom asked me.

"I'm from the Netherlands."

"Good," he answered. "So you have a Dutch passport." I nodded.

"As long as you carry your passport with you, you're always fine!" Tom said while he and Jesse walked away. Tim and I laughed.

"The first time I went to your concert must have been in 2004, which was the second concert in the Netherlands."

"That was just when *Somewhere Only We Know* saw its breakthrough outside of England," Tim said.

"It was in the early days of success, although you were together as a band already since 1995."

"I have been to most of the concerts until I moved to the United States to study in 2006. Since I live in Shanghai, there are fewer chances. I only went to the Hong Kong concert."

"You've been around Victor, but I'll have to go to the bathroom," Tim said.

"I start to feel the free flow of champagne pressing too," I laughed.

"It was so nice talking to you Tim, I appreciate you took the time to talk with me." Tim shook my hand and said:

"I think so too. Have a nice evening Victor!"

And he walked off. There I was, standing alone after just meeting my biggest idols. And they were so down to earth. Showing even interest in me, about where I came from, what I'm doing… I would have never expected this. I walked towards the exit, where Serena was waiting for me.

"Can you believe? I just talked twenty minutes with Tim from Keane! I feel so excited!" Serena was seemingly less impressed and excited than I was.

"I am glad you had a great night Victor," she said with a smile.

"Tim just took twenty minutes to talk with me. This will never happen anymore in my entire life."

I looked back into the hall, but nobody from the band was there anymore. For them, this was probably an hour of socialising after their concert which among other guests is probably nicer than alone in a hotel room. For me, this was a night I will never forget. Only Richard, Keane's drummer wasn't there. He might have been back in the hotel as I know he is more sensitive to jet-lags. More people were leaving the venue. Another look at the bar revealed that from an alcohol perspective, this party could last much longer.

"Let's go," I said to Serena while I took her hand. We walked the same way out, into the dark Beijing evening.

"Do you want to go somewhere for a drink? Or are you hungry?" I asked Serena.

"No, I'm fine. Let's just go back to the hotel," Serena said with a naughty expression on her face while she squeezed my hand.

"Alright," and while we walked, I pulled her slowly towards me, gave her a kiss the forehead and put my arm around her shoulders.

"Let's go back to the hotel."

30

Xinhu Riverside Apartments - 07:00

I woke up by the alarm fifteen minutes before seven, but it was not the first time. I did not sleep well last night, and neither the night before. I could not fall asleep, which usually never happen to me. Throughout the night, I woke up at least three times, opening my eyes and instantly thinking that I overslept. A look to my left confirmed that it was still too early to get up, as there was no visible daylight above the curtains. Each time it took me plenty of turns to fall asleep again. When I finally did, it must have been four or five in the morning already. Even though I had a night of disrupted sleep, I felt full of energy. After it was time to get up, I took a refreshing shower, made coffee and breakfast and be in the subway on the way to the office. I thought about it again. *Office*. That sounds nice. In fact, I did not have an office since I came back, which is now over a year ago. My office was either a classroom or my bedroom or a random coffee shop in Shanghai.

From today onwards, I would have my designated desk. This is what I have been dreaming of, working towards, and today it became a reality. I glanced around in the subway. As a result of my height, people always stare at me in public transportation, but today they do so in a different way. I sense that people can see my good mood. Now I can experience how public transportation is during rush hour. I usually had the luxury of travelling around rush hour. More people enter the subway from Zhenping Road Station onwards than they actually leave. Normally the crowd used to stay at a reasonable distance with me. Now they are standing basically against me. Personal space is a rare thing in Shanghai. Especially in the subway where people are not afraid of body contact with strangers. We were nearing Xujiahui station, interchange station between lines of the Shanghai Metro. It's usually a mingling of people. As I had to change to another line, I slowly moved closer to the subway car exit. The train entered the station, and we passed a few hundred people waiting at the platform for the train to stop and the doors to open. Do they all fit in? In the subway, I could feel people positioned towards the front of the door as I felt pressing against my back from two angles. The train slowly came to a stop, and the doors opened. Right now, it was just which side - platform or train pushed the hardest to decide who would be in or out first. Most often, team train wins. It still takes efforts, though.

Once I was on the platform, I found my way to the escalators while following a stream of people towards the exit. As the tallest man in line, I looked over a pyramid shape sea of people, answering to me with the backside of their head. I got up and followed the directions to line nine, which would lead me to Hechuan Road, the subway station right next to the Philips office. With the few business parks among the first stops, I could only imagine the people waiting at the platform. Once arriving there, my imagination became truth. Now I was on the other side - the platform side. I looked at the screens with a countdown till the next train would arrive. Similar to what I saw just now, people started to position to enter the train once it rolled into the subway station. Once the train came to a halt, exactly the same thing happened as minutes before, people push from both sides to get off and in an attempt to access the train. Despite a few pushing themselves from the platform into the train most of us, including myself, had to wait until the outgoing passengers were out. Once back on the train, the doors closed soon, and we were on our way. It would only be three stops until Hechuan Road. I had a girl pressing in my side, all most of us could do was just standing with our hands below our waist and wait till the next stop.

When I looked at my left, I noticed a guy wearing a blue Philips key-cord with on the lower end an employee pas. I smiled in the distance. Soon I would have one as well. Once we got closer to Hechuan Road, I pushed myself a little bit closer to the door. Without any issues, I got out and followed the signs to exit two, leading to street level. While I passed some breakfast stands on the side of the street, I almost immediately saw the building with the big glue illuminated Philips logo, and my heart filled with proud that finally, after trying so long I was part again of this company. I walked over the dusty street. Pieces of broken street tiles were all over the place. Was it still in construction or just the result of a lack of maintenance?

When I entered the business park, this changed. Here the streets were carefully maintained. The short cut grass looked fresh and green, with a visible perpetuated cut between the grass and the sideway. The hedges were carefully cut and surrounded me with a smell of pine trees. I walked around the corner of the building to the main entrance. Technically I could walk in, but I did not know where to go. HR only told me that I had to notice myself at the front desk, tell my name, and they would know what to do. I walked towards the reception area but had to wait as the reception lady was on the phone. I looked around. It seemed rush hour for employees to start working. They entered the office building with busloads.

"Hello sir, what can I do for you?"

The receptionist looked at me with a welcoming smile on her face.

"Good morning, I am starting today - HR told me to give a notice here once I arrived. The lady I have been in touch with is Diana."

"Sure, who can I tell her is here?"

"My name is Victor."

The receptionist dialled four digits on her phone and told Diana that a gentleman was waiting for her at reception. She hung up the phone and turned to me again.

"Please take a seat over there," she said while she pointed at a comfortably looking blue couch. "Diana will be here shortly."

I sat down and noticed a Philips magazine on the glass table in front of me. I browsed through it, absorbing some of the achievements made in the healthcare business unit. The magazine furthermore

He would not explain it this way, though. He would tell others that I achieved this by myself, based on the results of my internship and my persistence to get back into Philips. It took me over a year to get to this point, where I thought of giving up after reading his email where he told me that re-hiring opportunities were small or basically gone. The global financial crisis did not help either, causing human resources to freeze hiring budgets and constraining the chance for Gerald to grow his team.

"Here is your desk Victor," Diana said and pointed to a small cubicle in front of us. The desk had a long L shape and was right beside the window with a view over two factory roofs in a neighbouring business park. The desk itself was equipped with a small green plant, and a closed laptop, recharger, a blue map, notebook, business cards, a pen and pencil were carefully synchronically positioned among each other. Diana explained:

"The blue map contains a few policies you'll have to read and sign for IT, mobile phone and safety in the workplace. As well, it contains a copy of the employment contract as we agreed on by email and over the phone last week. Please read it carefully and return it back to me with your signature. You know where the kitchen is, so get yourself a nice cup of coffee first. I heard you like coffee."

I nodded with a smile on my face.

"Thank you, Diana."

Diana walked away, and I rolled the desk chair towards me, took a seat and opened my laptop. Coffee could wait for now. Inside was a little yellow sticky note with my username and password. I opened the blue map as well and read through the documents inside. One by one, I absorbed the information and signed the papers.

Then I saw Gerald walking out of his office. If he was on his way a meeting room or the kitchen for a coffee, he would pass my desk. Once he came closer, he noticed me.

"Hey Victor, good to see you here!"

"Hi, Gerald, thank you. It feels so good to be back here."

"I'm sure Diana told you about the meeting at ten-thirty? This will be the kick-off meeting for the project you're going to lead." From my internship, I still remember that Gerald was the type of contained an interview with a general manager, he seemed Dutch, but I did not know him. Shortly later, I heard:

"Hi Victor, welcome to Philips!" I turned up, and there was Diana, wearing a formal customised grey lady suit and a white blouse.

"Hi Diana," I said while I stood up and shook hands with her.

"How are you?" she asked.

"I am doing fine, thanks and you?"

"Good, thank you!" Diana sounded excited. She was now dressed much more formal than during the first occurrence we met two weeks ago, at the time of the interview. She continued:

"I have overseas visitors, so I will show you where your desk is on the fifth floor. Gerald advised me that there is a project kick-off meeting at ten-thirty this morning where he wants you to sit in so he can introduce you to the team." A rush of excitement ran through my body when I heard about the project kick-off meeting. I could not imagine a more hands-on start beforehand. We walked to the elevator and just fitted in. Without a single square centimetre space between all passengers, the elevator halted on every single floor until we reached the top of the building. Nobody said something, and with each stop, we got a little bit more space to breath. One colleague carried breakfast with her, spreading around a distinctive smell. Once we arrived on the fifth floor, I let Diana walk out first into the small gallery connecting the two elevator shafts. Walking either left or right would give us access to the office floor. Exactly as during the interview, we walked right. I was not sure which department was situated on the left side of this floor, but I assumed I would soon figure that out.

"Follow me please," Diana said, and we entered the office floor. The majority of colleagues was already at work, just like the last time I entered here. While we walked a corridor between a wall and a row of desks, I searched for Gerald's office. The door was open, but the window blinds were half-closed. I could not see him immediately. I owed this man so much. I should actually run in there with the most expensive bottle of whiskey I can afford and say thanks to him. Only because of his persuasion, I was offered this opportunity. Without him, the Philips door may have always remained closed.

manager who would give you tasks that are actually a bit out of your experience zone, but tasks of which he knew he could trust you to deliver well. He would not micromanage you but guide you in every step you needed his help. Sometimes he would stere you in the right direction, in case you digressed a bit away from the scope or objectives. He would always ask you the right questions to sometimes make you realise the need for change. During that time, I could not wish for a better manager. And I couldn't wait to get his feedback from now onwards again. Gerald shook my hand.

"I see you at ten-thirty."

And he walked indeed towards the kitchen to press the button for a freshly brewed coffee. Once he was out of the kitchen, I walked in to get myself a coffee too. The beans were still from the same brand. I walked back to my desk and completed the username and password for access to my laptop. Once I opened Outlook, I could see the meeting invitation from Gerald in my inbox, among some automatic generated welcoming emails from human resources and IT. I suddenly heard a male voice behind me.

"Hey Victor, are you back?" I turned around and saw Steve, one of the marketing colleagues I used to have lunch with pretty often. I stood up and shook his hand.

"In fact, I am! I just started eeeh…" and I looked at my watch, "Twenty minutes ago!" Steve laughed.

"Good to hear that, what will you be doing?"

"I will be working as an Integral Project Management Leader on a packaging related project. That's all I know, for now, we have a kick-off meeting later this morning. How are things with you?"

"Good Victor, we've been busy with launching new products continually. You remember we only had three products during your internship?" I nodded. Those products were the samples I showed to forty hotels in Shanghai, Hong Kong, Macau and Taipei.

"Now we have twelve products already. In just a couple of months. We have a deeper range in spots now."

"Wow, I can't wait to see them soon."

"Your essay on how hotels use LED lamps was a very good read. We've learned a lot from it for further marketing positioning."

"I'm glad I contributed my part," I said with a smile on my face.

"Let's catch up over lunch soon," Steve added.

"Lunch on average is still eeh... mama huhu, but they added a few new dishes to the menu."

"Perfect, let's do that!"

I followed Steve to the kitchen, where I got a cup of water.

"Let's talk soon," Steve said before he headed off.

I looked at my watch. I had still a bit of time until the meeting would start. I decided to quickly look over the papers in the blue map again to see if everything I had to sign was signed, scan a copy of it for my own reference and hand the originals back to Diana. After checking, I walked over to Diana's office. She wasn't in, but there was a box at the entrance of her office with "in" and "out". I slid the blue map containing all the documents in the "in" box. After that, it was time to collect my laptop, notebook and pen and make my way to the meeting room - but not without getting another coffee on the go.

Walking through the long corridor separating both sides of the office I found the meeting room, which was comfortably led up with a warm colour temperature light, a long table and what looked like an 80" TV screen at the far end of the wall. High room plants, looking like Kentia Palms, welcomed me from both corners in the meeting room. Three colleagues arrived already, but I did not recognise them. I introduced myself and walked to the seat on the far end, which was closest to the presentation screen. Soon after I sat down, more colleagues walked in. Gerald walked in as last, but exactly on time. He looked casual today, wearing jeans and a t-shirt. I remember from my internship that the only time he wore a suit was when his boss or any other high placed colleagues from oversees visited the Shanghai office. He had a notebook and his computer in his hand, and with a wide smile, he walked towards the screen. As if he had a big announcement to make. The LED spotlights from the ceiling above him, shined on his bold shaven head.

"Good..." He started. "I see we are complete. This is what I would like to call the kick-off meeting for a fascinating project. Some of you I have informed before, for some of you this is entirely new."

He looked around the table. I noticed some colleagues made notes already before something proper was discussed, but nobody was working on a laptop. Gerald seemed to have enough authority for people not to do this. Gerald continued:

"Before we move onto the details of the project, I would like to introduce a new member of our team - Victor. Some of you might still remember him as he completed an internship here one and a half year ago. He is an experienced project manager, and as this project needs a coordinator between all business functions, he will be an important connection point between you and your teams."

I actually did not consider myself as an experienced project manager, at least not practically. Theoretically perhaps yes. On paper, I knew at least what to do and how to execute it. Talks with the team leaders attending and their team members would provide me with the necessary information to fill the gaps and questions I have to successfully run this project. Gerald confirmed this:

"As he is the project coordinator, he will from time to time sit together with you and your team to inquire information and inform you about the next steps to take. Make sure you send out invitations for kick-off meetings this week Victor, so you are up and running as soon as possible." I nodded to confirm.

"Now let's move to the scope of the project," Gerald continued, and I listened carefully. I still had the idea that all of this could be a dream, and I was supposed to wake up soon. I pinched myself in the right arm to feel whether it would hurt, and it did.

After literally dreaming, trying, contacting Gerald, which sometimes felt like stalking, falling and standing up again to keep on believing in a good outcome, I can confirm that persistence eventually wins.

www.ingramcontent.com/pod-product-compliance
Lightning Source LLC
Chambersburg PA
CBHW021138080526
44588CB00008B/119